T0260769

Windows PowerShell™ 2

FOR

DUMMIES®

by Steve Seguis

WILEY

John Wiley & Sons, Inc.

Windows PowerShell™ 2 For Dummies®

Published by
John Wiley & Sons, Inc.
111 River Street
Hoboken, NJ 07030-5774
www.wiley.com

Copyright © 2009 by John Wiley & Sons, Inc., Indianapolis, Indiana

Published by John Wiley & Sons, Inc., Indianapolis, Indiana

Published simultaneously in Canada

No part of this publication may be reproduced, stored in a retrieval system or transmitted in any form or by any means, electronic, mechanical, photocopying, recording, scanning or otherwise, except as permitted under Sections 107 or 108 of the 1976 United States Copyright Act, without either the prior written permission of the Publisher, or authorization through payment of the appropriate per-copy fee to the Copyright Clearance Center, 222 Rosewood Drive, Danvers, MA 01923, (978) 750-8400, fax (978) 646-8600. Requests to the Publisher for permission should be addressed to the Permissions Department, John Wiley & Sons, Inc., 111 River Street, Hoboken, NJ 07030, (201) 748-6011, fax (201) 748-6008, or online at http://www.wiley.com/go/permissions.

Trademarks: Wiley, the John Wiley & Sons, Inc. logo, For Dummies, the Dummies Man logo, A Reference for the Rest of Us!, The Dummies Way, Dummies Daily, The Fun and Easy Way, Dummies.com, Making Everything Easier, and related trade dress are trademarks or registered trademarks of John Wiley & Sons, Inc. and/or its affiliates in the United States and other countries, and may not be used without written permission. Windows PowerShell is a trademark of Microsoft Corporation in the United States and/or other countries. All other trademarks are the property of their respective owners. John Wiley & Sons, Inc., is not associated with any product or vendor mentioned in this book.

LIMIT OF LIABILITY/DISCLAIMER OF WARRANTY: THE PUBLISHER AND THE AUTHOR MAKE NO REPRESENTATIONS OR WARRANTIES WITH RESPECT TO THE ACCURACY OR COMPLETENESS OF THE CONTENTS OF THIS WORK AND SPECIFICALLY DISCLAIM ALL WARRANTIES, INCLUDING WITHOUT LIMITATION WARRANTIES OF FITNESS FOR A PARTICULAR PURPOSE. NO WARRANTY MAY BE CREATED OR EXTENDED BY SALES OR PROMOTIONAL MATERIALS. THE ADVICE AND STRATEGIES CONTAINED HEREIN MAY NOT BE SUITABLE FOR EVERY SITUATION. THIS WORK IS SOLD WITH THE UNDERSTANDING THAT THE PUBLISHER IS NOT ENGAGED IN RENDERING LEGAL, ACCOUNTING, OR OTHER PROFESSIONAL SERVICES. IF PROFESSIONAL ASSISTANCE IS REQUIRED, THE SERVICES OF A COMPETENT PROFESSIONAL PERSON SHOULD BE SOUGHT. NEITHER THE PUBLISHER NOR THE AUTHOR SHALL BE LIABLE FOR DAMAGES ARISING HEREFROM. THE FACT THAT AN ORGANIZATION OR WEBSITE IS REFERRED TO IN THIS WORK AS A CITATION AND/OR A POTENTIAL SOURCE OF FURTHER INFORMATION DOES NOT MEAN THAT THE AUTHOR OR THE PUBLISHER ENDORSES THE INFORMATION THE ORGANIZATION OR WEBSITE MAY PROVIDE OR RECOMMENDATIONS IT MAY MAKE. FURTHER, READERS SHOULD BE AWARE THAT INTERNET WEBSITES LISTED IN THIS WORK MAY HAVE CHANGED OR DISAPPEARED BETWEEN WHEN THIS WORK WAS WRITTEN AND WHEN IT IS READ.

For general information on our other products and services, please contact our Customer Care Department within the U.S. at 877-762-2974, outside the U.S. at 317-572-3993, or fax 317-572-4002.

For technical support, please visit www.wiley.com/techsupport.

Wiley also publishes its books in a variety of electronic formats and by print-on-demand. Not all content that is available in standard print versions of this book may appear or be packaged in all book formats. If you have purchased a version of this book that did not include media that is referenced by or accompanies a standard print version, you may request this media by visiting http://booksupport.wiley.com. For more information about Wiley products, visit us at www.wiley.com.

Library of Congress Control Number: 2009931743

ISBN 978-0-470-37198-5 (pbk); ISBN 978-0-470-53577-6 (ebk); ISBN 978-0-470-53578-3 (ebk); ISBN 978-0-470-53576-9 (ebk)

Manufactured in the United States of America

10 9 8 7 6 5 4 3 2

WILEY

About the Author

Steve Seguis lives with his amazing wife, Annalene, in New York City, New York. He is a twelve-year Windows Systems Engineer veteran and specializes in systems automation. He was a Microsoft Most Valuable Professional (MVP) for Windows Server — Admin Framework from 2004–2007. He is also a contributing writer and technical editor for Windows IT Pro and, most recently, has published a book on Windows Server 2008 Administration.

Dedication

To my parents, Romeo and Lourdes, who gave me the opportunities that have allowed me to pursue my dreams and become who I am today.

Author's Acknowledgments

I've always been a fan of the *For Dummies* books, which has often resulted in one or two chuckles from my colleagues due to the incorrect perception that somehow reading a *For Dummies* book implies a lack of intelligence. The reality is that I'm a fan of making complex things simple and I like books that focus on getting me the information I need in an easy, digestible format. The *For Dummies* books have been doing this for years, and ever since I read my first *For Dummies* book (specifically *C For Dummies* by Dan Gookin, over a dozen years ago), I was captured by the ease at which I was able to gain knowledge while having the occasional laugh. I never in my wildest imagination thought I'd ever have the opportunity to write one myself . . . that is until my agent, David Fugate, got me in touch with the good people over at Wiley Publishing and got this journey started. Thanks David!

I'd like to thank Greg Croy, Executive Editor, for getting my proposal for this book approved. He actually retired before I was done writing the book, but kudos to him for getting the ball rolling. Thanks goes out to Blair Pottenger, Project Editor, for keeping me well-informed, answering all my questions, and putting in a lot of work to get the book finished. Of course, I'd also like to thank Katie Mohr, Acquisitions Editor, who took over Greg's role in this project after he retired. Katie went on maternity leave just before we got done with the book, so congratulations Katie on the new baby. The project had hit a bit of a plateau half way through, but when she took over we were able to regroup and get everything back on track.

I have to thank my very patient and supportive wife, Annalene, who puts up with me disappearing into the cubby hole I call my home office for late night writing sessions and generally dealing with all my quirks. We somehow work together to stay sane despite our lives going at 100 miles an hour.

I also have to thank my parents and my family for understanding how busy I get, generally staying out of my hair (what hair I have left), and letting me pursue my interests even though they continue to say that I need to slow down a bit and get some more sleep.

Finally, I'd like to thank the guys over at Microsoft for creating this awesome scripting language called Windows PowerShell. We've come a long way since batch files and as a long-time Windows administrator, I bow to your greatness. Windows PowerShell is truly empowering and more Windows folks in every company need to embrace it.

Publisher's Acknowledgments

We're proud of this book; please send us your comments through our online registration form located at *http://dummies.custhelp.com*. For other comments, please contact our Customer Care Department within the U.S. at 877-762-2974, outside the U.S. at 317-572-3993, or fax 317-572-4002.

Some of the people who helped bring this book to market include the following:

Acquisition, Editorial, and Vertical Websites

Project Editor: Blair J. Pottenger

Executive Editor: Greg Croy

Acquisitions Editor: Katie Mohr

Copy Editors: Virginia Sanders, Kathy Simpson

Technical Editor: David Dalan

Editorial Manager: Kevin Kirschner

Vertical Websites Project Manager: Laura Moss-Hollister

Vertical Websites Project Manager: Jenny Swisher

Supervising Producer: Rich Graves

Vertical Websites Associate Producers: Josh Frank, Marilyn Hummel, Douglas Kuhn, and Shawn Patrick

Sr. Editorial Assistant: Cherie Case

Cartoons: Rich Tennant (www.the5thwave.com)

Composition Services

Project Coordinator: Lynsey Stanford

Layout and Graphics: Melanee Habig, Melissa K. Jester

Proofreaders: Melissa Cossell, Christopher M. Jones

Indexer: Potomac Indexing, LLC

Publishing and Editorial for Technology Dummies

    Richard Swadley, Vice President and Executive Group Publisher

    Andy Cummings, Vice President and Publisher

    Mary Bednarek, Executive Acquisitions Director

    Mary C. Corder, Editorial Director

Publishing for Consumer Dummies

    Kathy Nebenhaus, Vice President and Executive Publisher

Composition Services

    Debbie Stailey, Director of Composition Services

Contents at a Glance

Table of Contents

Introduction

Welcome to *Windows PowerShell 2 For Dummies,* your ticket to the awe-some and magical world of Windows PowerShell. (Well, maybe it's not quite so magical, but at least your co-workers will think you're magical when you're done reading this book.) This book is a no-fluff, get-you-the-information-you-need-today kind of book, so if you like to read chapter after chapter of boring technical literature that keeps going around in circles, put this book back on the shelf, and walk away quietly. If, however, you want to read a book that is engaging, gives you the information you need to know rather than just a bunch of things you might want to know, and gets you up and running with Windows PowerShell as quickly as possible, then this book is for you!

About This Book

Windows PowerShell 2 For Dummies is an introductory guide to this relatively new and fascinating Windows scripting environment that's revolutionizing the way programmers think about Windows scripting. Before Windows PowerShell 2, there was Windows PowerShell 1.0 (what a shocker!). Windows PowerShell 2 takes the best elements of Windows PowerShell 1.0 and greatly improves on them, thanks in great part to the feedback from the Windows PowerShell community.

My goal in this book is to give you a concrete understanding of how things work in Windows PowerShell and fortify that knowledge with plenty of real-world examples that I'm sure you'll be able to relate to. In many cases, very short and quick examples are sufficient, but I also make sure to provide larger, slightly more complicated (yet infinitely useful) scripts whenever possible so that you can see how various concepts can be strung together into one cohesive unit.

This book is logically organized so that if you read it from cover to cover, you'll build on knowledge from earlier chapters to keep advancing your Windows PowerShell skills and level up (as they say in the role playing gaming world). Each chapter, however, is written as an independent unit that you can use as a reference for years to come as you find the need to go back and brush up on things.

Because Windows PowerShell 2 can be installed in different Windows operating systems, the examples are designed to be operating system–agnostic whenever possible. This way, you aren't going to miss anything, regardless of whether you run the program under Windows XP, Windows Vista, Windows Server 2003, Windows Server 2008, or even Windows 7.

After reading this book, you'll be able to piece together your own Windows PowerShell scripts that'll be sure to impress your boss, not to mention save you a ton of work and time. In fact, when you know how to use Windows PowerShell to your advantage, you'll have much more free time to do more interesting things, such as read this book again.

To mention briefly what this book is *not,* it's not an all-inclusive, everything-you'll-ever-want-to-know-about-Windows PowerShell reference. As you read this book, however, you'll realize how truly powerful Windows PowerShell is, because the book covers all the most important things you need to know.

This book is written to Windows PowerShell 2 CTP3. Windows PowerShell 2 has already come a long way since it was first announced to be under development, and I feel that any changes that Microsoft might make before the final release is out will be some bug fixes and perhaps some changes to some very advanced features (which this book doesn't delve into). That being said, we'll keep you up to date with any applicable changes through the *Windows Power Shell 2 For Dummies* Web site (`www.dummies.com/go/powershell2fd`), so keep yourself informed by visiting the site regularly.

Conventions Used in This Book

In this book, you enter a lot of commands at the Windows PowerShell command prompt or write scripts in a text editor such as Notepad. Scripts and code listings always appear in monofont, like this:

```
$str1 = "Hello "
$str2 = "World!"
write-output $str1 + $str2
```

Make sure that when you enter commands, you type them exactly as they appear in the book. Windows PowerShell is forgiving about things like spaces, but in general, if you encounter problems running any of the examples, first make sure that you've entered the example exactly as it appears in the book.

You'll be required to use your keyboard quite a bit with Windows PowerShell. Fortunately, you can make your life a bit easier by taking advantage of several keyboard shortcuts. When I direct you to use a keyboard-shortcut sequence such as Ctrl+S, press these keys on your keyboard simultaneously; then release them together. The plus sign is there to show that the keys are to be pressed together; you don't type the + sign.

What You're Not to Read

This book contains everything you need to know and a few things that are good to know. I've separated the good-to-know stuff into sidebars (which are shaded in gray) and paragraphs marked with the Technical Stuff icon. You can skip these sections and still survive the day, but feel free to read them; some of them contain some pretty useful information that you may need someday to win a game show.

Foolish Assumptions

Whenever I pick up a technical book, I want to know that it was written for someone like me, so I want to be clear about my assumptions of what you know and what you don't know before you dive into this book.

For starters, I'm assuming that you know how to use a computer. (Yes, if you haven't noticed already, you're holding a computer book. If you thought it was something else, such as a cookbook, feel free to nod a few times; put the book down; and walk a few aisles down to find the other *For Dummies* book you had in mind.)

You should also know how to use at least one of the operating systems supported by Windows PowerShell, such as Windows XP, Windows Vista, Windows Server 2003, Windows Server 2008, or Windows 7.

I don't expect you to know any kind of scripting or programming language (although it helps if you do). I go over everything you need to know, even if this is your first time. (It's okay; I don't bite.) Many of my examples cover ways to use Windows PowerShell to manage a Windows environment, including Active Directory, so preferably, you have some Windows administration under your belt. If you don't, don't worry; you still find plenty of useful information in this book.

Finally, although the title of this book is *Windows PowerShell 2 For Dummies,* I know that you're not a dummy (but I bet that guy who's staring at you for having a *For Dummies* book in your hand is). I know that you're a smart individual who knows that the best way to start any new topic (especially a scripting or programming language) is to pick up a *For Dummies* book.

So without attracting too much attention, give yourself a round of applause; then quickly move toward the counter and buy this book. While you're at it, get copies for your colleagues, too. It's the best compliment you can give them. Seriously, it is!

How This Book Is Organized

There are no surprises here. I've organized the book to make it easy for you to find what you're looking for. Whether you need to look up something quickly or feel like reading this book in your leisure time, you'll feel right at home. I've broken this book into seven parts so that you can pace yourself.

Part I: Getting a Bird's-Eye View of PowerShell 2

I find it easy to see trees and miss out on the entire forest, so I'm starting this book with a soaring, 10,000-foot (3,048-meter) view of Windows PowerShell 2. Chapter 1 helps you get your arms around Windows PowerShell by giving you an understanding of how it got where it is today. I show you how to customize the environment to best fit your style and some different time-saving techniques that help get you going faster in Chapter 2. Finally, Chapter 3 gives you your first taste of this amazing shell. Consider Part I to be your gateway to the world of Windows PowerShell.

Part II: PowerShell's Basic Structure and Syntax

Part I gives you your first taste of Windows PowerShell. Part II takes a step back by providing a detailed look at the structure and syntax that define Windows PowerShell. Think of this part as me showing you how to speak the Windows PowerShell language. Every scripting and programming language defines constructs for how to interact with it. Unfortunately, unlike humans (well, most humans), computers need precise instructions on what you want them to do, so getting this part right will pave the way for a smooth experience later.

Chapter 4 goes over Cmdlets, which are the basic commands that form the foundation of Windows PowerShell. I show you how to store data temporarily in your scripts using variables in Chapter 5. Chapter 6 goes on to show the different ways you can put some intelligence into your code by using logic expressions to control the flow of code within your script. Finally, Chapter 7 shows how you can make very effective command sequences by feeding the output of one command to the input of another command creating a command pipeline.

Part III: Complex Data Description and Sharing

Now that you know how to speak the language, Part III raises the bar and introduces more complex Windows PowerShell activities, such as interacting with Windows Management Instrumentation (WMI) in Chapter 8 and manipulating text in Chapter 9. You also get to see the power of numbers in Chapter 10. You discover how to take advantage of groups of data by using arrays in Chapter 11 and how to deal with reading and writing files in Chapter 12. Chapter 13 takes you on a journey through time by showing how you can use dates and times within PowerShell. The great thing about Windows PowerShell is that it makes even these relatively complex operations a breeze.

Part IV: Controlling Where and How You Operate PowerShell

Many of the features I cover in this part are, unfortunately, quite lacking in Windows PowerShell 1.0. After months of crying and whining (who said whining doesn't work?) from the Windows PowerShell community, the super-smart Windows PowerShell developers at Microsoft responded with some enhancements that really make Windows PowerShell 2 shine.

In this part, I go into the more advanced features of Windows PowerShell, including many new cool features introduced in Windows PowerShell 2. You create your own commands using Advanced Functions in Chapter 14 and obtain the ability to run scripts remotely in Chapter 15. I also show you how to make your scripts work with in an international setting in Chapter 16 and track down those ever-elusive bugs in Chapter 17. The enhanced capabilities for debugging your scripts in Windows PowerShell 2 are some of the best improvements in this new version of PowerShell.

Part V: Real-World Windows Administration Using PowerShell

I know that the main reason you're reading this book is to upgrade your skills and become more efficient in your job. This part is dedicated to showing the real power of Windows PowerShell through practical real-world examples. You get to see for yourself how you can tie everything that you've accomplished in the preceding four parts into some truly useful scripts that'll have your co-workers looking at you with pure awe and admiration.

In this part, you get to see some scripts to monitor your system in Chapter 18, meddle around in the Windows registry in Chapter 19, interact with Active Directory in Chapter 20, and monitor system status and manage security in Chapter 21. If you're an old-time script writer who's using Windows Shell Scripti-ng or Windows Scripting Host, you get a glimpse of how those scripts can be converted to Windows PowerShell in Chapter 22. Although this chapter is aimed mostly at IT pros, there's plenty of information in it for you, even if all you manage is your own PC.

Part VI: Configuring and Reporting Via PowerShell

In this part, I show you more real-world scenarios in which Windows PowerShell can make your job easier. You find out how to control your network configuration, such as TCP/IP and firewall settings in Chapter 23, and how to manage your hardware with nothing but Windows PowerShell in Chapter 24. You also find out how you can make your boss happier and your life easier by using the built-in features of Windows PowerShell to generate reports right from your script's output in Chapter 25.

Part VII: The Part of Tens

What would a good *For Dummies* book be without a good Part of Tens? After all, it takes weeks of perspiration to weed through mountains of information to bring you these lists of things you absolutely need to know. Find out in Chapter 26 what the top ten Cmdlets are; in Chapter 27, you see the top ten mistakes to avoid. It's okay — I know you're going to flip to the end of this book to take a sneak peek, so go ahead.

Icons Used in This Book

Tips highlight a point that can save you a lot of time and effort. Make sure that your eyeballs light up whenever you see one of these icons.

Warnings point out things you need to know to prevent something bad from happening. Imagine nuclear meltdown — or worse, such as running out of ketchup.

This icon marks the stuff you can skip because it goes into some pretty technical details. Although this material isn't critical to your understanding of how to use Windows PowerShell, some stuff in these sections will make you sound downright intelligent!

Remember to remember anything that has the Remember icon. Remember that!

What's on the Web Site

As much as I know how much you love typing lines and lines of code, I provide the code for all the code listings in this book right on the book's Web site (`www.dummies.com/go/powershell2fd`) for you to download and use. This site will save you time and also give you something to compare your code with if, for some reason, you type the code manually and it doesn't work correctly.

Again, this book is written to Windows PowerShell 2 CTP3. If there are any changes to Windows PowerShell 2 in releases after CTP3, I will put that up as errata on the *Windows PowerShell 2 For Dummies* Web site (`www.dummies.com/go/powershell2fd`), so if something in this book doesn't work quite right, check the Web site for any tips or code updates.

Where to Go from Here

Go forth and multiply! Wait — wrong audience. Now that the easy part is done, and I've got you salivating over Windows PowerShell, it's time to get you to do some work . . . err, have some fun! Sit down in front of a computer, get a can of your favorite energy drink, and get ready for hours of eye-opening goodness. Welcome to the world of Windows PowerShell. You'll wonder how you ever survived without it!

Part I

Getting a Bird's-Eye View of PowerShell 2

The 5th Wave   **By Rich Tennant**

Well, heck — that's just darn impressive! And you say it's programmed to sew up and dress the incision afterward as well?

1 In this part . . .

It's hard to really understand something without putting it in context. These first three chapters paint the scene for the rest of the book and give you a taste of what Windows PowerShell 2 is like. I like to think of this part as a quick tour of Windows PowerShell, past and present, so that you not only understand why Windows PowerShell is the way it is but also to demonstrate some of the things you can accomplish with it that I hope will create a thirst for more.

Chapter 1 helps you get your arms around Windows PowerShell by giving you an understanding of how it got where it is today. I show you how to customize the environment to best fit your style and some different time-saving techniques that help get you going faster in Chapter 2. Finally, Chapter 3 gives you your first taste of this amazing shell.

Chapter 1

The Windows PowerShell Rap Sheet

I'm a really lazy person by nature. I'm not lazy in the sense that I like to sit down and do nothing all day long, but rather I hate doing things over and over again. Whenever I find myself doing something very mundane, the first thing that pops into mind is "there has to be a way to automate this!" Computers are great work horses. They can run day in and day out and never complain. Logically, it makes sense to make your computer work for you rather than the other way around, so in my infinite laziness I'm constantly cooking up ways to make my computer work harder so I can have time to do more important things . . . like write this book for you.

Whether you're completely new to scripting or have done some level of automation in the past using other scripting languages, you'll really love Windows PowerShell. It gives Windows users a true shell that provides the same power over the Windows system that only people in the Unix/Linux community enjoyed previously. Microsoft has spent years and years trying to make Windows easier to use, and in the process of doing so have made some things quite frustrating for power users. (Remember when Microsoft was trying to force you to use wizards only?) Windows PowerShell is, in my mind, Microsoft's way of acknowledging that a significant number of users know what they want and don't want to sit around all day long clicking through dialog boxes to get their jobs done.

Addressing the Need for a Powerful, Windows-Focused Scripting Language

You've always had the standard Windows Shell, also known as the *command shell* or the *DOS prompt* (for those who can't let go of the past), to interact with Windows at the command line. You can automate various aspects of Windows from the command shell using built-in commands, other command line applications, and even string them together into Windows Shell *scripts* (or *batch files* for those still clamoring for the good old DOS days). If you want a bit more power and control, you can use Windows Scripting Host (WSH) and then use VBScript or JScript to automate your tasks. So the obvious question is "why add Windows PowerShell to this mix?" After all, can't you accomplish everything you need to do using these existing methods?

Sure, a good portion of everything you need to do in Windows can be accomplished by writing a Windows Shell or WSH script. I've been doing it for years with no problems, and when I first heard of Windows PowerShell being developed several years ago (when it was still under the codename *Monad*) I had mixed feelings. On one hand, it promised a whole new way of doing things, which was exciting, but on the other hand it just became one more thing I needed to learn. As Windows PowerShell came into maturity, I clearly saw that it really did live up to its promises, and I found myself jumping on the Windows PowerShell bandwagon.

Watching Monad morph into PowerShell

Windows PowerShell was architected by Jeffrey P. Snover back in August 2002, under the codename Monad. According to the original Monad Manifesto, it was designed as the next-generation platform for administrative automation. It was based loosely on the tried and proven approach for administrative automation in Unix.

In traditional command shells, you achieve a desired action by manipulating generally unstructured text output of a previous command to generate the desired output or effect using another command. In a regular Windows Command Shell, for example, you can use the following command sequence to find out if pinging www.whitehouse.gov returns any replies.

```
ping www.whitehouse.gov | find "Reply"
```

In the example, you pass the output of the ping command against www.whitehouse.gov into the find command because you want to filter the output so only the lines containing the word *Reply* get displayed. Monad tackled the limitations of this traditional method by devising a new approach for building commands by leveraging the .NET framework and its object model. Monad does this by defining an automation model where commands called *Cmdlets* (read as *command-lets*) can pass data to each other as structured objects rather than a loose collection of text.

My intent isn't to give you a history lesson on Windows PowerShell but rather to help you understand why it looks and acts the way it does. As you use Windows PowerShell, you might notice, for example, that the command syntax has a Unix feel to it. This isn't by coincidence but rather due to the language being modeled from powerful Unix shells with the added .NET twist. Don't be intimated, however — PowerShell is one of the easiest scripting languages to use and is very intuitive.

 If you want to read the Monad Manifesto as it originally appeared in 2002, you can view it on the Windows PowerShell team blog (`http://blogs.msdn.com/powershell/archive/2007/03/19/monad-manifesto-the-origin-of-windows-powershell.aspx`).

A little bit on Windows PowerShell 1.0

Windows PowerShell brings together the best parts of interacting with the traditional Windows Shell along with the power of writing WSH scripts. It creates a rich command line–based environment that puts more power into your hands by letting you run new PowerShell commands called *Cmdlets*. These are .NET class–based commands that give you the flexibility of high-level scripting while allowing you to access very low-level Application Programming Interfaces (APIs) through .NET wrappers.

Windows PowerShell 1.0 was the first full-production release of Windows PowerShell, and even though it delivered on many of the key elements needed to use it, it was adopted slowly for a few reasons:

- ✔ It wasn't built into any of the existing Windows operating systems, so administrators who wanted to use it had to make a conscious effort to deploy the PowerShell run-time.

- ✔ Administrators who had already mastered existing scripting languages didn't feel the need to use a new shell to accomplish the same tasks.

- ✔ As a new product, it took a while for enough people to start using it before the Windows PowerShell community became proficient enough to be able to demonstrate the more creative ways to use it.

Eventually Microsoft's own developers started taking advantage of Windows PowerShell 1.0, and it was soon adopted in their mainstream products like Microsoft Exchange 2007 and Systems Center Operations Manager (*SCOM,* formerly known as *MOM*). PowerShell 1.0 was then released with Windows Server 2008 as an installable, out-of-box feature. You and I should be excited about this because it really brings Windows PowerShell into the mainstream and also demonstrates Microsoft's commitment to bringing Windows PowerShell into the forefront of its systems management strategies.

Windows PowerShell 2, the Next Evolution

Despite the slow adoption of Windows PowerShell 1.0, a growing Windows PowerShell community emerged and put it through its paces. The Windows PowerShell developers at Microsoft took a lot of this feedback and criticism to produce what promises to be a much more production-worthy scripting environment — Windows PowerShell 2.

I'm sure enough time has now elapsed since you first heard about Windows PowerShell that it has piqued your curiosity (which is probably one of the reasons why you picked up this book). It's a great time for you to discover this scripting language because many of the limitations people faced while working with Windows PowerShell 1.0 have since been worked out. What you're all left with is a much more usable command shell that offers a host of different ways to do things. Your only real limit is your own creativity.

I know you're already asking the obvious: What's new in Windows PowerShell 2 that makes it so special? Here are some of the major changes and enhancements made to Windows PowerShell:

 ✔ **PowerShell remoting:** Gives you the ability to execute Cmdlets and scripts remotely. See Chapter 15.

 ✔ **Background jobs:** As the name implies, this improvement allows you to run commands in the background while you continue to work on other things. See Chapter 15.

 ✔ **Advanced functions:** Cmdlets used to be written only in C# and VB.NET. Now you can write your command pseudo-Cmdlets using Windows PowerShell itself. See Chapter 14.

 ✔ **Data language:** Gives you the ability to separate your code from the data, making it more portable and easier to share.

 ✔ **Script internationalization:** Helps scripts that have to accommodate multiple languages easier to implement. See Chapter 16.

- ✔ **Script debugging:** Finally, real debugging. You can set breakpoints in your scripts so you can halt execution to find out what's going on at a particular point in the script. See Chapter 17.

- ✔ **Some new operators and automatic variables:** Some new operators to make it easier to split and join strings and automatic variables for accessing user interface language information. See Chapter 5.

- ✔ **Additional new Cmdlets:** Mostly to support the preceding features.

- ✔ **Constrained runspaces:** Gives you the ability to constrain what commands and scripts Windows PowerShell can run within a given runspace.

- ✔ **Runspace pools:** You can think of these as ways to manage command execution by pooling together runspaces.

- ✔ **Integrated Scripting Environment (ISE):** A graphical version of the command shell that adds some cool new features such as multi-tabbed panes for working with multiple scripts at the same time. See Chapter 2.

- ✔ **Out-GridView:** You can output the results of your commands in an interactive table where you can then sort, search, and group the results. See Chapter 25.

- ✔ **New PowerShell APIs:** If you're a programmer, you can get to the new features provided in PowerShell directly using these APIs.

- ✔ **Some minor enhancements to existing commands and shell behavior:** Some additional parameters to existing commands have been added to increase functionality.

Even if you haven't used Windows PowerShell in the past, you can tell just by this list of new features that there are some significant enhancements to Windows PowerShell that go beyond the surface. I think Windows PowerShell 2 is a more complete product that still makes it easy for new users like you to master it while leaving plenty of room for you to grow.

What's really amazing is that while I'd classify many of the changes in Windows PowerShell 2 under an advanced feature category, discovering how to use them is a quick and easy thing even for a beginner. Before you know it, and with the help of this really cool book you're reading, you too will be taking advantage of these new features.

Installing Windows PowerShell 2

Words are just words. I know your heart is pumping already and you're about to scream at the top of your lungs "I want to use Windows PowerShell already, stop talking and tell me how!" Because Windows PowerShell 2 doesn't ship with any of the Windows operating systems except Windows 7, you'll generally need to install it first. Luckily, this task is relatively pain-free, so stick with me for a few seconds.

Windows PowerShell 2 is a replacement for Windows PowerShell 1.0. They can't co-exist on the same system, so if you already have Windows PowerShell 1.0 installed, make sure you uninstall it first. **Note:** To uninstall Windows PowerShell 1.0, you might have to select the Show Updates option in the Add/ Remove Programs control panel applet for it to be visible.

Windows PowerShell 2 can be installed on both the x86 and x64 platforms of Windows XP with SP3, Windows Server 2003 with SP2, Windows Vista with SP1, Windows Server 2008, and Windows 7.

You install Windows PowerShell 2 using these four simple steps:

1. **Download and install Microsoft .NET Framework 2.0**

2. **Download and install Microsoft .NET Framework 3.5.1.**

   Required for Windows PowerShell Integrated Scripting Environment (ISE) and Out-GridView.

3. **Download and install WinRM 2.0 CTP3.**

   This is required if you want to take advantage of the remoting and back-ground jobs features.

4. **Download and install Windows PowerShell 2.**

   I'm not going to give you step-by-step instructions here because it's a straightforward "next, next, next" installation.

Firing up the Windows PowerShell Command Shell

Congratulations! Now that you've got Windows PowerShell 2 installed, you can finally have some fun.

First, going forward, you might see me referring to Windows PowerShell 2 simply as PSH. Not only will this save me from carpal tunnel syndrome, but Windows PowerShell is often referred to as PSH within Windows PowerShell community, so don't be surprised if you see that abbreviation. (It's also some-times just called PS.)

Fire up the PSH command shell by choosing Start⇨All Programs⇨Windows PowerShell V2⇨Windows PowerShell V2.

If you're running Windows Vista, you may need to right-click the shortcut and choose the option to run as Administrator (running elevated) even if you have administrative rights on the system if you get access denied errors.

Windows PowerShell 2 launches and the command shell opens, as shown in Figure 1-1. It looks a lot like your old Windows command shell, except that by default the background is blue and the prompt is prefixed by PS. You can run some familiar DOS commands (such as DIR and CD), and they'll still work, but the output might look a bit different. Also, running some existing command line applications like XCOPY.EXE works too! I get into how this all works in future chapters, but the ability to run non-PowerShell commands is one of the greatest things about PSH — you can start using PSH today as a replacement command shell and run your old commands while getting familiar with the new PSH way.

PSH runs your regular command line applications as normal, but the built-in commands such as CD and DIR are actually aliases to new PSH Cmdlets. This is why the output of DIR looks a bit different. Also notice that you can't use the old switches (such as DIR /W) with DIR. The reason is because the underlying Cmdlet that DIR is mapped to uses different parameters. I talk more about aliases in Chapter 2.

Figure 1-1:
The
Windows
PowerShell
command
shell.

Going GUI: The Windows PowerShell Integrated Shell Environment (ISE)

The Windows PowerShell Integrated Shell Environment (ISE) is a bit of a mouthful, but it's really just a more graphically rich interface (see Figure 1-2) for interacting with PSH. You launch it the same way as the regular PSH command shell (see the preceding section), but you select Windows PowerShell ISE instead; select Start⟹All Programs⟹Windows PowerShell v2⟹Windows PowerShell ISE.

Script pane/Editor pane

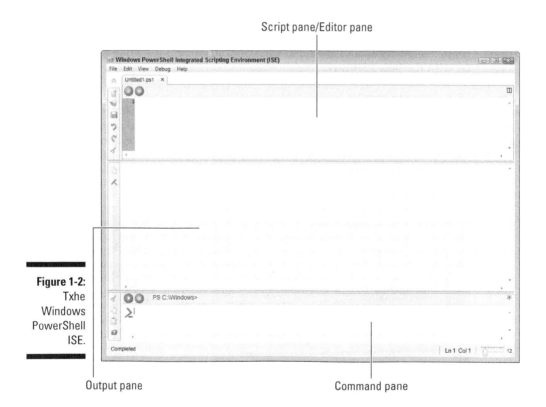

Figure 1-2:
Txhe
Windows
PowerShell
ISE.

Output pane   Command pane

Here's what you get with this handsome interface:

- ✔ **Script/Editor pane:** This is where you can view and edit your PSH scripts.

- ✔ **Output pane:** This is where the output of all your command or script is displayed.

- ✔ **Command pane:** You can enter commands in this pane just as you would in a regular PSH command shell.

You can also create PSH scripts by choosing File⇨New to display the editor pane above the output pane. If you're working on multiple scripts, a tabbed interface is displayed so you can easily switch back and forth between the different script windows, as shown in Figure 1-3.

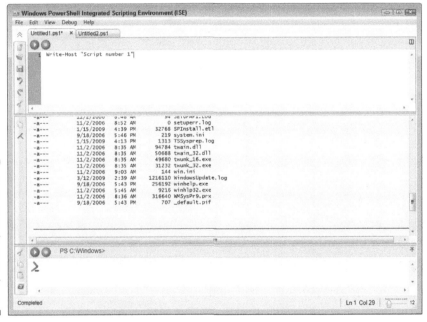

Figure 1-3:
The Windows PowerShell ISE window with the tabbed script editor interface.

You'll also notice that when you have a script open, you can run it simply by clicking the Run button (the right-pointing triangle, similar to the Play button on a CD player) on the toolbar. The toolbar has all the standard text-editing features as well as syntax highlighting, which makes editing your scripts a bit easier on the eyes. The best part is that the debugger is easily accessible from the Debug menu. (I cover debugging concepts in-depth in Chapter 17.) The ISE is an excellent tool for writing, running, and debugging your scripts in one easy-to-use environment. Think of it as a miniature Visual Studio for Windows PowerShell. I talk more about the ISE in the next chapter.

Although the ISE script pane is primarily designed for writing and editing scripts, it's a pure text editor, so you can use it to open or create plain text files and XML files.

Chapter 2

Customizing and Shortcutting the Environment

I like to watch people while they work in front of their computers. I find it fascinating. Call me weird (it's okay; plenty of people do), but it's interesting to see the different ways people choose to interact with their computers. For instance, I used to work with a Windows administrator who rarely used the keyboard shortcuts Ctrl+C and Ctrl+V to copy and paste items. He always used the right-click-then-copy-and-paste method because he felt he was more in control. (Yes, I make the same face you're making now.) I also used to work with someone who tried to do everything using the keyboard whenever possible and stayed away from the mouse as if it were the plague. I know others who are very finicky about what toolbars they use and some on the extreme end who even organize icons alphabetically. Whatever methods you use are a-okay — after all, it's always best to organize your work whichever way makes you the most efficient.

I thought that before getting started working with Windows PowerShell, you might find it useful to know different ways to customize the environment to best fit your style. After all, the more comfortable you are with the interface, the more intuitive and pleasant your experience will be. Also, following the whole "I'm a lazy guy" theme, I show you different time-saving techniques that help get you going faster. Does this sound interesting to you? Then read on!

Personalizing the Look and Feel of the Command Shell

If you're anything like me, you eventually find yourself with multiple command line windows open simultaneously because you, just like your computer, like to multitask. One of the problems with having multiple command shells open at the same time is figuring out which window does what. After all, they all look the same, right? Well, not necessarily. You can use a few handy tricks to make different windows more distinguishable:

✔ **Change the background and foreground colors.**

✔ **Change the window size.**

✔ **Change the window title.**

The following sections tell you how.

Adding color to your world

You can easily change the background and foreground colors to suit your preference. For example, you can change the background color to magenta and the foreground color (the color the text is displayed in) to blue by typing these commands at the PSH prompt.

```
$Host.UI.RawUI.BackgroundColor="magenta"
$Host.UI.RawUI.ForegroundColor="blue"
```

$Host is a special variable that is a reference to the current console object. You assign the appropriate color to the UI.RawUI.BackgroundColor and UI.RawUI.ForegroundColor properties of the console object.

Getting size-specific with your windows

The $Host.UI.RawUI object is actually pretty useful. You can query or manipulate additional properties through this object to affect the console's appearance besides the foreground and background colors. You can change the window size, the buffer size, and even change the window's title. (The following section covers how to change the title.)

The *buffer size* is the width and height of the window retained in memory where as the *window size* is the portion of the buffer that's visible. Because of this, the only real constraint is that your window size must be smaller than your buffer size. (PSH won't let you screw this up even if you try.) The buffer height is important because it controls essentially how far back you can scroll in your window as you run more and more commands. The default buffer height is 3,000, which means the buffer keeps up to 3,000 lines of output before it starts to discard older entries.

You change the window or buffer size by changing the value of either the BufferSize or WindowSize property of $Host.UI.RawUI. If you want to find out the current value, run the following PSH commands:

```
$Host.UI.RawUI.BufferSize
$Host.UI.RawUI.WindowSize
```

The output of either command is the width and height displayed in a tabular format. Now, you might be tempted to try something like this to change the window size:

```
$Host.UI.RawUI.WindowSize.Width = 110
$Host.UI.RawUI.WindowSize.Height = 40
```

Although PSH doesn't complain, the window size doesn't change, and if you query the value of WindowSize again, you'll find that the old values are still there. The correct way to change WindowSize is by assigning a new value to this property directly. Because WindowSize is an object, you need to somehow create an object of that type, set its width and height properties, then assign this new value to WindowSize. You can change the window size by using the following command sequence:

```
$size = $Host.UI.RawUI.WindowSize
$size.Width = 100
$size.Height = 25
$Host.UI.RawUI.WindowSize = $size
```

Here I store the value of WindowSize in a variable called $size. I don't really care so much about what the current value is, but I need to have an object that's the same data type as WindowSize so I can make the change. Now that I have such an object, I assign my new width and height values to it and then reassign this entire object back to WindowSize. If you want to change the buffer size, simply replace WindowSize with BufferSize.

I talk more about data types and objects in Chapter 5, so if you're eager to find out more about what these things are right now, you can mark this page and jump over to it if you want.

Window and buffer width and height dimensions aren't measured in pixels — rather, width is measured by the number of characters that fit on one row, and height refers to the number of rows it can accommodate.

A window by any other name . . .

Probably one of the easiest and most useful properties to modify is the WindowTitle property. You can change the title to something interesting like "Windows PowerShell Rules!" (see Figure 2-1) by running this line:

```
$Host.UI.RawUI.WindowTitle="Windows PowerShell Rules!"
```

Now you can easily distinguish one PSH window from another by quickly reading the window's title.

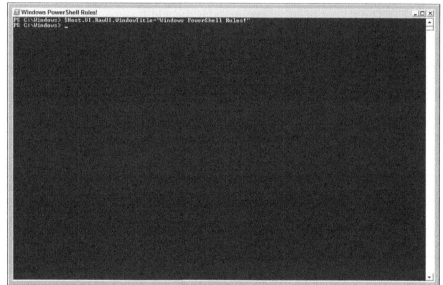

Figure 2-1:
Windows
PowerShell
with a
renamed
window
title.

Changing Your PowerShell Profile

I'm sure you had fun playing with colors and resizing your PSH window in the previous sections, but as you probably observed, the changes aren't preserved when you close the window. Sure, you can enter these commands each and every time you open a new PSH window, but that can get a bit tedious. What if you want these settings to be applied by default every time you open a PSH shell? No worries. Whenever you open Windows PowerShell, one of PSH's regular startup chores is to run your profile script (if it exists). Your *profile script* is a special script that runs every time you open a new PSH command shell. If it doesn't exist (which it doesn't, by default), PSH skips it and moves on.

You can find out where your profile is by running this command at the PSH prompt:

```
$profile
```

Yep, that's it! By default, the profile location should point to a file called `Microsoft.PowerShell_profile.ps1` in a folder called `WindowsPowerShell` in your `My Documents` folder. For example, on my workstation, it returns `C:\Documents and Settings\steguis.MONKEY\Documents\WindowsPowerShell\Microsoft.PowerShell_profile.ps1`.

The Windows PowerShell Integrated Scripting Environment (ISE) has its own profile script, which is in the same location (by default) as the regular profile script, except it's called `Microsoft.PowerShellISE_profile.ps1`.

If you happen to have an existing profile, open it up in Notepad; otherwise, create a blank text file using Notepad in the location pointed to by `$profile`. This profile is really just a PSH script that gets executed whenever a shell is launched.

Before you can create the profile file, you might have to create the `WindowsPowerShell` folder in your `My Documents` folder if it doesn't already exist.

You can stick any PSH code you want executed every time a shell is opened in your profile. Because you want to customize your interface, you can enter something like this:

```
$Shell = $Host.UI.RawUI
$Shell.WindowTitle="PowerShell Obeys Me"
$Shell.BackgroundColor="White"
$Shell.ForegroundColor="Blue"
$size = $Shell.WindowSize
$size.width=120
$size.height=55
$Shell.WindowSize = $size
$size = $Shell.BufferSize
$size.width=120
$size.height=5000
$Shell.BufferSize = $size
Clear-Host
```

Save this file and then open a new PowerShell window. Unless Windows Power Shell was installed and preconfigured for you by someone else, chances are good that all you get is an error that looks something like Figure 2-2.

What's this all about? Believe it or not, this error is Microsoft's way of looking out for you. Remember all those viruses that started spreading like wildfire when Microsoft started shipping Windows Scripting Host (WSH) with Windows

2000? That was because by having WSH installed, you automatically had the ability to run any WSH script, and a lot of malicious people out there took advantage of this behavior to get unsuspecting users to run their code. Well, the folks over in Redmond got a bit smarter this time around and have taken a bit of a more conservative approach. By default, Windows PowerShell won't let you run any script (not even your profile) unless it has been signed using a trusted certificate issued either by a Certificate Authority or a self-generated certificate using the Microsoft .NET Framework Software Development Kit (SDK).

This is really for your protection. Imagine if Windows PowerShell automatically executes a profile script without checking with you first. All a virus or worm writer needs to do is create or replace your PSH profile script, and the next time you open PSH, the malignant profile script will automatically do its nasty deeds.

I'm not going to discuss the creation of certificates or even how to sign scripts right now because I get to that in greater detail in Chapter 22. However, I strongly recommend that if you do decide to use PowerShell heavily in your environment that you take advantage of this security feature. For now, if you want to see how the profile works, you can change the default behavior of PSH and tell it to allow any script that's local to the system but still require any scripts run from other locations (such as network drives) to require a signature. You change this behavior by running this command:

```
Set-ExecutionPolicy RemoteSigned
```

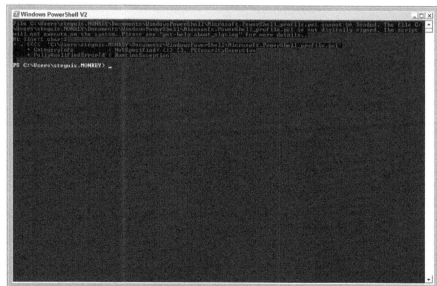

Figure 2-2:
Error
loading the
Windows
PowerShell
profile
script.

By default, the execution policy is *Restricted,* which means no scripts can be run and only interactive commands are allowed. When you change the execution policy to `RemoteSigned`, it eases up this restriction for locally stored scripts. Close your PSH window and open up a brand-new shell and watch how the title, color, and size all change before your very eyes.

Notice the `Clear-Host` command I added at the end of the profile script. All I'm doing is clearing the screen. This command is also useful if you have a lot of things on the screen and want to quickly clear it so you have a blank slate. You can also simply run `cls` to perform this task just as you could do in the traditional Windows shell.

Making the Windows PowerShell ISE Work for You

The Windows PowerShell ISE makes it really easy to work with Windows PowerShell. You launch the PowerShell ISE by choosing Start⇨All Programs⇨Windows PowerShell V2⇨Windows PowerShell V2. Because it's designed around very common Windows concepts, it doesn't take long to figure out how to use it. However, some improvements might not be directly obvious. For instance, getting help has never been easier. Just highlight the Cmdlet you want more help for, press F1, and the handy Windows help file showing the Cmdlet's syntax and all other kinds of useful information is displayed.

If you have the name of a Cmdlet in one of the panes and that pane is active (for example, the script pane or the command pane), pressing F1 automatically brings up the help for that Cmdlet without you selecting the Cmdlet name first.

In the command pane, if you want to enter multiple commands before running them in Windows PowerShell, you can press Ctrl+Enter to go to the next line without running the command in that pane. When you're ready, you can run the command sequence by pressing the green Run button or by pressing Enter.

If you want to run only part of a script or maybe even a single command within a script, you can do so by highlighting the section you want to run and then pressing the Run button. Only the portion of the script that's highlighted runs, rather than the entire script.

Customizing the ISE

Just as the Windows PowerShell console has a $host variable that you can use to access the console object, the ISE has a $psISE variable that lets you access the ISE host. Because you can access and even control the ISE through the $psISE variable, you can customize the color scheme of your ISE through the $psISE variable's options property.

Here's what I get when I check to see what the $psISE.options object contains:

```
PS C:\Windows>$psISE.options
TokenColors                     : {[Attribute, #FFADD8E6], [Command, #FF0000FF],
               [CommandArgument, #FF8A2BE2], [CommandParameter, #
                                  FF000080]...}
DefaultOptions                  : System.Management.Automation.Host.DefaultOptions
FontSize                        : 12
FontName                        : Lucida Console
OutputPaneBackground            : #FFF0F8FF
OutputPaneTextBackground        : #FFF0F8FF
OutputPaneForeground            : #FF000000
CommandPaneBackground           : #FFFFFFF0
ScriptPaneBackground            : #FFFFFFFF
ShowWarningForDuplicateFiles : True
ShowWarningBeforeSavingOnRun : True
LocalHelp                       : True
CommandPaneUp                   : False
ScriptPaneRight                 : False
```

You can change any one of those values to your liking. For instance, you change the output pane background to black by setting the OutputPaneBackground property to black:

```
$psISE.options.OutputPaneBackground="black"
```

As in the Windows PowerShell console, you can put any of these changes into your ISE profile script so that when you launch it, it has all the customizations you want.

Adding your own functions to the ISE menu

By far, one of the best features within the ISE is the ability add your own menu items. This feature allows you to add whatever kind of automation you want and make it available as both a menu item and a keyboard shortcut. To do this, you write your own function then access the $psISe variables's CustomMenu.Submenus collection using the Add method. Here's a very simple bit of code you can stick in your ISE profile script to demonstrate this functionality:

```
function My-Custom-Function
{
    Write-Host "Running my custom function!"
}

$psISE.CurrentPowerShellTab.AddOnsMenu.Submenus.Add("Run Custom Function",
          {My-Custom-Function},"Shift+Ctrl+f")
```

This code defines a simple function called `My-Custom-Function`, which displays the text "Running my custom function!" in the output pane. The `$psISE.CurrentPowerShellTab.AddOnsMenu.Submenus.Add` method takes three parameters. The first parameter is the name you see in the menu. The second parameter defines what to run, which in this case is the `My-Custom-Function` function. The last parameter is the keyboard shortcut you want to assign to it. Here, I assign Shift+Ctrl+F. When I press Shift, Ctrl, and F together on the keyboard, this key sequence causes the function to run as well. You can see how the ISE adds a Custom menu and then adds the submenu item you created using the `Add` method in Figure 2-3.

If you don't want to assign a keyboard shortcut to a menu item, you can just give the value `$null` in its place.

The Custom Menu

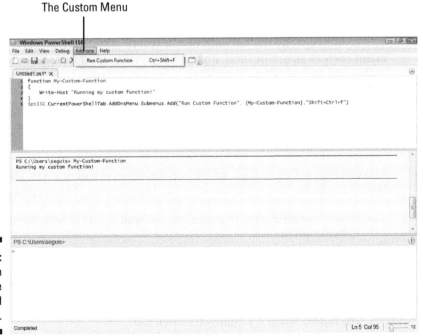

Figure 2-3:
The Custom menu of the PowerShell ISE.

Creating Aliases

As you work more in PSH, you'll notice that you use some commands more than others and, because all Windows PowerShell commands are in the verb-noun format (for example, `Set-ExecutionPolicy`), the length of these commands can get very tedious and error prone. This is where aliases come in handy. An *alias* acts as a second name to whatever command you designate to it. Remember, in the traditional Windows Shell you normally write a batch file to have this kind of behavior. In Windows PowerShell, the alias feature is built in.

For some reason, I find myself using Notepad and the Windows calculator a lot. If I'm in PSH, one of the easiest ways for me to start either of these programs is by typing **notepad** or **calc** in the command line and pressing Enter. Because I'm lazy and like to save myself time whenever possible, rather than typing **notepad** or **calc** I just want to type **np** for notepad or **cl** for calc. You can easily do this by running

```
New-Item alias:cl -value c:\windows\system32\calc.exe
New-Item alias:np -value c:\windows\system32\notepad.exe
```

This method also works for PSH commands such as `Set-Execution`. If you want to run `Set-Execution` by typing `se`, you run

```
New-Item alias:se -value Set-Execution
```

You need to specify the full path only if you're pointing to an external command such as an application. If you change your mind and want the alias `se` to refer to something completely different, you don't need to delete and recreate it. All you have to do is redefine it using the `Set-Item` command. Here's how you change the `se` alias to run a new, made-up command called `Show-Monkeys`:

```
Set-Item alias:se -value Show-Monkeys
```

You can also define various scope options when creating a new alias. A *scope* is just a definition for where an item can be accessed. The scope options are:

- ✔ None: A regular alias that you can use and delete at will. `None` is the default option.
- ✔ Constant: `Constant` aliases can't be deleted, nor have their values changed during the session.
- ✔ ReadOnly: `ReadOnly` aliases are like `Constant` aliases but can be deleted and have its value changed, provided you specify the `Force` parameter when it's changed or deleted.

✔ Private: Private scoped aliases can be seen only with the current scope.

✔ AllScope: AllScope is visible across all new scopes that are created.

You can combine options as well. For example, if you want to make the np alias ReadOnly while the cl alias is Constant with its scope set to AllScope, you can run this:

```
New-Item alias:cl -value C:\windows\system32\calc.exe -options
           "AllScope,Constant"
New-Item alias:np -value C:\windows\system32\notepad.exe -options "ReadOnly"
```

You can also use Set-Item to set the options for an alias after it has been created.

One more thing that you might need at some point is the ability to rename an alias. Suppose you have np defined as the alias for notepad but find that it sometimes gets confused with other commands. You decide that you now want the alias to be called note instead. The good news is you don't have to delete the alias and redefine it; instead, you can take advantage of the Rename-Item command. You can rename the np alias to note using the following command sequence:

```
Rename-Item alias:np -newname note
```

Another way to create and update aliases is using the New-Alias and Set-Alias commands. These are more straightforward than using the New-Item command. Using New-Alias, you can create the np alias with this command sequence:

```
New-Alias np c:\windows\system32\notepad.exe
```

Any alias you create during your PSH session is valid only for that given instance of PSH. As soon as you close that window (which in turn closes the session), all the new aliases you defined no longer exist.

Deleting Aliases

Needless to say, if you can create and update aliases, you also need the ability to delete aliases. Deleting aliases isn't difficult at all because the opposite of New-Item is Remove-Item. If you want to get rid of the se alias you created earlier for Set-Execution, you can run this line:

```
Remove-Item alias:se
```

You can also delete multiple aliases at once. For example, if you define a bunch of aliases such as `myalias1`, `myalias2`, and `myalias3` and now want to get rid of them, you can delete all aliases that start with `myalias` using the following command:

```
Remove-Item alias:myalias*
```

If the alias you're removing happens to be defined with the `ReadOnly` option, you have to use the `Force` parameter to get rid of it (otherwise PSH will spit out an error that it can't be deleted), like so:

```
Remove-Item alias:se -force
```

Accessing the Alias Drive

I'm sure you know that you can use any letter in the alphabet as a drive letter, but what's an alias drive? Drives in PSH have a bit of a different concept. You still have your usual drive letters that map to physical, logical, or network drives, but you can also interact with other special drives. Among them is the alias drive. The *alias drive* is a logical drive that stores aliases.

Think of the alias drive as a virtual drive that's used much like a database for your PSH shell. In this virtual drive, all your aliases are defined as items, where each item contains a name and definition. The *name* is the alias name, and the *definition* is whatever the alias is meant to represent. PSH has a long list of predefined aliases, most of which are there to help users like you to continue using familiar DOS-like commands to do traditional command line tasks. For example, if you run the `DIR` command in PSH, PSH gives you a directory listing, but the output looks a bit different. That's because `DIR` is actually an alias for the `Get-ChildItem` command, which is really different from the "old" `DIR` command but, in the case of listing files and folders, is functionally equivalent.

Want to find out what other aliases are out there? Easy! Run this:

```
Set-Location alias:
Get-ChildItem *
```

At the PSH prompt, the drive shows up as `Alias:\` rather than your usual drive letter. Also notice that there are lots and lots of predefined aliases, and if you browse through the alias list you'll notice a lot of familiar DOS and even Unix/Linux commands in the mix. Notice anything else interesting? Both `Set-Location` and `Get-ChildItem` have aliases, namely `CD` and `DIR` respectively. I know what you're thinking and you're right: This means that the following command sequence and the previous command sequence are equivalent:

```
CD alias:
DIR *
```

How's that for backward compatibility? With this information in hand, I'm sure the command you used for creating aliases (see the section "Creating Aliases," earlier in this chapter) makes more sense. The New-Item command is a generic command used for creating a new item in a given namespace, so when you create your alias you specify the path to the alias drive followed by a colon and then the alias name followed by the value for this item. That command creates an alias item in the alias drive.

The fact that alias definitions can be treated as a drive is also the reason why I chose to use New-Item in my examples for creating a new alias rather than New-Alias — I want you to see the alias drive concept being used.

Any alias you create during your PSH session is valid only for that given instance of PSH. As soon as you close that window (which in turn closes the session), all the new aliases you defined no longer exist.

Creating Persistent Aliases

Although creating aliases for each session is perfectly fine, most of the time aliases are most effective and useful if they're permanently available to you. After all, you spend the time creating an alias to make running Notepad as easy as typing np, but what's the point if you have to redefine this alias every time you open a new PSH window? What you need is a *persistent alias* — an alias that is always defined no matter how many times you close and open that PSH window.

This solution should be obvious to you if you read the "Changing Your PowerShell Profile" section earlier in this chapter. Yes, that's it; you can create persistent aliases by defining aliases in your profile script! Because the profile gets executed every time you open a new PSH window, it's a perfect location to define aliases so they're immediately available to you as soon as you open that window.

PSH also has two nifty commands that can assist you in making these aliases somewhat persistent. You can use the Export-Alias command to export all the alias information to a file and then import it using Import-Alias. This export-then-import method makes defining aliases in your profile very easy because you just need to import aliases from a file. It's also highly useful when you need to define the same set of aliases on multiple computers. You can define them on one system, export the alias definition, and then distribute it to all the other systems (or store it in a central location that can be read by all hosts).

You can easily export and import your aliases with the following command sequence:

```
Export-Alias c:\myaliases.txt
Import-Alias c:\myaliases.txt
```

That wasn't too difficult, was it? Export-Alias has some other useful options you can specify. By default, Export-Alias creates the output file, but if the file already exists the command overwrites the contents of that file. If you want to make sure this doesn't happen, you can use the noclobber parameter so the command returns an error if the file already exists:

```
Export-Alias C:\myaliases.txt -noclobber
```

You can also append to an existing alias file. This feature is great if you have aliases defined in different locations and are trying to consolidate them into a single file. Here's how:

```
Export-Alias C:\myaliases.txt -append
```

Getting to Know Tab Expansion

Tab expansion is one of those great, time-saving features in any command line–driven interface and is really nothing new. After all, this exists even in the traditional Windows command prompt. Windows PowerShell just extends its usefulness. Tab expansion occurs when you enter the partial name of a command, file, or folder and then press the Tab key to automatically complete it for you. As always, you can use Tab expansion to expand a path that you've started to enter at the prompt. If you are at the root of the C: drive and want to get to Windows\System32, an easy way to do this would be the following (assuming you are currently at the root of C:):

1. **Type** CD WIN **then press the Tab key.**

   Unless you have any other folder that starts with Win, the text should automatically expand to Windows.

2. **Immediately after WINDOWS, type** \SYS **and press Tab again.**

   This will automatically expand to the first folder in C:\Windows that starts with SYS. On a typical Windows installation, this will expand to C:\Windows\System.

3. **C:\Windows\System isn't what you want, so keep pressing Tab until it says C:\Windows\System32.**

4. **Now you can press Enter to execute the command and change to that directory.**

Although Tab expansion of file and folder paths is useful, Windows PowerShell now includes the ability to expand commands as well. Not only does expanding commands save time, but it also helps if you remember only the first part of a command and want an easy way to find what commands are available.

Suppose you want to export aliases and somehow forgot that the command is `Export-Alias`. You can open up a command shell, type in **Export-**, and then press the Tab key. Each press of the Tab key shows the next command that starts with the pattern you provided.

You can even use Tab expansion to display available properties or functions of a given object. Remember that code to store the current window size, which I explain earlier in the chapter? Here it is again:

```
$size = $Host.UI.RawUI.WindowSize
```

If you run this command in PSH, you have the current `WindowSize` object stored in `$size`. Now, if you want to change the `Width` property of that object, you would normally type

```
$size.Width = 100
```

With Tab expansion, you can save your delicate fingertips by skipping a few keystrokes. Rather than type **$size.Width**, you can just type **$size.w**, press the Tab key, and *voilà*, PSH automatically types **$size.Width** for you! See the Tab, embrace the Tab, love the Tab . . . it's simply Tabulicious!

If you're absolutely in love with Tab expansion and want more than what's offered out of the box, then you're in luck. Marc von Orouw (MVP Windows Admin Frameworks), otherwise known as the PowerShell guy, created Power Tab, which is an expansion of the Tab expansion feature. (Wow, that was a mouthful.) Think of it as Tab expansion on steroids. You can download it from his blog at `http://thepowershellguy.com/blogs/posh/pages/powertab.aspx`.

Chapter 3

A Pinch of Shell, a Pound of Power

. . . .

In This Chapter

▶ Getting your feet wet with Windows PowerShell

▶ Writing your first script

▶ Previewing a complex script that's as easy as pie

. . . .

*T*hroughout my career, I've found that many Windows administrators shy away from command line interfaces or any kind of scripting. Some reasons for this that have been mentioned to me are "it can be tedious," "there's a lot you need to remember," and "it's easier to make mistakes in a command line." I have to admit that these points have some validity, though this topic is highly debatable. I'm a bit of a 50/50 person myself, switching between command line and GUI tools, depending on the need.

I'm a firm believer that there's always more than one way to do things, and I always like to pick the best tool to get the job done. Some tasks are more efficient if you use a command shell, whereas others are far more convenient and less error-prone when you're using a GUI. If you're lucky, you're one of those who like to work in command line interfaces (CLI), but if not, don't let this bother you. Windows PowerShell is just another tool to help you get more done in less time.

In this chapter, I let you have a go at trying out a few Windows PowerShell scripts to see how easy it is even when doing something relatively complex such as connecting to Active Directory. More importantly, you get to see that scripts that do complex things can be just as short and simple as those that do very mundane things.

Getting a Taste of Windows PowerShell

In keeping with the tradition of understanding any new programming or scripting language, I want to get started with showing you how to display something on the screen. More specifically, I want you to make PowerShell (PSH) write Hello World! on the screen. Lucky for you, it doesn't take much effort — all you need to do is run this line:

```
Write-Output "Hello World!"
```

If you read through the list of predefined aliases by running the Get-Alias command (I cover aliases in Chapter 2), you might notice that the Write-Output command is aliased as echo for compatibility with the old Windows command shell, so the preceding command is equivalent to this:

```
echo "Hello World!"
```

While displaying Hello World! on the screen seems very trivial, ultimately displaying anything on the screen is the most fundamental thing you need to know. After all, no matter how complicated your script is, at some point you'll need to display something on the screen to inform the user about something such as the results of the script or status messages.

Although Write-Output is what echo is aliased to, if you want to output to the screen you can just use Write-Host because it has the added ability to output the text in a color of your choice.

Input and output are, after all, the two most critical things when it comes to computers, so now that you know how to display something on the screen, how can you obtain user input? Well, there's a lot of different ways PSH commands can receive input. If it's a script, you can use command line parameters. You can pass the output of one command as input for another command. You can also take input from the command line, as shown here:

```
$name = Read-Host "What's your name?"
Write-Host ("Hello " + $name)
```

In this example, you use the Read-Host command to prompt the user with the question What's your name? The user must then enter something at the command line in response to this question and then press Enter. The next line outputs Hello followed by the text you entered, as shown in Figure 3-1.

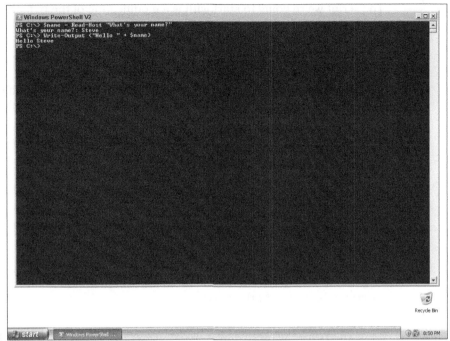

Figure 3-1:
A Windows
PowerShell
input/output
example.

Creating Your First Script

You can create PSH scripts using any text editor, such as Notepad or Graphical
PowerShell. When saving the script, give it a .ps1 file extension so PSH knows
it's a script and not some random text file. This file extension is used in
Windows PowerShell 1.0 and hasn't changed in Windows PowerShell 2 since,
for all intents and purposes, PSH 2 can run PSH 1.0 scripts with no changes to
either the code or the file names.

The file extension is the same for both versions of Windows PowerShell. So, if you
need to prevent someone who has only PSH 1.0 from accidentally running
your PSH 2–specific script, just add #REQUIRES Version 2 at the top of the
script, and you're golden!

The script we're going to start with is a modification of the DIR command and is shown in Listing 3-1.

1. It reads some command line parameter which should specify the path to a folder on your system.

2. It lists the contents of the folder just like DIR, except that you're going to display a color-coded output using green text for files and yellow text for directories.

Listing 3-1: Color-Coded Directory Listing

```
if ($args.count -ne 1) {
    Write-Host "Missing Parameter!" -foregroundcolor "Red"
    exit
}

$folderPath = $args[0]

Write-Host ("Directory listing of " + $folderpath)

# Process each item in the directory
foreach ($i in get-childitem $folderpath) {
    if ($i.mode.substring(0,1) -eq "d") {
        Write-Host $i.name -foregroundcolor "Yellow"
    } else {
        Write-Host $i.name -foregroundcolor "Green"
    }
}
```

To create your first script, follow these steps:

1. **Open Notepad or the Graphical PowerShell and enter the code from Listing 3-1.**

   You can download and use the code listings from the book's Web site (www.dummies.com/go/powershell2fd) instead of having to slog away at typing everything manually.

2. **Now save this on your system somewhere as** mydir.ps1.

   If you're using Notepad, make sure you change the Save As type to All Files before saving; otherwise, it will automatically append a .txt extension to your filename.

3. **Now in your PSH window, run:**

   ```
   c:\scripts\mydir.ps1 C:\
   ```

   This command lists the contents of the root of the C: drive using your newly created script. You see all your filenames displayed in white text, whereas all folder names show up in yellow text.

I'm using `C:\scripts` in this example, but you can change this path to wherever you saved your script.

If your script is in a path that contains one or more spaces, such as `C:\ Documents and Settings\Administrator\Desktop`, in order to run it you have to prefix it with an ampersand and then enclose the it in single quotes, such as `&'C:\Documents and Settings\Administrator\ Desktop\mydir.ps1'`.

If you're already in the directory where you saved your script and you try running it by entering just the script name (such as `mydir.ps1 C:\`), PSH complains saying that it isn't a recognized Cmdlet (the official term used when talking about PSH commands), function, program, or script file. This little complaint is another safety mechanism built into PSH. The current folder isn't automatically added to the search path when you're entering commands. This setup prevents malicious individuals from placing commands or scripts into your folders with the same name as common commands in hopes that you'll accidentally run their version instead.

To run a command that's in the directory you're currently in, you have to prefix it with `.\` (period followed by backslash), like this:

```
.\mydir.ps1 C:\
```

If you didn't change your execution policy to at least `RemoteSigned` (see Chapter 2) to get your profile script working, Windows PowerShell probably won't let you run this script. The command you'll need to run is `Set- ExecutionPolicy RemoteSigned` if you want to allow all local scripts to execute without requiring a signature.

Breaking Down Your First Script

Are you about ready to have a breakdown? Good, because I certainly am. I'm going to take a moment now to break down the script from the previous section and elaborate on how each of the different parts work. The first part of the code deals with handling command line arguments:

```
if ($args.count -ne 1) {
    Write-Host "Missing Parameter!" -foregroundcolor "Red"
    exit
}

$folderPath = $args[0]
```

The first line checks to see whether the number of command line arguments is not equal to 1 because you need to have the path of the folder specified as the first argument (otherwise, you can't do anything). If there isn't exactly one argument, PSH outputs the `Missing Parameter!` message on the screen in red and then exits. If there is exactly one argument, PSH takes the argument and stores it in the `$folderPath` variable. It then displays `Directory listing of` followed by the name of the folder as a heading for the rest of the output:

```
# Process each item in the directory
foreach ($i in get-childitem $folderpath) {
    if ($i.mode.substring(0,1) -eq "d") {
        Write-Host $i.name -foregroundcolor "Yellow"
    } else {
        Write-Host $i.name -foregroundcolor "Green"
    }
}
```

This section of code is a *loop* (a repeating section of code), and if you haven't done any programming before, it might seem a bit confusing. Don't worry; it's not as bad as it looks. The first line (the line starting with #), is a *comment,* which is a line in the script that Windows PowerShell ignores but is useful for someone reading the code.

If you start a line with the # character, you're telling Windows PowerShell that this line is a comment that it can ignore. Programmers use comments to explain what they're doing so it's easier to understand what's going on. It's always a good idea to leave comments in your script for yourself and for anyone else who might take a look at the script later. You can also add a # character at the beginning of a line of code to prevent it from being executed. This is called *commenting out* a section of code and it's something you might do if you're troubleshooting your script and need to prevent a few lines from running without having to delete that part of the code first.

The next line, which begins with `foreach`, establishes the loop. It's saying "for each of objects in the parentheses, perform the action that's defined within the curly braces." That stuff in the parentheses is sometimes called the *condition* for the loop, and in this case contains all the objects returned from running `Get-ChildItem` against the given folder path.

The `Get-ChildItem` command grabs a list of items in the specified path. In this case, it's the path the user of the script provides as a command line parameter. Every iteration of the loop brings back exactly one item, which it stores temporarily in the `$i` variable. Inside the loop it uses `$i` to refer to the single object returned by this particular iteration of the loop.

Each item in a folder contains a set of properties such as its `Name`, `Length` (size), `LastWriteTime`, and `Mode`. *Mode* refers to the various attributes of that item, such as directory (`d`), archive (`a`), read-only (`r`), hidden (`h`), and system (`s`). When you retrieve the value of the `Mode` property, it's returned as a sequence of five characters. Each attribute is given its specific spot within this sequence (`darhs`), and any attribute that isn't set is instead replaced with a dash. For example, a read-only directory would have a `Mode` value of `d-r--`, whereas a file that has the archive, hidden, and system attributes set would return `-a-hs`.

So now you know that if you query the mode property and the item is a directory, the first character in this value is `d`. And that's exactly what you do in your first script; you take the first character in the mode property and check to see if it's `d`. If it is, then the object is a directory, and you use the `Write-Host` command to display the name using yellow as the foreground color; otherwise, the object is just a file and you use green as the foreground color.

I'll leave the discussion about loops at that for now. I go over them in much greater detail in Chapter 6.

Sneaking a Peek at Complex Scripts

Occasionally I like to read fictional books, but I'm not a very patient man so sometimes I sneak to the end to find out what's in store. I don't see it as a spoiler — rather, it makes me more curious, and I want to read more and find out how the story ended up that way. Since the preceding section gives you a taste of an easy script, I thought it might be worthwhile to see Windows PowerShell do something a little more exciting, a bit more difficult, and hopefully a lot more useful. I certainly don't expect you to easily follow along this example, but I do hope that just like getting a peek of the end of a novel, you too will get excited about understanding how all this came to be. Don't worry; the rest of this book will cover all the details for you.

This script is going to be a bit more real-world and requires that you have an Active Directory domain to connect to. I'm also assuming you have some knowledge about Active Directory and Windows Management Instrumentation (WMI). This script queries a particular Organizational Unit (OU) in your Active Directory for a list of computers. It will then use WMI to query various properties of those computers and output it into table format. Take a look at the script in Listing 3-2.

Listing 3-2: Retrieving Computer Information from Computers Belonging to an Active Directory OU

```
$ou = [ADSI]"LDAP://ou=test,dc=testlab,dc=local"
$computers = $ou.PSBase.Get_Children()
$arrInfo = @()
foreach($node in $computers) {
    $arrInfo += Get-WmiObject -query "Select `
                Name,Manufacturer,Model, `
                NumberOfProcessors, `
                TotalPhysicalMemory `
            From Win32_ComputerSystem" `
            -computername $node.Name
}
$arrInfo | format-table Name, Manufacturer, `
        Model, NumberOfProcessors, TotalPhysicalMemory
```

Before I go any further, did you notice something fascinating? Compare this script with the previous script, which did far less than this one. They're practically the same length line-wise. That just shows you how powerful Windows PowerShell really is. With only a few lines of code, not only am I able to query objects in Active Directory, but I'm also able to query the object's properties through WMI and then output it in a nicely formatted table. I did all this without breaking a sweat or hurting my wrists from too much typing.

As you can see in Figure 3-2, this script lists the name, manufacturer, model, number of processors, and total amount of physical memory for each computer in the given OU. For now, I'm assuming that every item in the given OU is a computer. In a real production script, I would put in a lot more error checking between commands and also create filters for the Active Directory query because OUs can contain computers and other types of objects such as users, groups, and contacts.

If you want to see how this script runs on your own system, open your text editor and type it in (or use the file for this listing on the book's Web site). You have to change the LDAP path to and existing OU within your Active Directory, then save it as `complist.ps1`. Now run this script and watch the magic happen.

You'll see that some lines end with a backtick (`) character. This means that the next line is just a continuation of the current line and not a separate command. This is useful if you have very long commands that you want to break up into multiple lines rather than have them keep going on and on to the right.

Don't confuse the backtick (`) with the single quote ('). The backtick character is typically found to the left of the number 1 key on U.S. keyboard (usually above the tab key).

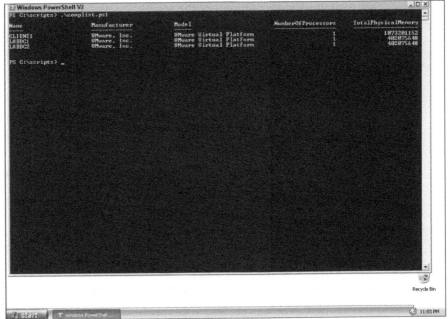

Figure 3-2:
Output from
the Active
Directory/
WMI query
script.

Examining the Nuts and Bolts of the Complist Script

The script in Listing 3-2 is made up of three parts. The first part connects to Active Directory and queries a list of computer names in a specific OU. The next part then queries each computer from that list to retrieve various computer properties using the `Win32_ComputerSystem` WMI class. Finally, the last part displays the results neatly on the screen.

Take a look at these two lines of code that make the up the first part:

```
$ou = [ADSI]"LDAP://ou=test,dc=testlab,dc=local"
$computers = $ou.PSBase.Get_Children()
```

The first line is the easiest way to establish a connection to Active Directory using the Active Directory Services Interface (ADSI). You must provide the correct path to an existing OU or container, or the script will return an error. The next step uses the `PSBase.Get_Children` function to return a *collection* (group) of objects that represent each item in the OU and store it in a variable called `$computers`.

Now examine the second part of the script:

```
$arrInfo = @()
foreach($node in $computers) {
    $arrInfo += Get-WmiObject -query "Select `
                    Name,Manufacturer,Model, `
                    NumberOfProcessors, `
                    TotalPhysicalMemory `
                From Win32_ComputerSystem" `
                -computername $node.Name
}
```

The first thing you do is declare an array called $arrInfo. Don't know what an array is? That's okay — for now, think of an *array* as a sequential grouping of items. (I discuss arrays in more detail in Chapter 11.) The second line starts a foreach loop where you perform one iteration of the loop for each item that's stored in the collection referenced to by the $computers variable. During each iteration of the loop, the current item is temporarily referred to as $node.

You then use Get-WmiObject to query the computer's Win32_Computer System name space and then add this to the $arrInfo array using the += operator. When this loop is done going through all the items in your OU, $arrInfo will essentially contain a collection of objects that in turn contain information regarding the various properties you queried through WMI.

Now take a look at the third and final part of the script:

```
$arrInfo | format-table Name, Manufacturer, `
            Model, NumberOfProcessors, TotalPhysicalMemory
```

In this last part, you feed the contents of the $arrInfo array into the Format-Table command, where you select which columns you want to display and in which order. Format-Table is then responsible for rendering these objects in a pretty table format (refer to Figure 3-2).

See how simple it is to go through all these steps using Windows PowerShell? If you've ever attempted to do to this in VBScript (or even just read through a VBScript or Windows shell script code that does something similar), for example, you'll notice how those scripts are longer than what you have in this powerful yet compact PowerShell script.

One of PowerShell's biggest appeals is that it can cater to people who want to automate things without having a strong programming background. If you have a good programming or scripting background, Windows PowerShell provides some very advanced features that give you much finer control over how you can implement your solutions.

Part II
PowerShell's Basic Structure and Syntax

The 5th Wave   By Rich Tennant

"We're here to clean the code."

Part II

PowerShell's

In this part . . .

You didn't learn to ride a bike or drive a car just by
having someone stick you in one and tell you to go.
Hopefully, someone knowledgeable sat down with you
and showed you the basics, such as where the brakes
were and how to use them before you got going. This part
goes over the really core functionality of Windows
PowerShell that really hasn't changed much since it was
first created. This stuff's the very foundation for almost
everything in Windows PowerShell, so if you had to pick
one part in this entire book to skip, this one isn't it.

Chapter 4

Shelling Out Commands and Scripts

. . . .

. . . .

*I*t's time for you to come face-to-face with Windows PowerShell commands, otherwise known as *Cmdlets* (pronounced *command-lets*). These commands are built on top of the .NET Framework. They are named in a very specific verb–noun format to make it obvious what action the Cmdlet is designed to perform, such as `Get-ChildItem` to retrieve the children of a specific object or `Set-Alias` to set an alias.

If you've been a Windows administrator for a while now, you undoubtedly have a few scripts in your virtual toolbox to make your day-to-day administrative tasks a bit more automated. Windows PowerShell also allows you to continue making use of many of these scripts without any modification right from within the Windows PowerShell environment.

In this chapter, you find out what's so special about Windows PowerShell commands that caused Microsoft to conjure up a completely new name for them. You'll also find out how to read command syntax and how to get help if you don't know what a command does. You get to see how you can run Windows Shell and Windows Scripting Host scripts right from within the PSH command shell.

Cmdlets: The Little Commands That Could!

The first time I ever saw the word *Cmdlet* was back when I started hearing about Windows PowerShell (when it was still called Monad). I thought that it meant something like a pseudo-command. In other words, I thought that Windows PowerShell was comprised of commands that really weren't commands but more like little mini-commands — and in fact, in some ways it is.

For all intents and purposes, Cmdlets are nothing more than Windows PowerShell commands.

Putting Cmdlets under a microscope

If Cmdlets are simply Windows PowerShell commands, it begs the question "Why give it a completely different name?" Yes, I guess it's cute to call commands Cmdlets, but there's more to this than you might think. Cmdlets are actually a bit different from the traditional concept of commands, in which people usually think of compiled console-based executable applications. Instead, Cmdlets are .NET classes usable only within the context of Windows PowerShell that implement some kind of action.

Unless you know a little bit about object-oriented programming (OOP), you may not be familiar with what the term *class* means when I say that Cmdlets are .NET classes. You can think of a class as being the definition or schema of an object. It describes what the object looks like and how it behaves. In this case, Cmdlets are defined within Windows PowerShell as classes that implement their functionality by using .NET code.

Cmdlets are really .NET classes compiled into Dynamic Link Libraries (DLLs) that are loaded by Windows PowerShell. They use the same memory space as the PowerShell process, which is one reason why they are more efficient than console applications.

A Cmdlet's action is very specific, usually targeting a particular kind of object. As a result, the developers of Windows PowerShell set some guidelines regarding how Cmdlets should be named. To ensure that command names are intuitive and descriptive, all Cmdlets are given names in the verb–noun format, in which the verb describes what the Cmdlet does and the noun describes what it acts on. Here are some examples of Cmdlets:

- ✔ Get-Service
- ✔ Set-Date
- ✔ Remove-Item
- ✔ Write-Host

I'm sure that you can guess from their names what the functions of these Cmdlets are. Get-Service retrieves information about services on the system. Set-Date lets you set the date on the system (actually, you use it to set the time as well). Remove-Item deletes an item; what it actually deletes varies depending on the context on which it is used. Write-Host writes something to the host (screen).

Being easy to understand is one of the biggest advantages of this kind of naming convention. The downside is that commands can get pretty long and tedious to type, which is why I cover shortcut techniques such as Tab expansion and aliases earlier in this book (Chapter 2, just in case you skipped it).

Checking out existing Cmdlets

You can find well over 200 Cmdlets defined within Windows PowerShell out of the box. Although the available Cmdlets give you plenty of flexibility in and of themselves, you can install additional Cmdlets from Microsoft (and even from other vendors) to provide more application-specific functionality. Microsoft Exchange 2007, for example, comes with the Exchange Management Shell, which is a set of Cmdlets built on top of Windows Power Shell to provide enhanced Microsoft Exchange management capabilities.

You can find all the Cmdlets that are at your disposal by running

```
Get-Command
```

The default output behavior of this Cmdlet probably doesn't help you much, though. The list of Cmdlets is so long that most of them just scroll right past you, and all you see are the last 40 or so at the end of the list, as shown in Figure 4-1.

You can use a couple of methods to get around this situation. For starters, if your window buffer is large enough, you can just scroll up to view all the commands. Your other alternative is to pass the output of this Cmdlet to the more command so that you see exactly one screen's worth of output at a time; then press the spacebar to go to the next page or press Enter (sometimes referred to as *CR,* for *carriage return)* to see one new line at a time. To pass the output of the Get-Command Cmdlet to the more command, run the following:

```
Get-Command | more
```

You can pass the output of any Cmdlet to another by using the pipe (|) character — a process that's called *piping* the output to another command. I cover pipes in greater detail in Chapter 7.

Figure 4-1:
Output of
the Get-
Command
Cmdlet.

You may have seen some of these Cmdlets in previous chapters and probably can guess what many Cmdlets do just by their names. But how can you find out more about what these Cmdlets are used for and, even more important, how to use them? The definition column to the right of the Cmdlet name (refer to Figure 4-1) is helpful because it shows some of the syntax, but the rest is cut off. Enter the Get-Help Cmdlet.

The Get-Help Cmdlet is your best friend, because if you forget everything you know about every Cmdlet out there, you're safe as long as you remember how Get-Help works. You run Get-Help against a Cmdlet such as Get-Alias by running

```
Get-Help Get-Alias
```

Replace Get-Alias with the Cmdlet name to display the description of that Cmdlet. The default output of Get-Help shows you the Cmdlet name, synopsis (short description), syntax, detailed description, related links, and remarks. Usually, if you've used this Cmdlet before, this level of information is all you need to jog your memory on how to use it.

If you're looking at a Cmdlet for the first time, you can use two other variations of Get-Help to get even more information. Continuing with the Get-Alias example, you can find more information by running one of these commands:

```
Get-Help Get-Alias -detailed
Get-Help Get-Alias -full
```

Both these variations provide a much higher level of detail regarding the Cmdlet in question. The -detailed switch provides more information, whereas the -full switch provides more technical information. For many Cmdlets, the output of Get-Help in conjunction with either of these switches results in the same output. This output not only gives you more information about the Cmdlet (such as detailed explanations of all the parameters it supports), but also gives you many examples to draw from.

Making Cmdlets understand you

When you use Get-Help to view a Cmdlet's information, you see the syntax for using that specific Cmdlet. A Cmdlet sometimes takes a different syntax depending on the context, however, and as a result, the parameters you can or must specify change too. I find that getting things into my head works best when I'm actually doing something, so I want you to use the Get-Service Cmdlet to get familiar with interpreting syntax notation. Enter the following:

```
Get-Help Get-Service
```

Running Get-Help on the Get-Service Cmdlet gives you the output shown in Figure 4-2. Notice that the synopsis tells you that this Cmdlet gets the services on a local or remote computer. The detailed description halfway down the screen expands on this synopsis to let you know that you can also use this Cmdlet to reference a specific service. From that, you gather that this Cmdlet is used to retrieve information about Windows services.

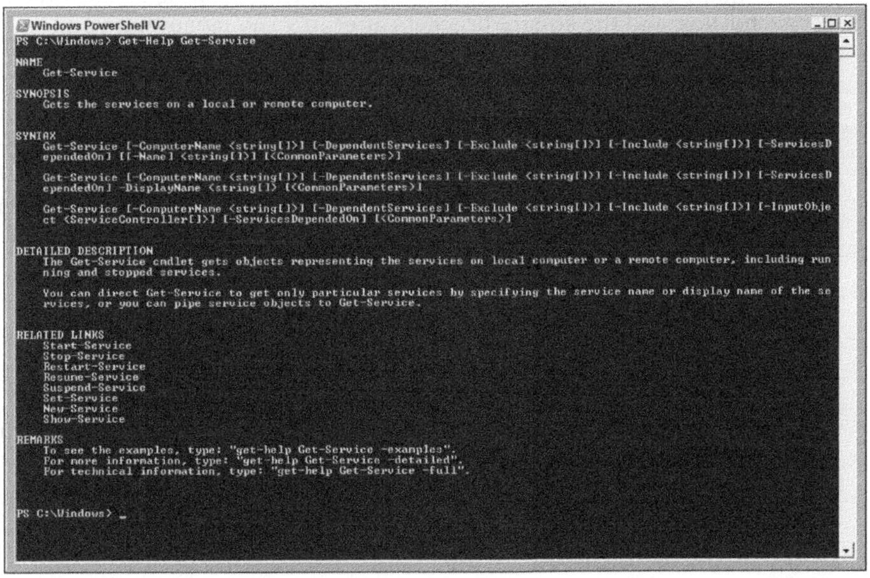

Figure 4-2:
Get-Help output for the Get-Service Cmdlet.

In the traditional Windows command shell, you normally rely on Windows Resource Kit commands such as SC.EXE to get this kind of information. In Windows PowerShell, this feature is built right in. You should also note that the Related Links section in Figure 4-2 lists other Cmdlets that are useful in this context. Not surprisingly, these are Cmdlets to stop, start, suspend, and resume services, as well as one to create a new service and to set various properties of a service. In this one screen, Get-Help gives you a wealth of information. The next step is actually using this command.

When you look at the Syntax section of the Get-Help output, you notice three different ways to use Get-Service, indicated by the three different syntaxes listed. Focus on the first syntax for now:

```
Get-Service [[-ComputerName] <string[]>] [-DependentServices] [-Include
            <string[]>] [-Exclude <string[]>] [-Name <string[]>]
            [-ServicesDependedOn][<CommonParameters>]
```

The names of the parameters typically start with a hyphen (–) so that the Cmdlet knows where a particular parameter starts and where it ends. Parameters in square brackets [] are optional parameters, whereas those in angle brackets <> are required. Then, of course, you see combinations such as [<CommonParameters>]. Is this parameter optional or required?

You have to look at which element encloses the other. In this case, the square brackets come first, which means that the parameter is optional. The angle brackets inside the square brackets mean that the parameter is required, but in this case it's required only in conjunction with certain other specified parameters. To make matters more confusing, you also see those square-bracket pairs after the word string[]. *String* is just a technical word for *text,* and the square brackets after string mean that you can enter one or more strings.

Also, some parameter names are required, whereas others aren't. Take a look at the -Name parameters versus the -ComputerName parameter, and notice the extra set of square brackets enclosing -Name. This extra set of square brackets means that you have the option to leave off -Name when specifying service names. This option usually applies only to parameters that come first in the list. Run these two commands, for example, and notice that they are equivalent:

```
Get-Service -Name eventlog,spooler,wuauserv -ComputerName PC1
Get-Service eventlog,spooler,wuauserv -Computername PC1
```

Because all the service names show up at the beginning of the parameter list, Windows PowerShell can infer that you mean for that list to apply to the -Name parameter. This is why -Name is enclosed in square brackets: to indicate that you can leave it out, just as I did in the previous example.

Although you can save some time by omitting optional parameter names such as -Name for the Get-Service Cmdlet, it's good practice to specify them anyway so that your intentions for those parameters aren't ambiguous.

One Shell to Rule Them All

Whenever a new product or technology is released, there's usually a period in the beginning when the adoption rate of the technology is slow. I usually attribute this slowness to people who aren't willing to let go of their old ways and/or aren't taking a good-enough look at the new stuff to appreciate what's been done. In the case of Windows PowerShell, I think that some users (and by *users,* I mean Windows administrators) have a notion that using it will force them to switch back and forth between PSH and the Windows command prompt to use older scripts or commands.

This is far from the truth. Windows PowerShell is actually smart enough to let you run all your traditional Windows Shell scripts and batch files, as well as scripts based on Windows Scripting Host right from within the Windows PowerShell console. (I cover WSH in more detail later in this chapter.)

Windows Shell scripts

Windows Shell scripts and batch files have existed forever. I'm sure that you already have a whole slew of them sitting all over your hard drive. People who are looking at Windows PowerShell for the first time, though, and are starting to understand Cmdlets and aliases sometimes think that Windows PowerShell is no longer capable of running Windows Shell scripts.

If you recall, most (if not all) of the built-in commands for the traditional command prompt are aliased in Windows PowerShell to a Cmdlet, such as DIR being aliased to Get-ChildItem and Echo being aliased to Write-Output. If you run DIR /W at the Windows PowerShell prompt, it won't work because the /W switch isn't valid for Get-ChildItem, even though it's valid for the real DIR command. Given that information, it's easy to see why people don't think batch files will work in Windows PowerShell: Windows Shell scripts that rely on these commands won't work. Or will they?

Open Notepad, enter the following Windows Shell script, and save it as test.cmd:

```
@ECHO OFF
ECHO My Old Windows Shell Script
Set X=0
for /f "tokens=*" %%i in ('DIR /B C:\') do call :output "%%i"
ECHO Script Complete!
goto :EOF

:output
Set name=%1
Set /A X=X+1
echo %X% - %name%
goto :EOF
```

I don't know how well versed you are in Windows Shell, but basically, this script takes a list of file and folder names at the root of C:\ and then displays it onscreen with a prefix. This prefix is a sequential number starting from 1 followed by a space, a dash, and then another space. Knowing how this Windows Shell script works really isn't important, but I want to show you how it behaves in the traditional command prompt and in Windows PowerShell.

Now that you have the test.cmd script saved somewhere (such as C:\scripts), open a Windows command prompt (cmd.exe) and then execute this script by running

```
C:\scripts\test.cmd
```

Again, change the path to wherever you saved test.cmd, and enclose it in double quotes if the path contains a space. Figure 4-3 shows the Windows command-prompt output.

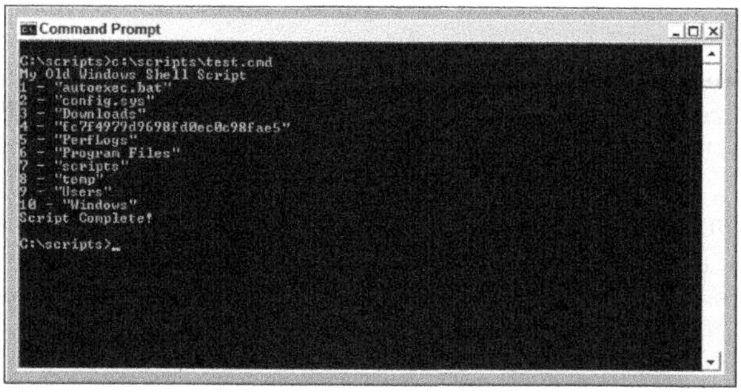

Figure 4-3:
Output of
test.cmd in
a Windows
command
prompt.

Now open Windows PowerShell, type the same command (`C:\scripts\test.cmd`), and press Enter. Take a look at the output in Figure 4-4.

Figure 4-4:
Output of
test.cmd in
a Windows
PowerShell
window.

Do you notice any differences (besides the different-color backgrounds)? Hint: There are none!

Going back to the source code for `test.cmd`, notice the call to `DIR /B C:\` that's used to return the list of names of files and folders at the root of `C:\`. Go back to your Windows command prompt, and run `DIR /B C:\`. The command returns the list of file and folder names as expected, right? Now switch over to your Windows PowerShell window, and run the same command. Windows PowerShell spits out the following error:

```
Get-ChildItem : Cannot find path 'C:\B' because it does not exist.
At line:1 char:4
+ DIR <<<<  /B C:\
```

That's strange! If the command doesn't run in Windows PowerShell, how is it that the Windows Shell script works? I'm not going to blurt out the answer. Instead, I want you to see for yourself. Close out of any Windows command prompts you have open. Open Windows Task Manager (just right-click the taskbar and choose Task Manager); then go to the Processes tab and click Image Name to sort the list of processes alphabetically. Make sure that no `cmd.exe` processes are running.

Open `test.cmd` in Notepad again, and replace the `ECHO Script Complete!` line with the word `PAUSE` so that the script looks like this:

```
@ECHO OFF
ECHO My Old Windows Shell Script
Set X=0
for /f "tokens=*" %%i in ('DIR /B C:\') do call :output "%%i"
PAUSE
goto :EOF

:output
Set name=%1
Set /A X=X+1
echo %X% - %name%
goto :EOF
```

Save the changes, and rerun `test.cmd`. This time, the script stops with the prompt `Press any key to continue . . .`, due to the newly added `PAUSE` statement within the Windows Shell script. Don't do anything inside the PSH window, and go back to your Task Manager's Processes tab. Notice something interesting? Yes, a new `cmd.exe` process is running, as shown in Figure 4-5.

Go back to the Windows PowerShell window, and press any key to continue. Take a look at Task Manager again. The `cmd.exe` process is gone. Do you have any idea now what's going on?

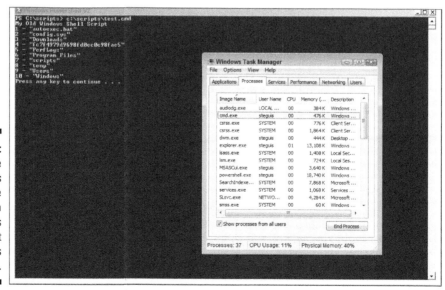

Figure 4-5:
Cmd.exe
process
shown while
running a
Windows
Shell script
in Windows
PowerShell.

Well, it turns out that Windows PowerShell is performing some magic in the background. It *spawns* (starts) a new cmd.exe process, which is the old Windows command prompt, in the background and executes the Windows Shell script in there. Windows PowerShell acts as a host, redirecting any input to or output from this hidden command prompt to the Windows PowerShell display, and what you're left with is the illusion that Windows PowerShell did all the work for you.

Yes, I know that Windows PowerShell is really faking it and running your Windows Shell scripts and batch files in a hidden Windows command prompt, but here's the cool part: You can still run your Windows Shell scripts as you always have for years without ever leaving Windows PowerShell. Now you can just keep working in your PSH console, running your old scripts the way you always have, and then, when you feel like it, using some Cmdlets for other things. This practice is a great way to get yourself started using PSH without feeling by having to switch between different command shells.

Windows Scripting Host

Windows Shell scripts are great because they're easy to put together, but you're limited to the built-in commands and any other command line applications you can get your hands on. Usually, when you're creating more powerful scripts that do things like manipulate databases or Active Directory, you use Windows Scripting Host (WSH), because you can use VBScript or JScript to interact with some of the rich interfaces that WSH exposes.

These scripts are saved in files with names ending in a .vbs extension for VBScript source files and .js for JScript source files, and are run with WScript.exe or CScript.exe. Examine this very simple WSH script written in VBScript:

```
WScript.Echo "Starting WSH Test Script..."
For i = 1 to 5
        WScript.Echo i
End
WScript.Echo "WSH Test Script Complete!"
```

Even if you've never written any VBScript before, I'm sure you can guess that this script displays a count from 1 to 5 onscreen, preceded and followed by some other miscellaneous text. Type this script in Notepad, save it as C:\scripts\samplewsh.vbs, and run it in Windows PowerShell by typing C:\scripts\samplewsh.vbs at the PSH prompt and pressing Enter.

The output of this script depends on the default host you've set for WSH. WSH supports two hosts: `WScript.exe` and `CScript.exe`. These two scripting hosts aren't too different; the main difference involves the way they display output. When you use `Cscript.exe`, it uses a command shell to display output, just as a regular Windows Shell script does. `WScript.exe`, on the other hand, is a graphical host and displays the output in dialog boxes. *Note:* WScript opens a dialog box for every `WScript.Echo` statement in your script, and you must acknowledge the dialog that pops up by clicking the OK button before the script continues.

You can change the default host in Windows PowerShell just as you do in a command prompt. To change the default host to cscript, run `CSCRIPT //H: CSCRIPT`. To change it back to wscript, run `WSCRIPT //H:WSCRIPT`.

This behavior is no different from running WSH scripts from a command prompt, which is exactly what you want. Running any WSH script causes it to be executed with either Wscript.exe or Cscript.exe and then runs as it normally would. Again, this doesn't change the way you work with WSH scripts, so you can continue using your old WSH scripts (or any new ones you want to create) just as you would before. You no longer have an excuse to stay away from Windows PowerShell.

Chapter 5

When Dollars Turn into Variables

. . . .

. . . .

*V*ariables are one of the key building blocks of any scripting and programming language. Without them, you wouldn't be able to store values,
easily manipulate objects, or use Windows PowerShell for anything more
than simple tasks.

For some reason, every time I think of variables, I'm taken back to the dark
days of high school algebra. Don't get me wrong; I actually ended up doing
quite well in algebra, but in the beginning I had an unusually hard time getting the idea that some letter such as x could represent some seemingly
arbitrary value. Once I finally grasped this enlightening idea, the rest of my
mathematical learning experience was smooth sailing. (Okay, I admit it; cal-
culus did throw me a curve ball, but I got through it!)

Variables in Windows PowerShell are just like variables in other scripting and
programming languages in that they are names of things that represent some
value, just as the almighty x in algebra always represents something else.
Without variables, it would be difficult to make any useful scripts because
you wouldn't be able to store any state information or preserve any values.
In short, you wouldn't have any ability to know what happened in any other
part of the script. In this chapter, I discuss what variables are as well as how
they're represented and used in Windows PowerShell.

Discovering Variables: They Vary Very Much

Variables are names of things that represent some value or object. In Windows PowerShell, all variable names are prefixed with the dollar sign ($). The variable names themselves can contain a mix of letters, numbers, and symbols, including spaces. Although you can get away with using symbols and spaces in variable names, I recommend against it whenever possible — if you use symbols and spaces, you have to remember to enclose the variable name in curly braces. Here are some examples of variables:

- ✔ `$MyVariable`
- ✔ `$AVariableWithANumber6`
- ✔ `${A variable with spaces}`
- ✔ `${A variable with special characters @#%%}`

The use of curly braces around the variable name gives you the flexibility to use almost any name you can come up with. Although you may be tempted to use variable names with spaces to come up with more descriptive variable names, the use of camel case notation, such as what I did with `$MyVariable`, can be just as effective without the extra drama.

Camel case notation is the practice of combining words without spaces by capitalizing the first letter of each word and using lowercase for subsequent letters in that word, as in `ThisIsAnExampleOfCamelCase`. This is especially useful for variable names because it allows you to use very descriptive names without having to resort to using spaces and still maintains legibility.

If you're familiar with other scripting languages, such as Perl, the syntax of prefixing variable names with dollar signs is very familiar to you. This is the easiest and most direct method for defining a variable. You can also explicitly define a variable using the `Set-Variable` Cmdlet to get additional control over the advanced properties of the variable, such as its scope and description. You can find out more about this Cmdlet by running the following command at the PowerShell prompt:

```
Get-Help Set-Variable
```

Getting to Know Data Types

You can use variables in Windows PowerShell to store practically any kind of value, whether it's a number, character, string, or even an object (more on this in the section "Working with Objects through Variables," later in this chapter). These different kinds of values are known as *data types*. Variables that can take on any data type are called *variants,* and most scripting languages use them because they offer ease of use and overall flexibility.

Windows PowerShell actually contains a potentially infinite number of data types. *Basic* data types cover all of what are called primitive values. *Primitive values* are values you would typically expect to store as data and are the fundamental building blocks of the more complex data types. The basic data types are

✔ Boolean: True or false condition.

✔ Byte: An 8-bit unsigned whole number from 0 to 255, such as 32.

✔ Char: A 16-bit unsigned whole number from 0 to 65,535. For example, 1,026.

✔ Date: A calendar date, such as January 1, 2009.

✔ Decimal: A 128-bit decimal value, such as 3.14159265.

✔ Double: A double-precision 64-bit floating point number. In effect, this is another kind of decimal value but has a narrower range of values than a decimal.

✔ Integer: A 32-bit signed whole number from –2,147,483,648 to 2,147,483,647, such as 152 or –1839.

✔ Long: A 64-bit signed whole number. This is like an integer but holds far more values, such as 9,233,372,036,854,775,807.

✔ Object: Any kind of object. Sound a little vague? Okay, let me discuss this a little further.

The object data type is a bit misleading because it's really a way of referring to practically all the other data types that can exist. This is where that "potentially infinite number of data types" comes into play. Anyone can create new data types by defining their structure in the form of a class. A *class* is simply a definition of this new data type.

For example, if you want to have some data type that represents an address, you can create a class called Address with various properties such as street, city, state, country, zip, and so on. When you actually create things (well, virtual things in memory) from this class, the thing created is called an *object.*

To sum it all up, an object is an instance of a class, just like the number 2,432 can be an instance of an integer.

✔ Short: A 16-bit unsigned whole number. This is like an integer but holds far fewer values. It can only hold values from –32,768 to 32,767.

✔ `Single`: A single-precision 32-bit floating point number. This is like a `double` but holds far fewer values, such as 20.3654.

✔ `String`: A grouping of characters that most people just call text.

Programmers use the word *string* a lot, but if you don't have a programming background you might not know what it means in this context. In programming terminology, it simply means a consecutive grouping of characters (what the rest of the world simply calls text). I'm fairly certain there's some history around why it's called a string and who came up with it, but I just like to think it's because a consecutive grouping of characters form a string of characters hence the name *string* to keep it short. A string can have zero or more characters. A string with no characters is called an *empty string* or a *null string*. In general, you define a string by enclosing it in double quotes, such as `"This is a string"`.

Dealing with data types

Data types can be a double-edged sword. Sometimes knowing or being able to specify exactly what you intended the variable's contents to be interpreted as can make a whole world of difference when you use them. Likewise, not knowing what the data types are can lead to some very strange effects. For example, take this very simple Windows PowerShell code snippet:

```
$a = 1
$b = 2
$c = $a + $b
write-output $c
```

Even if you've never written a single line of code before, you can probably guess what this script displays. (Here's a clue . . . the answer is 3!) But what if 3 isn't what you intended it to display? Windows PowerShell uses the plus (+) operator not only to add numbers together, but also to combine strings (in other words, put two pieces of text together).

In the example, I added two numbers to produce some output. What if I actually intended to combine the two numbers as two individual characters so that the output isn't 3 but rather 12; in other words, the character 1 followed by the character 2. With the way it's written in the example, PowerShell tries to be smart and sees that I'm using the + operator to combine two numbers, so it logically assumes that I want these values to be added as two numbers. If you want to combine the previous two as strings, you run the following code instead:

```
$a = "1"
$b = "2"
$c = $a + $b
write-output $c
```

By enclosing the numbers in quotes, you're telling PowerShell that you want them treated as string literals rather than numbers. *String literals* is the term used for a string that's explicitly defined by enclosing the text in quotation marks. When you then combine them with the + operator, PowerShell sees you want to combine two strings, so it *concatenates* (joins) the two together, and in this example, the output is 12.

If you combine a number and a string, the number is automatically converted to a string, and the two are combined. Taking the preceding snippet as an example, you only really need to put one of the values in quotes, and Windows PowerShell automatically converts the value of the other one when it tries to combine the two.

Explicitly defining the data type

The example in the preceding section is one way of explicitly telling Windows PowerShell the data type of the value for ambiguous data types such as numbers. Another way of defining a data type is to actually restrict the type a variable can store. You can even convert a value to another data type.

Out there in the programming world, the terms *data type* and *type* are used interchangeably. For the this book, I stick with just the term *data type*. That's less confusing for both you and me!

Why in the world would you ever want to limit the type of values that a variable can store or explicitly convert a value to another data type? At first, it seems like an unnecessary step, especially when PowerShell is more than capable of figuring out the data type of the value you're assigning to each variable, but there are quite a few good reasons to do so:

- ✔ **Surprise! Unexpected values:** One of the best reasons for limiting the data type is to safeguard the variable from inadvertently being assigned a value of an unexpected data type. In a real-world script that can contain hundreds of lines of code, it's very easy to accidentally assign a value to a variable that you didn't intend to. This usually introduces bugs that are very difficult to track down (the ones that you smack yourself on the head for later when you find them!).

- ✔ **Clarity:** Defining the data type eliminates ambiguity for the variable so that PowerShell performs the operation you actually want it to do rather than what it *thinks* you wanted it to do.

- ✔ **Improved performance:** Defining the data type can help performance a little bit by allowing PowerShell to make certain optimizations during its execution because it doesn't need to guess what the variable might contain.

Here's a simple example. Suppose you want to define a variable called $IntegerOnly that you want to be able to store integers and only integers. This is done by declaring the variable as an int data type. The following code snippet shows how you can accomplish this and also what happens if you try to assign another data type to this variable:

```
[int]$IntegerOnly = 100
$sum = 2 + $IntegerOnly
write-output $sum
$IntegerOnly = "PowerShell Rules!"
write-output $IntegerOnly + " Yes, it does!"
```

When I declare $IntegerOnly, I prefix it with [int], telling PowerShell that this variable can store only values of data type int. When I output the value of $sum, it displays the expected value of 102. I then try to assign the value "PowerShell Rules!" to $IntegerOnly, and the next output statement should display "PowerShell Rules! Yes, it does!" If you run this code snippet, you'll see that doesn't quite work. Why not?

Windows PowerShell complains about assigning the string "PowerShell Rules!" to $IntegerOnly. This is because I used the [int] prefix to instruct Windows PowerShell to allow only integer data types to be stored in $IntegerOnly. Because Windows PowerShell can't automatically convert a string to an integer, it throws an error that it can't convert the value "PowerShell Rules!" to data type "System.Int32".

There's a really easy way for you to find out the type of value that a variable contains. You can use the GetType() method on the variable, which returns data type information about the value stored by it. Going back to my earlier example, to verify that $IntegerOnly is indeed an integer you can run this line:

```
$IntegerOnly.GetType().Name
```

Windows PowerShell is built on top of the .NET Framework, so it isn't any surprise that variables in PowerShell are objects just as they are in the .NET Framework. This means that while they're used for storing and retrieving values, they also have their own set of properties and methods. GetType() is one of them and actually returns an object that contains more than just the data type name. It also includes the following information: IsPublic, IsSerial, Name, and BaseType. I use the .Name property of the object in the preceding code because I'm interested only in the data type name, but you can simply run GetType() on the variable without specifying a property, and Windows PowerShell retrieves all the information for you.

Also, as I mention earlier in my discussion about the different data types and objects, the data types that each variable can represent are endless (essentially, any data type that can be defined in .NET). You can simply put the data type name in the square brackets, such as [System.Text]. Because it would be insanely tedious to use this full name for the most common data types, PowerShell defines many *data type shortcuts* which have much simpler abbreviated names. Table 5-1, lists some of the more commonly used data type shortcuts.

Table 5-1	Common Data Type Shortcuts	
Data Type Shortcut	*Description*	*Full Type Name*
[bool]	True or False	System.Boolean
[byte]	8-bit unsigned character	System.Byte
[char]	16-bit unicode character	System.Char
[int]	32-bit signed integer	System.Integer
[long]	64-bit signed integer	System.Long
[decimal]	128-bit decimal value	System.Decimal
[single]	32-bit floating point value (single precision)	System.Single
[double]	64-bit floating point value (double precision)	System.Double
[string]	A string of unicode characters	System.String
[array]	An array of values or objects	System.Array
[xml]	An XML object	System.Xml.XmlDocument
[wmi]	Windows Management Instrumentation object	System.Management.ManagementObject

Casting values

When I say I'm "casting values," I'm not trying to start new Broadway musical. *Casting* refers to the process of changing a variable's data type from one value to another. For example, what happens when you try to add an integer to a double? Going back to the simple plus (+) operator, when you try to combine two or more data types, Windows PowerShell internally performs a series of steps for you to make it all work:

1. PowerShell compares the two (or more) data types being combined. If they match, it simply continues.

a. If the data types are different, PowerShell attempts to cast (convert) the values to a common data type.

b. PowerShell attempts to look for a data type that can store the values being converted without losing its original value and tries to convert the values to this data type.

   Because PowerShell does this, you don't lose any data during the conversion. For example, when combining an integer and a double, PowerShell converts the integer to a double because the double is the larger data type. If PowerShell can't find a data type that can accommodate all values being combined, it throws an error.

2. When all the data types are the same, PowerShell combines the values and returns the resulting value.

   The resulting data type is the data type all the values were converted to.

In the previous section, you define a variable using the square brackets to assign it a specific data type. Well, you can also use the square brackets to force Windows PowerShell to cast a data type to a different data type. You've seen how an integer and a string are combined automagically. Naturally, if you want to combine a double and a string, you can run the following commands:

```
$MyString = " Windows PowerShell "
$MyDouble = 2.0
$outstring = $MyString + $MyDouble
write-output $outstring
```

Not surprisingly, the output of the preceding commands is `Windows PowerShell 2.0`. For fun, I'm going to switch the order by which the two variables are combined by changing the `$outstring` line with this command:

```
$outstring = $MyDouble + $MyString
```

When you run this, it gives you an error saying it can't convert the string to a data type `System.Double`. It was just working, so what's going on here? Although a double can easily be converted to a string, Windows PowerShell tries to convert the string to a double because it appears first in the order of evaluation. It obviously can't do this because the string doesn't contain a valid double value, hence an error is thrown.

You can get around this by explicitly casting the double to a string, so in effect you're controlling what data type the variables get converted to rather than relying on Windows PowerShell to get it right:

```
$outstring = [string]$MyDouble + $MyString
```

You cast a value by prefixing the variable name or value with [*data_type*]. This is the same syntax for defining a variable of a fixed data type, but in this context you aren't redefining the variable but rather temporarily converting it to a new data type. **Note:** Windows PowerShell tries its best to make this happen for you, but some things just won't work. For example, you can't try to cast a string that doesn't contain purely numerical characters into a number.

You can also cast a variable using the -as operator:

```
$outstring = ($MyDouble -as [string]) + $MyString
```

There are some differences between the two methods, but for the most part they're interchangeable. You should use the -as operator because it's the preferred method for casting values, but if you want you can shorthand it by simply prefixing the value or variable with the data type as you did earlier.

Windows PowerShell performs quite a lot of operations when combing values and more so when you ask it to do data type conversion. It's all really dependent on the data type of the current value and what you're converting it to. If you want to see what happens when you explicitly cast a $MyDouble to a string before combining with $MyString, you can run this line:

```
Trace-Command -Name TypeConversion -pshost {[string]$MyDouble + $MyString}
```

You can see what the debug information looks like in Figure 5-1. This command is very useful as you can see in great detail every step Windows PowerShell takes as it combines the two values. You can enclose any expression you want in the curly braces to have it debugged. You can also use the Trace-Command Cmdlet to debug other tasks, not just Type Conversion. Read the Type Conversion help using the Get-Help Cmdlet to find out more.

You should try to get yourself very well acquainted with data types. You can probably get away with not knowing all the possible data types, but you at least should be comfortable working with the most common ones. Specifically, you should understand what values are valid for each data type and also how they behave when combined with other variable types. For example, if you combine an integer with a string, the integer gets converted into a string, and these two are then joined (concatenated) together as strings to produce a new string. Not understanding this can lead to bugs in your scripts that can become very difficult to troubleshoot.

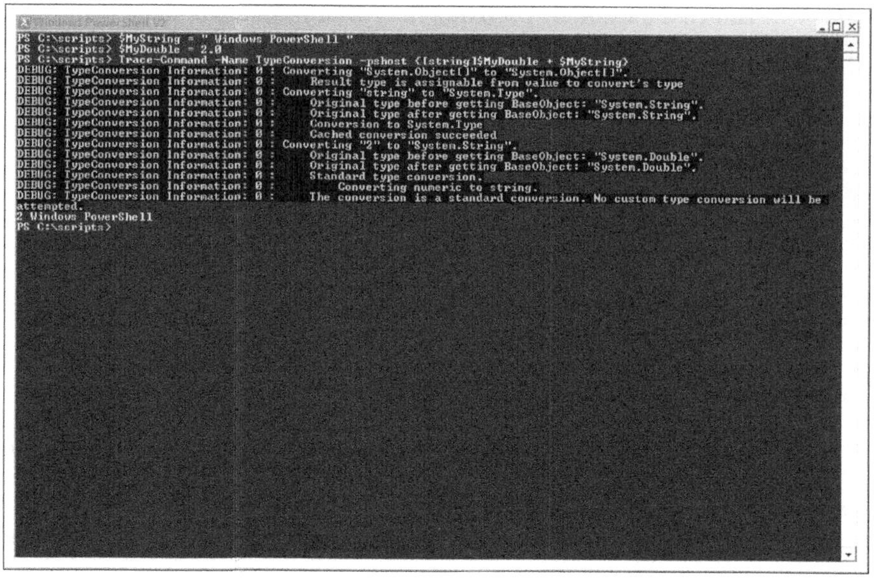

Figure 5-1:
Debugging
Type
Conversion.

Constant and Read-Only Variables

Variables are (by virtue of their name) variable, so having a constant or read-only variable seems like quite an oxymoron. In most scripting and programming languages, these are simply called *constants* or *named constants,* but essentially they're actually special variables that are marked to hold a constant value set during their initialization, in effect making them read-only. Windows PowerShell takes it one step further and makes a distinction between constant and read-only variables.

There is a distinct difference between a constant variable and a read-only variable even though they're functionally equivalent. The two are similar in that constant and read-only variables are both initialized with a value upon declaration and that they maintain that value. The difference is that while you can't change a read-only value, you can delete it, whereas constant variables can't be change or deleted and exist for the duration of the session (until you close the PowerShell window).

You must use the `Set-Variable` Cmdlet in order to set a constant or read-only variable. You can then use `Remove-Variable` to delete a read-only variable. (**Remember:** You must exit the Windows PowerShell console completely before a constant variable is released.) The following example shows how you can define and use constant and read-only variables and also how to clear a read-only variable:

```
Set-Variable PI 3.14159265 -option Constant
Set-Variable Author "Steve Seguis" -option ReadOnly
$radius = 3
$area = $PI * $radius * $radius
write-output "Area is: " + $area
write-output "This book is written by: " + $Author
Remove-Variable Author -force
```

You use the `-option` switch for the `Set-Variable` Cmdlet to specify if the variable being defined is constant or read only. The first parameter is the name of the variable, and the second parameter is the value to assign to it. Notice how you don't use the dollar sign character ($) in the variable name. When using `Set-Variable`, you simply specify the variable name without using the dollar sign.

Dollar signs are only required when defining variables without using the `Set-Variable` Cmdlet.

After the constant or read-only variable is defined, you can use them as you would any other variable except you can't change its value. The last line in the example shows how you use the `Remove-Variable` Cmdlet to get rid of a read-only variable. `Remove-Variable` is a Cmdlet used to remove any variable. If you don't specify the `-force` parameter, PowerShell won't let you remove a read-only variable and will throw an error if you try.

I prefer using read-only variables rather than constant ones unless it's a variable I want to ensure remains in effect throughout my entire session. Read-only variable types are extremely useful in scripts where you want to define some fixed values (such as the value of PI or a buffer size) and protect them against accidental changes during the script's execution. They're also highly efficient because Windows PowerShell knows not only what data type the value is, but also that it won't change and can allocate and store it in memory most efficiently.

Understanding Automatic Variables

You can call a variable almost anything you want. The "almost" part of that sentence is because some variables are special to Windows PowerShell and are reserved for its own use. They're called *automatic variables* because PowerShell is in charge of managing them for you. Not only are they one less thing you have to worry about (other than remembering not to try redefining them yourself), but they're also extremely useful variables that you'll undoubtedly use time and time again. You can see a list of all the automatic variables and what they contain in Table 5-2.

I didn't magically know all these variables. I got this information thanks to Windows PowerShell's really cool `help` command. If you want more information about automatic variables, you can run the following command and to get more details about each of these variables:

```
get-help about_automatic_variables
```

Table 5-2	Automatic Variables
Variable Name	**Description**
`$$`	Contains the last token in the last line received by the shell.
`$?`	Contains the state of the last operation. True when successful, false otherwise.
`$^`	Contains the first token in the last line received by the shell.
`$_`	Contains the current object in the pipeline object.
`$Args`	An array of undeclared parameters or values passed to a function, script, or script block.
`$ConsoleFileName`	Stores the filename of the most recently exported console file.
`$PSCulture`	Contains the current culture used by the OS.
`$Error`	An array of error objects representing the most recent errors.
`$ExecutionContext`	Contains an `EngineIntristics` object that represents the execution context of the Windows PowerShell host.
`$False`	This one's a shocker. It contains the value `FALSE`.
`$ForEach`	Contains the enumerator of a `foreach-object` loop.
`$Home`	Stores the full path to the user's home directory.
`$Host`	Current host application for Windows PowerShell.
`$Input`	Contains the object currently in the pipeline in the `Process` block of a function.

Variable Name	Description
$LastExitCode	Contains the exit code of the last Windows program executed.
$MyInvocation	Contains information about the current command. Useful for dynamically retrieving the filename and path of the current script.
$NestedPromptLevel	Stores the current prompt level for nested prompts. This is a bit advanced, so you may want to run the get-help about_automatic_variables command for additional information.
$NULL	Contains NULL or empty value.
$PID	Contains the process identifier of the Windows PowerShell process.
$Profile	Stores the full path to the Windows PowerShell user profile for the default shell.
$PSHome	Stores the full path to the installation of Windows PowerShell.
$PSVersionTable	A hash table containing details about the version and build of the current Windows PowerShell console.
$Pwd	Stores the full path to the current directory.
$ShellID	Contains the identifier for the current shell.
$True	Contains TRUE.
$PSUICulture	Stores the name of the UI culture currently in use.

As you can see, quite a few automatic variables get created and are managed by Windows PowerShell during its execution. Some of them seem pretty useless at first glance. For example, you have the two opposing variables, $True and $False. You might be wondering why you would need to have these variables when you can simply use the words True and False for the values like many other scripting languages. The reasoning is because it's possible to mistake the string as False with the value True. I've got you scratching your head, haven't I? In short, it's because the word False can get confused as a string, and any non-empty string is True.

Why would False ever evaluate to True? In scripting languages such as VBScript, you usually assign `True` or `False` values simply by using those words directly. The danger with the word False is that if it's somehow misinterpreted as the string `"False"` rather than the Boolean meaning of False then it evaluates to `True`. This is because any number that is non-zero and any string that is non-empty is automatically treated as True in a Boolean statement. This is also the same reason why the automatic variable `$NULL` is defined. The string `NULL` is supposed to mean nothing (undefined/empty) but it can be misinterpreted as the string `"NULL"`, which is a non-empty string and would evaluate to `True` instead. Yes, it is a bit overkill, but by defining these values as automatic variables that have permanent and definite meaning, Windows PowerShell can safeguard their values so there is no ambiguity in their use.

You can see many of these automatic variables used throughout this book, and I hope that gives greater meaning to them. If you just take a moment and go over them, you can see how they can be quite useful. Suppose that, at some point in the future, a new version of Windows PowerShell is released, and you write your script to take advantage of those new features and want to protect it from being executed against unsupported versions. You can query the values in the `$PSVersionTable` hash table and get all the information you need (from the running Windows PowerShell console all the way to the build number) and compare it with what you want the environment you designed the script to run in to be. For example, you can check whether the version and build number are greater than a certain value.

`$Pwd` is another great variable to have. If you've ever had to write a Windows shell script (batch file) to find out the current path that you're in, you know how convoluted that process is. Typically, you have to run the `DIR` command in a loop, parse out the current directory, and assign it to a variable. In PowerShell, all you need to do is read the `$Pwd` variable and you're done! It's so easy, it makes me feel guilty using it.

Working with Objects through Variables

Because variables point to objects, you can treat them as the object itself — which also means you can manipulate and retrieve information from the referenced objects through the variable name. A simple object to deal with is a string. A *string,* which is nothing more than text, has many properties and methods that are quite interesting. You can retrieve how long the string is (how many characters it contains). You can find out what character is in a given position or likewise the position of a certain character within the string. You can even manipulate the string in different ways, such as returning its value in all upper or all lowercase.

I have a whole chapter dedicated to strings (see Chapter 9), but I use some quick examples here to give you a feel for how this manipulation takes place using variables. Consider the following code snippet:

```
$firstname = "Dan"
$lastname = "Daman"
$fullname = $firstname + " " + $lastname
write-output $fullname
```

As you can see, there's nothing special going on here, and the output is clearly going to be Dan Daman. What if you want to display how many characters are in $fullname and you want to display the value of $fullname so that all characters are in uppercase? Not a problem; it's really easy. String objects conveniently have a property called length that dynamically stores the length of the string at any given time. String objects also have a method called ToUpper() that returns the string object all in uppercase letters. With these two pieces of information, you can then solve this problem by running the following code:

```
$firstname = "Dan"
$lastname = "Daman"
$fullname = $firstname + " " + $lastname
write-output "Length of full name: " + $fullname.length
write-output "Full name is: " + $fullname.ToUpper()
```

Notice how I use length without the parentheses and I use parentheses for ToUpper. That's because properties are generally directly accessible values, whereas ToUpper is a method that internally converts the text to uppercase before returning its value. The dot between the variable name and the property or method name is commonly referred to as the *dot operator*. It is used to tell Windows PowerShell that what comes after the period is a property or method that belongs to the object directly preceding it.

Objects are instances of classes. You can think of a *class* as a definition, schema, or type. It defines what the object will look like. For example, a class called Dog might be defined as having the properties of color, size, and breed, and might have methods such as bark, eat, and sleep! Because an object is an instance of a class, an instance of class Dog might be your neighbor's dog Fluffy. (I made this up, so if you're neighbor has a dog named Fluffy it's a pure coincidence — I don't know your neighbor!) In the virtual world, an object is the instance of a class that you can actually interact with. Object properties are directly accessible using the object.property_name syntax. Methods usually involve the class having to do something rather than just get an internally stored value, so they're called *like functions*. The string's ToUpper method doesn't take any parameters which is why it doesn't have anything in the parentheses — but some methods do require parameters. For example, if you want to replace part of a string with another string, you use the string's replace method:

```
$fullname = "Johnny Goodman"
$newname = $fullname.replace("Good","Bad")
write-output $newname
```

This replaces any occurrence of the word "Good" with "Bad" in the string stored in the variable $fullname. As a result, the output of this snippet is "Johnny Badman".

Chapter 6

A Bit of Logic to Save the Day

Computers are simply oversized and overpowered calculators. Sometimes it's hard to explain this to the average nontechie, but everything we do on our computers — sending and receiving e-mail, browsing the Web, watching movies — all comes back to numbers! In fact, everything comes down to two numbers: 0 and 1 (nothing and something).

Take away all the fancy processor architecture, bus speeds, and cool case lights on a computer, and you have a machine that's good at adding ones and zeroes and also at comparing true and false. Everything else that you see, hear, and interact with on your computer is some sort of representation of these fundamental units.

In this chapter, you give your Windows PowerShell scripts a little more intelligence by building on these concepts of true and false to direct the flow of information through your scripts.

A Logic Primer

Logic is built around the premise of true and false values, which are known as *Boolean values*. In general, the digit 1 represents true, and the digit 0 represents false. Windows PowerShell, however, also has automatic variables that define the values of true and false — namely, $TRUE and $FALSE.

When working with Boolean values, you can use a set of operations to combine and compare them. These operations are

> ✓ AND: When you compare two values by using the AND operator, the result is true if, and only if, both values are true.

 ✔ OR: The OR operator, on the other hand, returns true if either value
   is true.

 ✔ Exclusive OR (XOR): The Exclusive OR operator returns true if, and
   only if, one of the values is true.

 ✔ NOT: Finally, the NOT operator negates the value, so not true is obviously
   false, and vice versa.

Take a look at Tables 6-1 through 6-4, which illustrate how Boolean values are
evaluated.

Table 6-1	Boolean AND Operator	
Value 1	*Value 2*	*Result*
True	True	True
True	False	False
False	True	False
False	False	False

Table 6-2	Boolean OR Operator	
Value 1	*Value 2*	*Result*
True	True	True
True	False	True
False	True	True
False	False	False

Table 6-3	Boolean XOR Operator	
Value 1	*Value 2*	*Result*
True	True	False
True	False	True
False	True	True
False	False	False

Table 6-4	Boolean NOT Operator
Value	*Result*
True	False
False	True

A lot of this information may seem to be very basic, but as you start building complex logic statements to control how your scripts flow, it's good to remember how true and false get evaluated when they're combined, because often, those evaluations are the places where bugs start to creep in.

This discussion won't be complete until I show you how all this stuff works in Windows PowerShell. Take a look at this bit of code:

```
$a = 1; $b = 2
($a -eq 1) -and ($b -eq 2)
($a -eq 1) -or ($b -eq 2)
($a -eq 1) -xor ($b -eq 2)
-not ($a -eq 1)
```

In this code, -eq means the equal sign and is one of the operators used to compare two values. If you work out the logic in your head (or simply run this code in Windows PowerShell), you see that the results of these commands are the values True, True, False, and False.

You can use a semicolon (;) to put multiple commands on the same line, as in $a = 1; $b =2. This behavior applies to scripts, but you can also use a semicolon on the command line, so typing something like this at the PSH prompt on one line and then pressing Enter is perfectly valid:

```
$color = "Blue"; Write-Host ("I like the color" + $color)
```

Table 6-5 shows the different operators you can use in PSH to compare values.

Table 6-5	Comparison Operators
Operator	*Description*
-lt	Less than
-le	Less than or equal to
-gt	Greater than

(continued)

Table 6-5 *(continued)*

Operator	*Description*
-ge	Greater than or equal to
-eq	Equal to
-ne	Not equal to
-is	Returns true if the value is a certain data type
-isnot	Returns true if the value is not a certain data type
-like	Like (uses wildcard for pattern matching)
-notlike	Not like (uses wildcard for pattern searching)
-match	A match using regular expressions
-nomatch	Not a match using regular expressions
-contains	Used to see whether a collection or group of items contains a given item
-notcontains	Used to see whether a collection or group of items does not contain a given item

By default, the comparison of values isn't case sensitive. If you want a case-sensitive comparison of two values, you prefix the comparison with c. Likewise, if you want to explicitly make the comparison case insensitive, prefix it with i, as in this example:

```
$a = "test"
$b = "Test"
# This returns False
$a -ceq $b
# This returns True
$a -ieq $b
# This behaves the same as -ieq and returns True
$a -eq $b
```

Branching Using If/Else

The most basic way to control how your script flows is to use if/else statements. This method is very natural because it's generally how you make decisions on a day-to-day basis: *If* I eat this banana chocolate chip muffin for breakfast, I'll be in a good mood the rest of the day; otherwise *(else)*, my coworkers will see my dark side. Take a look at this simple `if` statement, and try to figure out what it does:

```
$a = 6
if ($a -gt 5) {Write-Host "Greater than 5!"}
```

If you guessed that it writes `Greater than 5!` on the screen, you guessed correctly. The `if` statement evaluates the condition in the parentheses. If the resulting value is true, whatever is inside the curly braces gets executed.

Any nonzero value also evaluates to true, so sometimes script writers and programmers use this fact as a shortcut. Look at the following code snippet. Both `if` statements are functionally equivalent; the only difference is that the second version takes advantage of this behavior to simplify the code.

```
$a = 1
if ($a -ne 0) {Write-Host "Non-zero value entered"}
if ($a) {Write-Host "Non-Zero value entered."}
```

Using `if` by itself is useful if you have a segment of code that you want to execute only if a certain condition is true — if a file exists or the number of command line arguments is greater than zero, for example. Sometimes, you want one segment of code to execute if a condition is true and a different segment of code to execute if the condition isn't true. This situation is where the `else` statement fits into the picture:

```
$name = "Steve"
if ($name -eq "Steve") {
    Write-Host "Hello Steve!"
} else {
    Write-Host "Hello Anonymous!"
}
```

This example outputs `Hello Steve!` to the screen, because $name equals Steve. If you change $name to any other value, the script displays `Hello Anonymous!` instead.

A common use for `if`/`else` statements is to have your script perform a sanity check before doing something and then use the `else` statement to display an error message. You could have a script check to see whether a file exists and, *if* it does, to read the contents and do something fun, or *else* use `Write-Host` or `Write-Warning` to display a message onscreen to tell the user that the input file can't be found.

Now comes a strange-looking statement: `elseif`. This statement looks like a hybrid of `else` and `if` because it is. Take a look at the two code segments in

Listing 6-1. One of them uses a combination of *nested* (one statement inside another) if/else statements, and the other one uses if/elseif/else combinations.

Listing 6-1: Different Approaches for Performing a Nested Value Comparison

```
# Size comparison version 1.0
$size = "M"
if ($size -eq "S") {
    Write-Host "Small"
} else {
    if ($size -eq "M") {
        Write-Host "Medium"
    } else {
        if ($size -eq "L") {
            Write-Host "Large"
        } else {
            if ($size -eq "XL") {
                Write-Host "Extra Large"
            } else {
                Write-Host "Unknown Size"
            }
        }
    }
}

# Size comparison version 2.0
$size = "M"
if ($size -eq "S") {
    Write-Host "Small"
} elseif ($size -eq "M") {
    Write-Host "Medium"
} elseif ($size -eq "L") {
    Write-Host "Large"
} elseif ($size -eq "XL") {
    Write-Host "Extra Large"
} else {
    Write-Host "Unknown Size"
}
```

You can download and use the code listings from the book's Web site (www. dummies.com/go/powershell2fd) instead of having type everything manually.

The first size-comparison code snippet uses nested if/else statements. Even when I use indentation to help make code a bit more readable to the human eye, the code is still a bit unwieldy, and making a mistake in that sea of curly braces and parentheses is very easy.

The second version uses the `elseif` statement to compact the code by creating a sort of conditional `if` statement that gets evaluated only if the previous `if` statement returns false. This method not only saves me a bit of typing, but also makes understanding this code snippet a whole lot easier.

Using the Switch Statement

Using `if/else` and `if/elseif/else` statements works quite well a majority of the time. When you have a large set of values, however, and want to compare it with another value to determine what code you want to run next, even the `if/elseif/else` method is a bit clunky. The answer is the `switch` statement, as demonstrated in the following code:

```
$size = "M"
switch ($size)
{
   "S"    {Write-Host "Small"}
   "M"    {Write-Host "Medium"}
   "L"    {Write-Host "Large"}
   "XL"   {Write-Host "Extra Large"}
   default {Write-Host "Unknown Size"}
}
```

This code snippet is functionally equivalent to the `if/elseif/else` version, but notice how much cleaner it looks. It also makes adding extra choices much easier; you simply add more values that `$size` can match and then put whatever code for that match inside the curly braces. The `default` statement is optional; it's the catch-all option if no matches exist for any of the other defined values.

Doing It Over and Over and Over Again with Loops

Most of the time, I resort to writing a script whenever I feel it's not worthwhile to perform a repetitive task manually. Sometimes, writing that script takes as much time as doing the job manually, but a script offers the benefit of repeatable results. Also, I can reuse that script as is or use it as a framework for a similar task.

The theme that I see most frequently in scripts is repeating a particular task over and over on different objects. Your script might go through a list of files in a given folder and rename the files with a different file extension, for example. Another script might query Active Directory for a list of users who have a particular attribute set and then modify that attribute. I'm sure that you can come up with many examples of tasks that you'd love to automate.

You automate tasks in Windows PowerShell by using loops. A *loop* is nothing more than a code block that can be run repeatedly many times depending on a certain condition you provide it. You can choose among several kinds of loops — namely, `for`, `foreach`, `while`, `do while`, and `do until` loops. Although they all do the same thing (repeat a code segment over and over), they have slightly varying uses that make some loops more ideal than others in different situations.

Looping with For

You typically use the `for` loop is when you want to loop through some code a finite number of times. Yes, you can make the code loop forever, but as a rule of thumb, if you want to run something a known number of times, the `for` loop is the ideal choice. The `for` loop looks like this:

```
for ($i = 1; $i -le 5; $i++)
{
    Write-Host $i
}
```

The corresponding output is the digits 1 through 5 displayed onscreen, one digit per line. The interesting part is inside the parentheses, because that part controls the loop. If you examine that part of the code closely, you'll notice three distinct parts separated by semicolons.

The code within the curly braces of a loop is called the *loop block*.

The first part, `$i = 1`, is the *initialization expression,* which it sets up the loop. The expression in the initialization portion gets executed only once: at the beginning of the loop. In this case, it initializes `$i` with the value 1.

The next part, `$i -le 5`, establishes the condition that must return true for the loop to continue and is evaluated for each iteration of the loop. When this expression returns false, the loop is done. In this case, the code says that as long as `$i` is less than or equal to 5, keep going.

The last part, $i++, is a *counting section;* it also is executed once per iteration of the loop after each loop-block execution is complete. $i++ means to increase the value of $i by 1.

Although theoretically, you can put whatever you want in any of these three sections, the way you see it in the example is the typical way you'd use it. I use the letter i in the example because the variable used in the for loop statement is called the *iterator.* This variable gets this name from its job, which is to iterate through items.

The code inside the curly braces can be anything you want. Many times, you use the current value of the iterator, for several reasons such as using it as an index into an array (which I talk about in Chapter 11) or for combining with other values to generate some output (perhaps by using it in a calculation).You can refer to it inside the curly braces as you would any other variable. Just remember that the value of the iterator changes during each pass of the loop, based on the code you have in the counting section.

Using Foreach to loop through collections

The foreach loop is a cousin of the for loop, in that it too executes for a finite number of times. Unlike the for loop, however, it doesn't have to be told how to increment its values. Instead, you give foreach a collection of objects and the variable name for the iterator, and foreach automatically loops through each item in the collection one by one. Have a look at this code snippet:

```
foreach ($i in Get-Alias)
{
    Write-Host $i.name
}
```

The statement in the parentheses, $i in Get-Alias, is where you define the iterator, which I call $i in this example. Then you tell the iterator what collection of items to point to — in this example, the return value of Get-Alias. Get-Alias returns a collection of AliasInfo objects that defines all the aliases currently defined in the system. For each iteration of the foreach loop, $i refers to one of these objects; then you can reference whatever you want from these objects within the body of the loop. In this case, the loop is just displaying the name of the alias.

Using foreach loops is always ideal when you're going through a collection of objects, due to the ease of establishing and using the loops.

Looping for a While

Sometimes, you want to repeat a process many times and don't know exactly how many times it'll run, but you do know the condition that must exist for the loop to terminate. This situation is where a `while` loop comes in handy. The `while` loop checks to see whether a particular condition you specify evaluates to true; then it executes a block of code and continues to repeat that block of code until the value in the `while` condition evaluates to false. Take a look at this code:

```
$objRandom = New-Object Random
$val = $objRandom.Next(1,10)
while ($val -ne 7)
{
    Write-Host ("You got a " + $val + "...")
    $val = $objRandom.Next(1,10)
}
Write-Host "Congratulations, you got a 7!"
```

This code is a pretty good demonstration of a situation for which a `while` loop may be appropriate. This code snippet generates a random number between 1 and 10 and displays the number it receives until it finally gets a 7. Because you don't know how many random numbers might need to be generated before you get a 7, the `while` loop allows you to continue searching until you do.

The first two lines initialize a new `Random` object and grab the first random value. The `Random` object is what allows you to generate random numbers. You use the `Random` object's `Next` method to specify the lowest and highest number you want the code to return to generate a random number.

The `while` loop checks the conditions in the parentheses to determine whether it should go into the loop. In this example, I'm checking to see whether `$val` is not equal to 7. If it isn't, the code displays the value and then generates a new random number from 1 to 10. The condition for the `while` loop is reevaluated, and the cycle continues. When `$val` contains the value 7, the code stops looping and then displays the congratulatory message.

Running a loop at least once with Do While

A slight variation of the `while` loop is the `do while` loop. You can do exactly the same thing with `do while` that you can with the `while` loop, so why have another version of the same thing? Well, actually, the two loops have subtle differences. For starters, `do while` loops evaluate the condition *after* the code in the loop block has executed. The side effect of this fact is that the code in your do while loop is guaranteed to run at least once. Take this code for example:

```
$objRandom = New-Object Random
do
{
    $val = $objRandom.Next(1,10)
    Write-Host ("You got a " + $val + "...")
} while ($val -ne 7)
Write-Host "Congratulations, you got a 7!"
```

Notice the subtle differences between this do while version and the while loop version. Because the code block is guaranteed to execute at least once, you can change the order of the random-number generation and the output, and eliminate the need to generate a number before the loop. Although these variations perform the same task, notice that they're not functionally equivalent. The do while version actually says You got a 7 . . . before it says Congratulations, you got a 7!, whereas in the while version, the code jumps straight out of the loop.

Taking a look at Do Until

The do until loop is (not surprisingly) very similar to the do while loop. The two loops are the same in that they evaluation the condition after the first iteration of the loop block, but they're different in how the condition controls the loop. In a do until loop, when the condition in the parentheses evaluates to true the loop is done, whereas in a do while loop the condition in the parentheses must evaluate to false to end the loop. Look at this example:

```
$objRandom = New-Object Random
do
{
    $val = $objRandom.Next(1,10)
    Write-Host ("You got a " + $val + "...")
} until ($val -eq 7)
Write-Host "Congratulations, you got a 7!"
```

As you can see, the do until version of the preceding do while code is exactly the same. The only difference is I changed the condition from $val -ne 7 to $val -eq 7. To make remembering the differences easy, I just think of do until as being the negative version of do while. You can use both methods interchangeably, but pay attention to the condition you write for the loop.

Avoiding loop pitfalls

Loops cause many of the bugs that cause runaway scripts. It's very easy to write a loop in which the condition you set to end the loop is a value that'll never be attained. Consider this `for` loop:

```
for ($i = 1; $i > 0; $i++) {
    Write-Host $i
}
```

Notice anything wrong? This `for` loop keeps going and going because it initializes `$i` to 1 and keeps incrementing this value, but the condition for the script is that `$i` is greater than 0, which is always true.

I have to admit that this example is a bit contrived. Infinite loops occur frequently in variations of the `while` loop because you usually use a `while` loop when you don't necessarily know how many times the loop block will need to be executed. Here's a variation on the random-number check code that results in an infinite loop:

```
$objRandom = New-Object Random
$val = $objRandom.Next(1,10)
while ($val -ne 11)
{
    Write-Host ("You got a " + $val + "...")
    $val = $objRandom.Next(1,10)
}
Write-Host "Congratulations, you got a 11!"
```

Again, the code is generating random numbers from 1 through 10, but the condition I set won't exit the loop until the value is 11, which is impossible, so this loop will run forever. This bug is an obvious one, but this kind of stuff happens if I initially write the script so that I'm looking for 11 and generate numbers from 1 through 20. The code works, but then I realize that I want to go only from 1 through 10 and update the random code generation — but forget to update the loop condition. In very long scripts, this mistake is very easy to make, especially if you get really lazy and use the search-and-replace feature in your text editor to make changes.

So whenever you find your scripts going crazy (such as using 100 percent of CPU), the problem usually is a runaway loop. The first thing you should do is check the conditions of all your loops; most of the time, you'll find the culprit in a loop.

Chapter 7

Working on a Pipeline

In This Chapter

▶ Using pipelines to become more efficient

▶ Piping commands together

▶ Working with data and displaying results

*I*f you take a moment to look around you, I'm sure that you can find a lot of inefficiencies. I see some of the biggest inefficiencies when I'm dealing with any kind of government agency. I'm not a political kind of person, but having worked with various government entities throughout my career, I can say that the bureaucracy that's designed to create clear lines of responsibility and authority also typically creates some very inefficient processes as a side effect.

Typically, getting anything done involves going to one department, filing some paperwork, getting something back, and then going to another department and filling out some more paperwork (usually, with the same information) — and this process can go on and on. Departments and even agencies rarely share information. Wouldn't it be nice if you could submit a request somewhere, and that request would automatically flow through all the relevant departments or agencies and give you your results at the end? This scenario is a pipe dream for most of us. Luckily, though, it's closer to reality in Windows PowerShell. You don't have to deal with the same kinds of problems because you can take advantage of pipelines.

In this chapter, you see how information is passed from one PSH command to another using pipelines. Unlike pipelines of the past, PSH pipelines are much more sophisticated and, in my opinion, much more effective. Once you read this chapter, you'll see why this new way of passing information between commands makes so much sense and you'll never want to do it using any other method ever again.

Using Pipelines to Streamline Your Commands

Command line interfaces can suffer the same kinds of inefficiencies that you see in the real world. If you want to query some information from one computer, that process is straightforward in Windows PowerShell; you just use Windows Management Instrumentation (WMI) to query that information. What if you want to query a bunch of computers? Now you somehow have to provide Windows PowerShell a list of computer names. You may have this information in a file, or you may have to query Active Directory. Well, querying Active Directory for a list of computers is a completely different command, so what are you supposed to do? Run the query command, get a list, and then run a command to query WMI?

The problem can get even more complex as more data sources are required. The solution is a pipeline.

A *pipeline* occurs when you take the output of one command and direct it to the input of another command. When you do, you don't need to act as the middleman; rather, you string together the commands you want to work together to produce a given output. This process is called *piping* the output of one command to another.

Pipelines have existed forever. They started showing up in some of the early Unix shells, and even MS-DOS had support for pipelines. So what's so great about Windows PowerShell if this isn't a new concept? To understand better, take a look at this regular command line sequence, which you can run in the traditional Windows command shell:

```
ipconfig | find "IP Address"
```

This sequence uses `ipconfig` to list the IP configurations of all the network adapters on your system and then pipes that output to the `find` command, where it filters the output and displays only the lines that contain the string `"IP Address"`. The result is a simple command sequence that gives you all the IP addresses on your system.

The problem with this method (and, frankly, with all the methods that exist today) is that it relies on manipulating the text output of the preceding command. If the output of `ipconfig` changes so that the string `"IP Address"` is changed to `"IPv4 Address"`, for example, this command sequence won't return any results. If you have a lot of scripts that depend on this output, you have to go back and fix them all.

Windows PowerShell continues to use the same convention of using the pipe (|) character to denote piping the output of one command to another, but in the background, the behavior has changed significantly — fortunately, for the better. The designers of Windows PowerShell realized that relying on text output is far from being a good idea. A good example of why relying on text output can cause some complications is if the command output is in a localized language. If you work in a global IT shop, you have to accommodate every language variation of this output in each of your scripts.

Windows PowerShell doesn't pass text between commands; it passes objects. This arrangement is significant because the receiving command can access the various attributes of the object directly, rather than trying to parse out strings to interpret the data. This point may seem to be trivial, but it's not. Objects have a specific structure that is well defined and easy to access, so you never have to worry that the text will change on you.

Stringing Commands Together

If you've piped commands together in MS-DOS or in the Windows command prompt, or have even gone as far as writing scripts that take advantage of piping commands together, you'll need to change the way you think about pipes when working in PSH.

Here's a typical command that works fine in the Windows command prompt:

```
dir c:\windows\system32 | find ".exe"
```

The command performs a directory listing of `c:\windows\system32` and then pipes the output to the `find` command to filter for lines that contain the string `".exe"`. Now try running the same command in Windows PowerShell. Strangely, it returns an error message, stating that the parameter format isn't correct.

If you remember, `DIR` is just an alias to `Get-ChildItem`, so you'd probably try running `Get-ChildItem` or `DIR` directly without the pipe to make sure that it actually returns some information. Just running `DIR` by itself against `c:\windows\system32` returns a slightly different-looking output from the regular Windows command prompt, but you do see full filenames. So the `find` command should work because it just looks for a particular string in the given input. What's going on?

Although `Get-ChildItem` displays the results in a pretty format onscreen when you run the command, that format isn't how the information is transferred to another command when it's directed through a pipe. The output that you see when you run a Cmdlet is just the default representation of the objects that it returns. To see this concept in action, take a look at these three commands:

```
Get-ChildItem c:\windows\system32 | Format-Table
Get-ChildItem c:\windows\system32 | Format-List
Get-ChildItem c:\windows\system32 | Format-Wide
```

You see the output of these commands in Figure 7-1, Figure 7-2, and Figure 7-3, respectively.

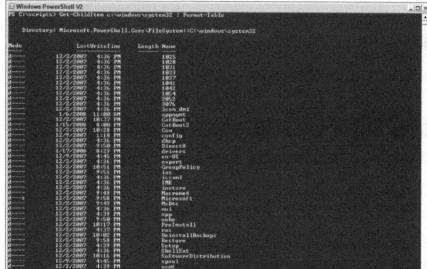

Figure 7-1:
Piping Get-ChildItem through Format-Table.

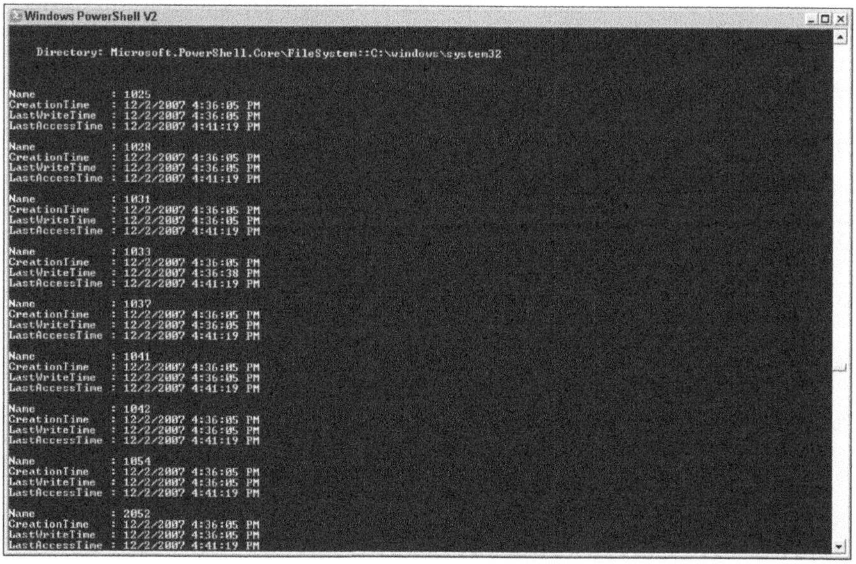

Figure 7-2:
Piping Get-ChildItem through Format-List.

Figure 7-3:
Piping Get-
ChildItem
through
Format-
Wide.

Get-ChildItem continues to return the same data, but the Format-Table, Format-List, and Format-Wide Cmdlets are changing the way the data is displayed. The formatting Cmdlets do this without having to parse the original output of Get-ChildItem (which happens to be the same as Format-Table). Instead, it takes the collection of objects returned by Get-ChildItem and just rearranges them for output in the specified format.

The reason why all this fancy stuff works is that data and the presentation of data are completely separate concepts in Windows PowerShell. All the actual objects returned by the different Cmdlets are pure data, and Cmdlets don't care how this data is presented to the user.

This situation has two significant side effects:

✔ It allows Cmdlet authors to focus on the functionality of their Cmdlet and return the data they want without having to worry about who or what will use the data.

✔ Because Cmdlets return just data, authors can format the data any way they want without first manipulating the format defined by the original Cmdlet author.

All this begs the question "If Cmdlets return just data, why is it that when I run Cmdlets that return data, the output on the screen still looks pretty?" It's a fair question, because the author of the Cmdlet really doesn't care about the output format and certainly doesn't write that code in the Cmdlet to begin with. The answer is a Cmdlet called Out-Default.

`Out-Default` is in charge of figuring out how to render the output of a given command if no formatter is specified. Every command that you type in the PowerShell console is automatically piped to `Out-Default` in the background. Then the final output is based on the kind of object stream `Out-Default` receives. You can think of a *stream* as being the flow of data.

Every known object has a view that is registered to it and that defines which formatter to use. When you run a command interactively in the Windows PowerShell console, `Out-Default` automatically redirects the output to `Out-Host`, which automatically selects the appropriate output formatter for you (in the case of `Get-ChildItem`, `Format-Table`). Then you can easily see the result you want in a default view. If you want to change the way that the output is displayed, you can use one of the available formatters or, if you're bold, create your own scripts or Cmdlets to do this job for you.

Getting the Right Output

Usually, the default output of the Cmdlets is enough to give you the information you want. Defaults are designed to cover the general use of a given command but sometimes give too much or too little information. The solution is to tailor the output to your needs. Consider the `Get-Process` Cmdlet. By default, it displays a nice tabular list of running processes as well as information such as the number of handles open, the amount of memory being used, the amount of CPU time spent on it, and the process ID. All this information is very good. If you want the output to display only the process ID and process name in a tabular format, however, you can run

```
Get-Process | Format-Table -property id,name
```

Here, you give `Format-Table` the list of object properties you're interested in. When `Format-Table` displays the list of objects returned by `Get-Process`, it displays only those properties that you specify. It also respects the order in which you specify the property names, so if you want to display the process name before the process ID, you can switch the property names around like this:

```
Get-Process | Format-Table -property name,id
```

Do you want to see something else really cool? Because Cmdlets return objects (are you sick of me repeating that yet?), you can do other really cool things to filter the output. If you want to find out which processes have a process ID greater than 1000, for example, only want to display only the name of the process, the amount of CPU time it's received, and the process ID, you can do that easily with this pipeline (Figure 7-4 shows the output):

```
Get-Process | Where-Object {$_.Id -gt 1000} | Format-Table -property Name,CPU,Id
```

Windows PowerShell V2

PS C:\scripts> Get-Process | Where-Object {$_.id -gt 1000} | Format-Table -property name,CPU,id

Name	CPU	Id
alg	0.109375	2012
ctfmon	0.734375	1204
powershell	32.78125	1264
spoolsv	0.265625	1400
svchost	738.953125	1036
svchost	1.8125	1088
svchost	1.4375	1188
VMwareService	465.515625	1664
VMwareTray	0.46875	1032
VMwareUser	2.3125	1120
wuauclt	0.09375	1184

PS C:\scripts>

Figure 7-4:
Filtering the output of the Get-Process Cmdlet.

You use the Where-Object Cmdlet whenever you want to filter the objects that passed along the pipeline.

The Where-Object Cmdlet takes a script block that defines how the objects should be filtered. The block is enclosed in curly braces. If you examine the script block I use to filter for process IDs greater than 1000, you see something new: the $_ symbol. The $_ symbol is an automatic variable (I talk about variables in Chapter 5) that refers to the current object in the pipeline. In plain English, {$_.id -gt 1000} means that for every object the Where-Object Cmdlet receives from the pipeline, Where-Object takes the Id property of the object and checks to see whether it's greater than 1000. Only those objects that meet this criterion get passed along the pipeline to the next command.

Where-Object is aliased as where, so don't be surprised if you come across pipelines that use just the word where to filter objects.

I use Format-Table in the preceding examples, but you can use the Select-Object Cmdlet as a more generic method of specifying the object properties you want to retrieve in a pipeline. Another useful Cmdlet for working with pipelines is Sort-Object, which sorts the incoming objects. You can sort by one or more object properties; Sort-Object first sorts by the first property you specify, and then by the next property, and so on. You can also tell it to sort in ascending or descending order.

Here's a slight variation on the Get-Process example. This time, I'm using Select-Object to specify the fields I want and Sort-Object to sort the objects first by CPU time and then by Id:

```
Get-Process | Where-Object {$_.Id -gt 1000} | Select-Object Name,CPU,ID | Sort-
        Object CPU,Id
```

I hope that you already see how powerful the simple change of returning objects rather than text really is. Doing something like this in Windows shell scripting or even in Windows Scripting Host (WSH) would take many lines of code, but here, everything happens on one line.

Part III
Complex Data Description and Sharing

In this part . . .

*N*ow that you know the basics, it's time to shift gears and start having some real fun. I'm going to build on some of the concepts I talk about in the previous part, but now it's time to bring in slightly more complex concepts. Chapter 8 addresses working with Windows Management Instrumentation (WMI) to query information from Windows. I delve deeper into concepts like manipulating strings in Chapter 9 and working with numbers in Chapter 10. In Chapter 11 I cover data structures like arrays and hash tables which will allow you to group data together. I discuss methods for reading from and writing to plain text files and even XML or HTML files in Chapter 12. Finally, I address working with dates in Chapter 13.

Chapter 8

Working with Windows Management Instrumentation

I've been managing Microsoft Windows–based networks for a fairly long time now, and I still remember how much manual effort it took to perform even simple systems management tasks before Windows Management Instrumentation (WMI) came about. I remember during the year leading up to Y2K, a company I did some work for had to bring in a small army of technicians just to visit each and every workstation to find out their BIOS version in order to determine which ones needed to be flashed to become Y2K-compliant. If WMI was accessible to me back then the way it is today, I'm certain I'd still have a lot more hair on my head. Those times have come and gone, and many of the systems management tools today are built to take advantage of WMI. PowerShell is no exception!

In this chapter, you run some commands that allow you to interact with Windows through WMI. It's something that's very easy to do but packs a big punch, so once you understand how to talk to Windows through WMI, you'll be increasing your effectiveness in controlling Windows exponentially.

Getting Familiar with Windows Management Instrumentation

Windows Management Instrumentation (WMI) provides a standardized interface for interacting with a Windows-based system regardless of the underlying hardware manufacturer and specific Windows version. Prior to WMI, different hardware vendors might have provided different Application Programming Interfaces (APIs) that you could have used to write some code and get this information yourself, but if you happened to have hardware from different vendors you were forced to learn different APIs. This disparity applied not only to hardware, but even to the different version of Windows operating systems. There just wasn't one cohesive way to access the information you needed quickly.

This lack of a unified approach made automating systems tasks (such as querying installed hardware, software, and other operating system properties) very time consuming — if not nearly impossible. WMI is the answer to all this because it provides a set of non-proprietary specifications and standards for interacting with various components of a system.

WMI is now officially the term used by Microsoft when referring to what was once called Web-Based Enterprise Management (WBEM) for Windows. WBEM is a set of standard technologies created and managed by the Distributed Management Task Force (DMTF). The DMTF is an industry organization that collaborates with thousands of technology companies worldwide to develop management standards and integration technology for enterprise and Internet environments. The DMTF also has a Common Information Model (CIM) that specifies a common definition of management information relating to systems and services. WMI is fully compliant with the CIM and WBEM specifications and continues to maintain that compliance as these standards evolve.

Examining the WMI architecture

WMI isn't all that complicated, but it does have a few moving parts. At the bottom of the WMI architecture are the *managed objects* — the things you typically interact with, such as physical devices on your systems (your motherboard, memory, cup-holder . . . err . . . DVD-ROM drive); your Windows Registry; and basically anything that can be accessed using the Windows API.

On top of the managed objects layer are a bunch of WMI *providers*. You can think of the WMI providers as pieces of bilingual software capable of speaking WMI and the native language of whatever managed object they're designed to manage. This is your middle man, so to speak, in your transactions with the operating system through WMI.

The actual thing you interact with is the WMI Management Infrastructure, which is comprised of two components: CIM Object Manager (CIMOM) and the CIMOM Repository (see Figure 8-1). The *CIMOM Repository* contains a list of objects you can use to interact with the system, whereas *CIMOM* is in charge of providing you with a standard method for interacting with the system. CIMOM is the broker for all your WMI transactions.

WMI is built around classes that create an abstract representation of the managed objects. *Instances* are the actual objects in memory that you interact with. For example, you have a `Win32_Process` class that represents a process; each running process is then an instance of the `Win32_Process` class.

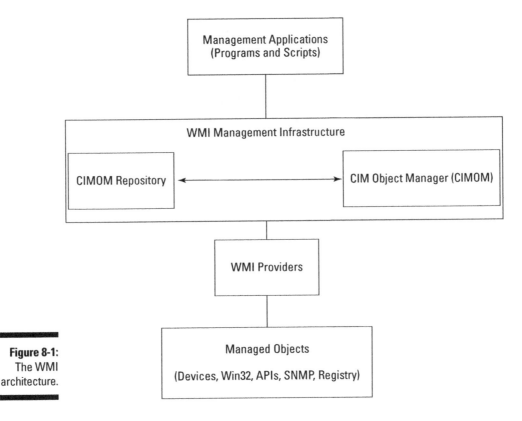

Figure 8-1:
The WMI
architecture.

Management Applications
(Programs and Scripts)

WMI Management Infrastructure

CIMOM Repository ←——————→ CIM Object Manager (CIMOM)

WMI Providers

Managed Objects

(Devices, Win32, APIs, SNMP, Registry)

Poking around in WMI namespaces

Each object that WMI exposes is made available through a specific namespace. You can think of a *namespace* as a naming convention that uniquely identifies a class (the definition of an object). Namespaces also help group related classes together. Most of the core WMI classes you'll typically work with are stored in the `root\CIMV2` namespace. However, if you have other applications that define their own WMI classes, they'll usually define their own namespace. For example, if you have Microsoft Exchange installed on the system, you'll have a WMI namespace called `root\MicrosoftExchangeV2` that you can use to query various Microsoft Exchange properties. There are similar namespaces for products like IIS (`root\MicrosoftIISv2`) and SQL Server (`root\Microsoft\SqlServer`).

One way to find out what WMI namespaces are defined in your system is to open the Windows Management Instrumentation MMC snap-in. You can do this by following these steps:

1. **Choose Start⇨Run.**

2. **Enter** `wmimgmt.msc` **and press OK.**

   This will open up the WMI MMC snap-in.

3. **Right-click WMI Control (Local) and choose Properties.**

   This brings up the WMI properties dialog box.

4. **Click the Security tab.**

5. **Double-click the Root folder (or click the plus symbol to the left of it) to see the entire namespace tree (see Figure 8-2).**

Figure 8-2:
You can view the WMI name-spaces available on the local host.

Securing WMI

Because WMI gives you the ability to query and, where applicable, even make changes to managed objects both locally and remotely, security is a big concern. Fortunately, WMI namespaces have their own set of Access Control Lists (ACLs) that define which accounts can perform what kind of action on classes in that namespace.

You set the security using the same WMI MMC snap-in. You simply need to select the namespace you want and click the Security button (refer to the previous section). You usually won't be touching these permissions, but sometimes you might have to in order to get something to work. For example, some namespaces don't allow you to interact with them remotely, so you have to explicitly allow this. You can allow or deny any of the permissions listed in Table 8-1.

Table 8-1	WMI Permissions
Permission	*Description*
Execute Methods	Allows running of methods provided by WMI classes.
Full Write	Full permission to read, write, and even delete all WMI classes and instances.
Partial Write	Write access to static WMI objects.
Provider Write	Write access to objects provided by providers.
Enable Account	Read access to WMI objects.
Remote Enable	Remote access to WMI objects.
Read Security	Can view WMI permissions but not change them.
Edit Security	Can view and modify WMI permissions.

Making Windows PowerShell Interact with WMI

Working with WMI using Windows PowerShell is as easy as sipping cool lemonade on a hot summer's day. You need to know only one Cmdlet, and that is `Get-WMIObject`. In its simplest form, you need to give `Get-WMIObject` only the name of a class, and it gladly spits out information about all the instances of that class along with any properties it has. To find out information about your BIOS, you can run this line:

```
Get-WMIObject Win32_BIOS
```

If you want to know some general information about the computer you're on (such as the name, manufacturer, and model), run this:

```
Get-WMIObject Win32_ComputerSystem
```

These commands query the local host to return this information, as shown in Figure 8-3.

WMI allows you to get information remotely as well. You can query the same BIOS information off a computer called REDLINE by using the Get-WMIObject Cmdlet's -computername parameter:

```
Get-WMIObject Win32_BIOS -computername REDLINE
```

An easy way to see all the classes available to your disposal is by using Get-WMIObject to list them out for you. Simply enter this:

```
Get-WMIObject -list
```

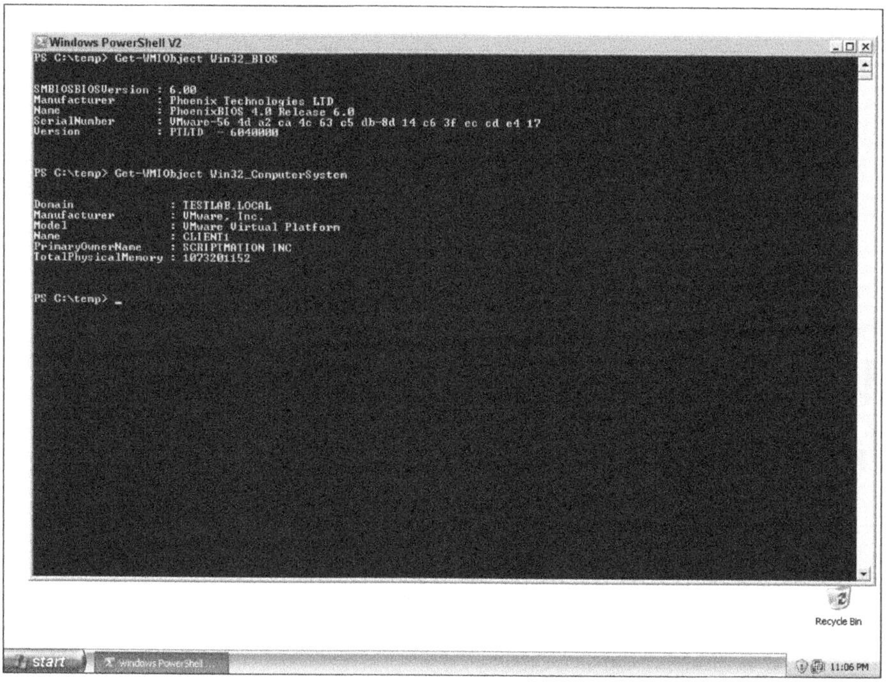

Figure 8-3:
I got this output after running Get-WMIObject against common WMI classes.

Most of the time, you'll only be dealing with core WMI classes that directly interact with various Windows or system components. The names of these WMI classes all start with `Win32_`, so by taking advantage of pipelines (see Chapter 7), you can use the following sequence of commands to filter out only those WMI classes:

```
Get-WMIObject -list | where {$_.name.startswith("Win32_")}
```

Notice how many classes are available for you to interact with. The reality though is that while there is practically a WMI class to interact with almost any imaginable part of Windows, you'll only typically interact with a subset of these classes on a regular basis. Table 8-2 lists some of the more commonly used WMI classes.

Table 8-2	Commonly Used WMI Classes
Class	*What it Represents*
Win32_BIOS	Various properties related to the system BIOS
Win32_ComputerSystem	Various properties related to a computer running Windows
Win32_Directory	A directory/folder in Windows
Win32_Environment	System environment variables
Win32_LogicalDisk	Storage devices on a system
Win32_NetworkAdapter	A network adapter on a system
Win32_NetworkAdapterConfiguration	The configuration of a network adapter on a system
Win32_NTLogEvent	An event log entry
Win32_OperatingSystem	The operating system including things such as build number and service pack level
Win32_Printer	A printer installed on the system
Win32_PrintJob	A print job running on the system
Win32_Process	A process running on the system
Win32_Processor	A CPU on the system
Win32_QuickFixEngineering	Small patches to the operating system

(continued)

Table 8-2 *(continued)*

Class	What it Represents
Win32_Registry	The Windows registry
Win32_ScheduledJob	A task scheduled on the system
Win32_Service	A service installed on the system
Win32_Share	A shared resource on the system
Win32_TimeZone	The time zone for the system

You can find out more about a specific WMI class (such as what it represents and what properties are available to you) by looking them up on the Microsoft Developer Network (MSDN). You can find a list of all the WMI classes at http:// msdn2.microsoft.com/en-us/library/aa394084(VS.85).aspx.

The default namespace in Windows is root\CIMV2. In general, you're not going to want to change this unless you have a very specific reason because all the WIN32_ classes fall into this namespace. The Get-WMIObject commands you issued earlier all work because it just so happens that the WMI classes you queried all belong to root\CIMV2. If you want to query a class outside of this namespace, you need to explicitly define it using the -namespace parameter. Here's an example where you can query the IISWebService class of root\MicrosoftIISV2 if you have IIS installed:

```
Get-WMIObject IISWebService -namespace "root\MicrosoftIISV2"
```

By explicitly specifying the -namespace parameter, you'll see all the properties available to you, not just what it returns by default. This means if you want to find out all the properties available in the Win32_ComputerSystem class, you can run this line:

```
Get-WMIObject Win32_ComputerSystem -namespace "root\CIMV2"
```

Using SQL Syntax in WMI to Get WQL

Structured Query Language (SQL) is a language for interacting with relational database management systems (RDBMS), such as Microsoft SQL Server. So what happens when SQL and WMI collide? The product is WMI Query Language, more commonly known as WQL. The use of SQL-like syntax to query WMI is very natural because when you think of WMI, you can loosely translate it into regular database terminologies.

A relational database consists of data organized into tables. Each table has a set of columns *(fields)* and rows *(records)*. For example, in your SQL database you can have a table called tblUsers that consists of four fields: FirstName, LastName, Username, and Password. Each row is a record that represents a different user. Table 8-3 illustrates how this table might look like.

Table 8-3	Sample SQL Database Table — tblUsers		
FirstName	*LastName*	*Username*	*Password*
Joseph	Bradshaw	jbradshaw	S3kD2#g
Sean	Black	sblack	J42D@fg3
Nicole	Anderson	nanderson	p!nk35T

In SQL, if you want to query the database, you use the SELECT statement. If you want to query tblUsers for the FirstName and LastName of a user with a Username of sblack, you run the following query:

```
SELECT FirstName,LastName FROM tblUsers WHERE Username = 'sblack'
```

You just give the SELECT statement the fields you're interested in, the table you want to query, and (optionally) a condition that filters the results. You can do a whole lot more than this using SQL's SELECT statement, but I won't elaborate on it much more since this isn't a book about SQL (although, if you're interested in SQL you can also pick up *SQL For Dummies,* 6th Edition, by Allen Taylor).

Okay, so now that you know everything there is to know about SQL (yea right!), here's how it is similar to WMI. Remember your good friend, the Win32_ BIOS class? Instead of thinking of it as a class, think of it as a database table. The Win32_BIOS class has a bunch of different properties such as Manufacturer, Name, SerialNumber, and Version. Think of these properties as fields in your Win32_BIOS table. Because every computer has only one BIOS, this table has only one record — but still it has a record.

This striking similarity is exactly why the synergy between SQL and WMI is so natural. Now to put all this together, if you want to find out the manufacturer and version of your BIOS, all you need to do is run this command:

```
Get-WMIObject -query "Select Manufacturer,Version From Win32_BIOS"
```

That's it! The cool thing is that you're still using the Get-WMIObject Cmdlet, which means you can still use all the other parameters such as -computer to run it against another computer. **Note:** I didn't have to add a WHERE clause in my query, because I wasn't filtering for anything specific.

Harnessing the Power of WMI

If you haven't been taking advantage of WMI, you've really been missing out. Because practically everything in Windows is represented by a WMI class, it opens up a whole world of opportunity to automate almost anything you want in Windows. Now that you've had a look at how querying WMI works in Window PowerShell, it's time to look at some real-world scenarios where WMI becomes really handy.

In this scenario, you get a call from a user stating that one of the applications she uses doesn't work. You begin to get other calls about the same application, so you believe this has to be a server-side issue since their other network-based applications continue to work fine. You're not normally the administrator for this application, but you need to get this resolved quickly. How can Windows PowerShell and WMI help you?

Normally I do two things in situations like this:

   ✔ I check for any services that are set to automatic startup but are not currently running — this might point out that a service this application is dependent on has crashed.
   ✔ I check the application's event log for any errors.

Not-so-coincidentally, I explain how to do those two things in the following sections.

Querying service status

To find out which services are set to automatic startup and aren't running, run the following command pipeline:

```
Get-WmiObject Win32_Service | Where-Object {($_.StartMode -eq "Auto") -and ($_.
          State -ne "Running")} | Select-Object DisplayName,Name,State
```

This command queries the `Win32_Service` WMI class for all services on the system and filters it using the `Where-Object` Cmdlet for services that have the `StartMode` property equal to `Auto` and the `State` property not equal to `Running`. Because you're interested only in the name of the service, the display name, and the state of the service, you then use `Select-Object` to select just those properties.

Sometimes this is enough to resolve the problem. If it's a Web-based application and you see that the World Wide Web Publishing service is stopped, then most likely you just need to start it back up again to get things running.

You can start a service using the `Start-Service` Cmdlet. The reason I added the `Name` property in addition to the `DisplayName` property when querying for stopped services is because you need to specify the `Name` property of the service when starting it up. So if you had to start up World Wide Web Publishing Service (W3SVC), you actually have to run this line:

```
Start-Service W3SVC
```

Looking for event log entries

The other troubleshooting step you can take is to comb the event logs for any possible errors. The `Win32_NTLogEvent` WMI class gives you access to all the Windows event log entries, so that's a good place to start. You can use the following command pipeline to query the application log for all the `Error` events:

```
Get-WmiObject Win32_NTLogEvent | Where-Object {($_.LogFile -eq "Application")
              -and ($_.Type -eq "Error")} | Select-Object Category,Computer
              Name,EventCode,Description,Message,TimeWritten | Sort-Object
              TimeWritten
```

You just use `Get-WmiObject` to query all the items in `Win32_NTLogEvent` and pipe it to the `Where-Object` Cmdlet to filter for entries where the `Logfile` is equal to `Application` and the `Type` is equal to `Error`. You then pass these results to `Select-Object` to specify the fields you're interested in and then sort the results by the `TimeWritten` field.

In reality, it might be faster (or even easier) to just use the Event Viewer to get this information rather than typing out long command sequences just to get the same information. In a real-world scenario, you really wouldn't be putting these commands together on the fly to troubleshoot an issue. The best way to take advantage of WMI is by creating a toolkit of scripts for common troubleshooting tasks.

An even more ideal situation is for the application expert or administrator to describe a set of troubleshooting steps to follow if there's a problem with the application. More likely than not, you can automate many of these troubleshooting steps that relate directly with the operating system through Windows PowerShell WMI scripting.

Changing WMI Authentication Levels

In my brief discussion about WMI early in this chapter, I left out a very important aspect of WMI — *authentication levels*. Authentication levels control when and how authentication is performed when connecting to a WMI provider. This is very important because WMI permissions are very distinct, and in some cases just being an administrator of the computer doesn't automatically give you access to query a provider.

Microsoft IIS is one of those providers. Due to the added risk associated with running a Web service, the Microsoft IIS WMI provider (root\ MicrosoftIISv2) requires all data sent between the server and the client to be authenticated, verified, and encrypted. To find out the major and minor IIS version numbers of an IIS instance running on a server called web01, you can run this command sequence:

```
Get-WMIObject -class iiswebinfo -namespace "root\MicrosoftIISv2" -computer web01
             -authentication 6 | Select-Object MajorIISVersionNumber,MinorIISVe
             rsionNumber | Format-List
```

The key portion of this code snippet is in the Get-WMIObject call. In particular, you now have to explicitly specify the namespace because MicrosoftIISv2 doesn't exist in the default root\CIMV2 namespace. The class you're interested in is iiswebinfo because this class contains information related to the IIS version number. If you're running this command on a computer other than the Web server, you have to specify the Web server's computer name with the -computer switch to run the query.

The most interesting part is the -authentication parameter. This is new to Windows PowerShell 2. Without specifying this -authentication parameter with the value of 6, Windows PowerShell (well, actually the underlying WMI provider) returns an Access Denied error message. The value of 6 sets the authentication level to PacketPrivacy, which authenticates, verifies, and encrypts data transferred between client and provider.

As you can see in Table 8-4, you can choose from seven authentication levels. In Windows PowerShell 1.0, you were limited to only the default settings, so this a nice new feature in Windows PowerShell 2. Well, actually, it's beyond nice. Without this added feature, there would be no way you could use PowerShell to interact with the Microsoft IIS provider using WMI.

Table 8-4	WMI Authentication Levels	
Name	*Description*	*Authentication Parameter Value*
Default	Authentication uses the default settings.	0
None	There is no authentication being used at all.	1

Name	Description	Authentication Parameter Value
Connect	Authentication happens only during the initial connection between client and provider.	2
Call	Authentication happens at the beginning of each call but subsequent data isn't signed or encrypted.	3
Packet	Authentication happens against all data received from the client but data packets are still not signed or encrypted.	4
Packet Integrity	All data transfer is authenticated and verified. All data packets are signed but not encrypted.	5
Packet Privacy	The highest level of authentication: All data is authenticated, verified, and encrypted.	6

Pretending to Be Someone Else Using Impersonation

When you connect to a WMI instance, you can also tell it how it can use your credentials in order to perform a certain action. You specify the impersonation level with Get-WmiObject using the -ImpersonationLevel parameter. You can choose between five different impersonation level values, as listed in Table 8-5.

Table 8-5	WMI Impersonation Levels	
Name	Description	ImpersonationLevel Parameter Value
Default	Uses the default value of the remote host.	0
Anonymous	Hides your credentials from the WMI provider.	1

(continued)

Table 8-5 *(continued)*

Name	*Description*	*ImpersonationLevel Parameter Value*
Identify	Enables WMI objects to query for your credentials. Default for WMI pre-version 1.5.	2
Impersonate	Enables WMI objects to use your credentials when running, thereby impersonating you. This level is the default for WMI version 1.5 and later.	3
Delegate	Lets WMI objects impersonate you and additionally use your credentials to access other objects on other systems.	4

You won't normally have to specify the impersonation level. However, if you're connecting to a WMI provider on a different computer, you might have to set the impersonation level to 3 (Impersonate), especially if you don't know the WMI version of the remote host ahead of time. This is because prior to WMI version 1.5, the default impersonation level is Identify, which is good enough for local WMI queries but insufficient for running remote WMI commands.

You can use the Delegate impersonation level only if all the accounts involved in the WMI query have been given *trusted-for-delegation* permissions in Active Directory. This is a safeguard for using Delegate access because it allows a remote computer to impersonate you on yet another remote computer. Needless to say, with sufficient privileges and malicious code, this can potentially be very harmful, so be careful when using the Delegate impersonation level.

Using the New WMI Cmdlets

The authentication parameter of the Get-WMIObject Cmdlet isn't the only new WMI feature for Windows PowerShell 2. In fact, three new Cmdlets specifically dealing with WMI are now available to you. These newbie Cmdlets are Invoke-WMIMethod, Remove-WMIObject, and Set-WMIInstance, which I describe in the following sections.

Making things happen with Invoke-WMIMethod

WMI isn't all about being able to query properties. You can also use WMI to take action through different WMI providers by invoking methods defined in the WMI class. *Methods* are code blocks that are designed to perform a specific action. For example, the `Win32_Service` class has a `StartService` and `StopService` method that you can use to start and stop services. For example, to stop the World Wide Web Publishing Service (`W3SVC`), run this command:

```
Invoke-WMIMethod -path "Win32_Service.Name='W3SVC'" -name StopService
```

You use the `-path` parameter to specify a specific instance of the `Win32_ Service` class to run this method on. In this case, you tell it to run against the `Win32_Service` instance where the `Name` property is equal to `W3SVC`. The `-name` parameter gives it the name of the method you want to call.

Some methods require arguments to be specified so that it knows what to do. A good example of this is the `Create` method for the `Win32_Process` class. The `Create` method is used to create a new process, but to so it needs the name of the executable that you want it to run. If you want to use WMI to start Internet Explorer, you can run this command:

```
Invoke-WMIMethod -class Win32_Process -name Create -argumentlist "C:\Program
             Files\Internet Explorer\iexplore.exe"
```

Notice how you use the `-argumentlist` parameter to give the `Create` method the argument it needs to perform its task.

WMI classes can define their methods as being instance- or static-based:

- ✔ An **instance method** relies on a specific instance of a class to act upon. The `StopService` method of the `Win32_Service` class is a good example of an instance method. You can call `StopService` only on a specific service instance. Just telling the `Win32_Service` to `StopService` doesn't work because it doesn't know which service you're talking about.

- ✔ A **static method** can be run on a class regardless of instance. The `Create` method of the `Win32_Process` class is a good example of a static method. You don't need a specific `Win32_Process` to call `Create` — you're creating a whole new process anyway, which in general is not dependent on any other process.

Deleting objects using Remove-WmiObject

You can use the Remove-WmiObject to send a WMI object to its virtual grave. Of course, this works only on objects that you can actually delete — for instance, you can't use Remove-WmiObject to make your RAM magically disappear. You'll typically use this Cmdlet to get rid of objects such as files, printers, registry keys, and processes.

This Cmdlet has about as many arguments as Get-WmiObject, so it's quite flexible. In practice, though, there's a much easier way to use this Cmdlet. You simply use Get-WmiObject to get the list of objects you're interested in and then pipe it into Remove-WmiObject, and *voilà,* they're done.

Here's a good little exercise that shows how cool this Cmdlet actually is:

1. **Open Notepad on your computer.**

2. **Run the following code:**

   ```
   Get-WmiObject -query "Select * from Win32_Process where name='notepad.exe'"
   ```

   If you have Notepad open, it returns all the information you ever want to know about the notepad.exe process.

3. **Now run this code:**

   ```
   Get-WmiObject -query "Select * from Win32_Process where name='notepad.exe'"
            | Remove-WmiObject
   ```

   Notepad is no longer running on your computer, all thanks to Remove-WmiObject.

 Remove-WmiObject is quite powerful, and because it's designed as a fairly destructive Cmdlet you should make sure the objects you want to remove are in fact the ones you really want to get rid of. The best way to do this is by querying for the WMI objects and making sure the right objects are returned before piping it into Remove-WmiObject.

Setting WMI properties using Set-WmiInstance

The Set-WmiInstance Cmdlet is used for setting read-write WMI properties. Although a vast majority of WMI class properties are read-only, quite a few aren't, and this Cmdlet lets you take advantage of those properties. An example of a class that has a read-write property is the Win32_Environment class. It defines all the environment variables on the system.

You can see all the environment variables defined on your system by running this line:

```
Get-WmiObject Win32_Environment
```

Each environment variable consists of three properties: Name, Variable Value, and UserName. The Name and VariableValue properties contain the names and values of these variables, and the UserName defines the user where the variable applies to. An entry of <SYSTEM> means it's a system variable, but if you see a specific username in there then those represent user variables.

To create a new system environment variable called MyVariable with a value of MyValue, you use the Set-WmiInstance Cmdlet like this:

```
Set-WmiInstance -class Win32_Environment -argument @{Name="MyVariable";VariableV
        alue="MyValue";UserName="<SYSTEM>"}
```

The -argument parameter is where you specify the name/value pairs that will be created. The argument value is in the format of a *hash table*. I go over hash tables in greater detail in Chapter 11, but for now suffice it to say that a hash table is data structure that maps keys to values. In the Set-WMIInstance command you issue in this section, an example of a key would be Name, and MyVariable is an example of a value.

Chapter 9

Bringing Strings into the Limelight

*W*hether you're writing e-mail or browsing the Web, you're constantly interacting with some form of text. Besides the spoken word, text is one of the most common ways we communicate with one another. In fact, I'm communicating with you right now through text. Even though computers are really just oversized and overpowered calculators, when it comes to interaction between humans and computers, text is the natural choice for communication. I mean, how useful would it be for the computer to display `1101000 1100101 1101100 1101100 1101111` to greet you instead of writing `Hello` onscreen?

Interacting with computers by using text is important, which is why displaying, reading, and manipulating text are key features of any programming or scripting language. PowerShell provides all the bells and whistles to make all this work easy for you. In this chapter, you find out just how surprisingly capable PSH is at dealing with and manipulating text. Armed with this knowledge, you'll be parsing, filtering, and doing all kinds of fun stuff with text in no time.

Taking Your First Look at Strings

The technical name for text is *string*. Although you normally think of text as having some meaning, a string is really nothing more than a consecutive sequence of characters. It doesn't matter what characters are placed next to one another; they all form strings. Some examples of strings are

```
This is a string
Ldf3rj814
@@fdfds338adsvk
f
SDf sdfdki weird string
```

As you can see, a string can contain any character you want, can be any length, and can include any white space such as spaces and tabs. Theoretically, string length is unlimited, but in the real world, the length of a string is limited to the amount of memory you have.

Differentiating between empty and null strings

You can have a string that has zero length, which is a string that doesn't contain any characters, called an *empty string*. You can also have a string with no length. Wait — isn't a string with zero length the same as one with no length? Well, not exactly. A *null string* is a special kind of string that hasn't been defined yet, so it doesn't contain anything and doesn't have a length. Its value is the special automatic variable called $null.

If a variable has a data type of string and is defined but initially isn't given a value, it contains a null string instead. If empty strings are merely strings that don't contain anything, why can't null strings just initialize to an empty string so we can do away with the null-string concept altogether? The answer is that this concept exists so that you can differentiate a string that hasn't been initialized yet from a string that is purposely set to have no value.

If the string is part of a command line parameter, for example, you can check to see whether the value is equal to $null, which means that the user didn't provide a value for this parameter. This string is very different from an empty string, because even though it's just an empty (blank) string right now, the user provided a value for it.

Creating literal strings

Strings are everywhere in Windows PowerShell. They exist as properties for various objects. Also, they can be returned by different object methods. The most direct way to create a string is to define what's called a *literal string*.

You create literal strings by enclosing a sequence of characters in double quotes. This way, you are literally defining the string. A literal string looks like this:

```
"This is the definition of a literal string"
"...and here is another string"
"and a string with some random characters 35vndaa3$%@32"
```

 Sometimes, strings are created for you automatically. When you combine a string with another data type, for example, Windows PowerShell automatically tries to convert that data type to a string for you.

Simplifying using Here-Strings

When you have to define a string that has line breaks or special characters such as double quotes, you can do so by joining multiple strings like this:

```
$regularString = "First line of string`n" +
                 "Second Line`n" +
                 "Third Line"
Write-Host $regularString
```

As expected, you get this output:

```
First line of string
Second Line
Third Line
```

Although this code works, typing all those plus signs and `n characters to generate a new line gets tiresome, especially if you're trying to define a string that is many more lines long. To make your life easier, you can use a Windows PowerShell feature called Here-Strings. You create a Here-String by starting it with an at (@) sign followed by a double quotation mark and then a new line. You end a Here-String by using a double quotation mark followed by the @ sign, and this needs to be done on a new line by itself. Windows PowerShell treats all the text in between those symbols like a literal string. This means that if you put a new-line character in that space, that new line is preserved when you use the string. The Here-String version is the exact equivalent of the preceding string example. See how much simpler it looks:

```
$myHereString = @"
First line of string
Second Line
Third Line
"@
Write-Host $myHereString
```

The best part about `Here-Strings` is that (because Windows PowerShell treats everything between the start and end of a `Here-String` literally) you can even include quotation marks in a `Here-String`, and PowerShell won't get confused. Here's an example:

```
$noProblemString = @"
This is a Here-String with quotation marks.
I can enter "I am in quotes" here and it will
Display correctly if I output this string.
"@
Write-Host $noProblemString
```

Make use of `Here-Strings` whenever you find yourself defining a very long string that includes new-line characters or quotation marks.

Performing String Surgery

You often need to manipulate strings to create new ones, such as splitting them apart, combining them, or grabbing particular segments of a string. Luckily, Windows PowerShell can provide a rich set of methods for string manipulation because it's built on top of the .NET Framework.

Combining strings

Because you often want to put strings together dynamically (as needed when the code runs), combining strings is one of the most common string operations. A typical use is when you want to output some information onscreen by combining some literal strings with variable values, as in this example:

```
for ($i = 0; $i -lt 5; $i++) {
    Write-Host ("The current value is: " + $i)
}
```

You simply use the plus (+) operator to combine two strings. You can combine more than two strings by using the plus operator between all the strings you want combined, as shown here:

```
$a = "Windows PowerShell " + "For Dummies"
Write-Host $a
$b = "Windows " + "PowerShell " + "For " + "Dummies"
Write-Host $b
```

Combining strings with nonstrings

You can combine strings with other data types that aren't strings, provided that those data types can be converted either *implicitly* (automatically by PSH) or *explicitly* (by first casting the value as a string). (For more about data types, see Chapter 5.) When you combine a string with a nonstring value, and the string shows up first when you're reading the values from left to right, the nonstring value is implicitly converted to a string and then combined using the usual method. Does this process sound confusing? It's easier than it sounds. Take a look at this code snippet:

```
$myString = "You are number "
$myNum = 1
Write-Host ($myString + $myNum)
Write-Host ($myNum + $myString)
```

As expected, the first call to `Write-Host` displays `You are number 1`. Windows PowerShell sees that you're combining a string and a number (in this case, an integer), so in the background, it first converts the number 1 to the string 1 and then continues to combine the two strings.

The second call to `Write-Host` results in an error message saying that it can't convert `"You are number"` to a type `"System.Int32"`. Here, Windows PowerShell sees that you're combining a string and a number as well, but because the first value it sees is a number, it tries to convert the second value to the same data type. Because the string `"You are number"` doesn't represent a number, Windows PowerShell spits out an error.

The solution to the problem of combining a string and any other value, even though the first value is not a string, is explicitly converting the other value by *casting* (changing) it to a string. To do this, you add `[string]` before the variable name to tell Windows PowerShell that you want this value to be treated as a string (which forces the conversion). This modified version of the second `Write-Host` statement works the way you want it to:

```
Write-Host ([string]$myNum + $myString)
```

To force a value that isn't a string to be treated as a string, prefix it with `[string]` to tell Windows PowerShell that you want to cast it into a string data type.

Splitting strings

If you can combine strings, you have to have a way to split them apart. You might have quite a few reasons for wanting to take a string apart. You may want to take a string that's delimited by a certain character, such as a line from a comma-separated value (CSV) file, and get the individual strings that represent different columns of data. Sometimes, you need to take just a portion of a string, such as the first three characters of a name.

To split strings, you use nothing other than the (drumroll, please) `split` method. The `split` method, in its simplest form, splits a string into an array of strings by using spaces and tabs as delimiting characters. I discuss arrays in Chapter 11, but for now, you can consider an *array* to be a group of similar items that you can reference with an index. Think of an array as being a line of schoolchildren, with each child (element) standing behind another. Then you can refer to a child in that line based on his or her position, such as the fifth child (counting from the front of the line).

Here's a code snippet that takes a string with spaces and uses the `split` method to break it into multiple strings:

```
$str = "This book is fantabulous!"
$str.split()
```

The output of that command sequence is

```
This
book
is
fantabulous!
```

Although that code is pretty cool and a neat trick, it doesn't seem to be very useful. To put some meat on the bone, have a look at the next example. You have an IP address as a string, and you want to split the IP address so you can find out the value of any of the four octets of that IP address. The `split` method comes to the rescue again:

```
$myIP = "192.168.10.100"
$ipArr = $myIP.split(".")
Write-Host ("Number of elements in ipArr" + $ipArr.length)
Write-Host ("First octet: " + $ipArr[0])
Write-Host ("Second octet: " + $ipArr[1])
Write-Host ("Third octet: " + $ipArr[2])
Write-Host ("Fourth octet: " + $ipArr[3])
```

Notice a few interesting things in this example? Look at the call to the `split` method, which takes a string as a parameter that specifies what characters to use as delimiters. By running `$myIP.split` with `"."` as the parameter, you instruct the `split` method to take the string stored in `$myIP` and split it into substrings, using a period as a delimiter.

An array has a property called `length` that defines how many items are stored in it. The example displays the number of elements to show that after the `split` method is called, `$ipArr` indeed has an array for four elements, just as expected. To grab the individual elements of the array, you reference it by using the array's index notation, which is in the format `$arrayname[index]`.

Arrays are *zero-index based,* meaning that the first element is referred to as `$arrayname[0]`, so to find out the second element you need to specify `$arrayname[1]`; to find the third element, you use `$array-name[2]`; and so on. To get to any index you want, you have to specify `$arrayname[position - 1]`.

When specifying the delimiter in the `split` method, you're not limited to one character. If you use multiple characters as delimiters, you can simply combine them all and provide a string of all the delimiters. This code snippet is functionally equivalent to the preceding code snippet, because it treats a period, a colon, and a semicolon as delimiters in the given string:

```
$myWierdIP = "192.168:10;100"
$ipArr = $myWeirdIP.split(".:;")
Write-Host ("Number of elements in ipArr" + $ipArr.length)
Write-Host ("First octet: " + $ipArr[0])
Write-Host ("Second octet: " + $ipArr[1])
Write-Host ("Third octet: " + $ipArr[2])
Write-Host ("Fourth octet: " + $ipArr[3])
```

Snipping off a piece of a string

Another common string operation is grabbing a particular portion of a string, called a *substring.* A substring can be a portion of the beginning or end of the string, or somewhere in between. If the string is delimited, you can use the `split` method for this operation, but in general, if you have a string and want to grab any given substring from it, you use the `substring` method. Have a look at this piece of code:

```
$name = "Steve Seguis"
$part1 = $name.substring(0,3)
$part2 = $name.substring($name.length-4,4)
Write-Host ($part1 + $part2)
```

Here, I define my full name as a string. Using the `substring` method, I tell Windows PowerShell to return the first three characters of `$name` and assign it to `$part1`. Then I tell it to grab the last four characters of `$name` and assign it to `$part2`. Finally, I combine these two substrings to generate the output *Steguis*.

The `substring` method of a string takes two parameters. The first parameter is the offset from the first position (start from the left) of the string to where you want to start grabbing characters. The number 0 is used to denote the first character. The second parameter is the `length` of the substring. It defines how many consecutive characters you want to retrieve starting from the offset provided in the first parameter.

Whenever you want to grab a certain number of characters starting from the beginning of a string, just use `$stringvariable.substring(0, length)`, where *length* is how many characters at the beginning of the string you want to return.

All strings also have a `length` parameter that tells you how many characters are in the string. To get a substring of a given length starting from the end of a string, you have to perform some math, using the string's length and the number of characters you want to determine the starting point that the `substring` method requires.

Whenever you want to grab something from the end of a string, just use `$stringvariable.substring($stringvariable.length - count, count)`, where *count* is the number of characters you want, starting from the last character.

As I mention earlier in this section, you're not limited to taking just the first or last part of a string. You can use the `substring` method to grab any portion of a string, as in this example:

```
$test = "The sky is cloudy!"
Write-Host $test.substring(4,6)
```

This code snippet outputs `sky is` because it takes the substring starting with offset four (which is really the fifth character in the string) and returns the next six characters.

When using substrings, it's very easy to introduce errors into your code, so you should employ some defensive programming to protect yourself. If you write a script and assume that a given string variable will always contain a string that is more than six characters and use the `substring` command to return the first four characters, what happens if the script suddenly encounters a value that has only three characters? The result is an error that causes the script to quit. To guard against this error, you can wrap the `substring` statement in an `if/else` clause to make sure that the length of the string is at least the number of characters you want to extract, as in this example:

```
$a = "abc"
if ($a.length -ge 4) {
   Write-Host ("First four characters are: " + $a.substring(0,4))
} else {
   Write-Host ("String has less than 4 characters: " + $a)
}
```

Here, you check whether the length of $a is greater than or equal to four. If it is, you display the first four characters; otherwise, you tell the user that the string has fewer than four characters and just output the entire string.

Performing string substitutions

There's a common saying among management staff: "Everyone's replaceable!" Although this saying is true, I've always found it to be a bit disturbing. Unfortunately for poor little strings, the saying is true even for them. You can replace any part of a string with another string by using the string's replace method. Consider this code snippet:

```
$str = "Steve is Evil!"
$newstr = $str.replace("Evil","Good")
Write-Host $newstr
```

This example literally replaces Evil with Good. The replace method takes two parameters. The first parameter is the string you want to replace in the string, and the second parameter is the string you want to replace it with. If the string you want to replace doesn't exist, nothing is replaced.

Working with String Positions

Sometimes, you need to find the position of a string in another string, most commonly to calculate the starting position for grabbing a substring. Suppose that you have an e-mail address as a string. Now you need to extract the user and domain information based on the e-mail address. You can do this operation easily in your head, because you know that the username is whatever comes before the @ sign and the domain name is what comes after the @ sign. You can perform this operation in Windows PowerShell just as easily by using something like this code snippet:

```
$email = "someone@dummies.com"
$atpos = $email.IndexOf("@")
$user = $email.substring(0,$atpos)
$domain = $email.substring($atpos+1, $email.length-($atpos+1))
Write-Host ("Username: " + $user)
Write-Host ("Domain: " + $domain)
```

As you can see in the code snippet, you can find out the position of a string in another string by using the IndexOf method. You call the IndexOf method on the string you're searching in (which in this case is $email), and the parameter of IndexOf is the string you're looking for. The value this code returns is the index within the string that contains the first occurrence of the given search string. If the search string isn't found, the return value is -1.

This example returns a value of 7, which is stored in $atpos. Notice, however, that the @ sign is the eighth character in the string. Why does the code return 7? Remember that when you're referring to string indices, the first character is always index 0; the second character is index 1; and so on. Because the @ symbol is the eighth character in the string, the corresponding index is 8-1, or 7.

Getting the username is very easy, because you just use the template for pulling substrings that start from the beginning of the string. You start by using the substring method and have it start at the beginning by using 0 as the first parameter. To get the length of the string, you can just use the value of $atpos because it already contains the value that's equal to the length of the string that comes before it.

You can extract the domain name in a similar fashion, but the process requires a tiny bit more math. You have to set the starting point of the substring to $atpos+1 because you want to exclude the @ sign from the string that the code returns. To get the length of this substring, you need to take the length of the string and subtract the position you start with.

Another really good and common use of the IndexOf method to get the string position is performing comparisons of partial strings. Suppose that you're writing a script that expects the value of a certain variable to contain a valid e-mail address. A simple check for this value is to make sure that the string contains an @ sign. In the real world, of course, this check isn't enough to validate an e-mail address, but for the purpose of this example, you can create a simple test to see whether the value might conceivably be an e-mail address. To make sure that a string contains an @ sign, you can do something like this:

```
$email = "my_invalid_email_address"
if ($email.IndexOf("@") -lt 0) {
   Write-Host "Invalid email address!"
} else {
   Write-Host "Valid email address!"
}
```

The IndexOf method always returns a value greater than or equal to 0 if it finds the given search string in the string where this method is called; otherwise, it returns -1. You can take advantage of this fact by checking to see whether the return value of IndexOf is less than 0 to determine whether a match wasn't found.

Changing the Case of Strings

Strings come in all shapes and sizes, and sometimes, you want to create some uniformity in their display. One way to keep string output uniform is to make sure that all the characters are uppercase or lowercase. This feat is easy to accomplish; strings have the built-in capability (with the ToUpper and ToLower methods) to change the case of all their characters. Here's an example:

```
$str = "My MiXed CaSE stRInG"
Write-Host $str.ToUpper()
Write-Host $str.ToLower()
```

Coding really doesn't get any easier than that. Although this example is convenient, its limitation is that these two methods convert the entire string to uppercase or lowercase. What if you only want the first character to be uppercase and force the remaining characters to be lowercase? A good example of this scenario is if you're displaying first names and want the characters to be in that specific format. This task is doable, requiring just a little bit more effort, as in this example:

```
$name = "sTEvE"
$a = $name.substring(0,1).ToUpper()
$b = $name.substring(1,$name.length-1).ToLower()
Write-Host ($a + $b)
```

Here's where substrings really come in handy. Because the ToUpper and ToLower methods affect the entire string, you just split the string into substrings, apply the appropriate case-changing methods to the substrings, and then recombine.

Using Regular Expressions

I've always found the term *regular expressions* to be a bit funny, because I find nothing "regular" about them at all. Also, this term begs the question "Are there irregular expressions?" (There aren't, by the way).

A *regular expression* (*RegEx,* for short) is nothing more than a string that describes a search pattern. The best part is that as simple as they sound, regular expressions really give you a lot of power to define very specific search patterns. Before you can use regular expression in Windows PowerShell (which turns out to be very easy), you need to know how to create regular expressions (which, unfortunately, turns out to be more difficult).

Again, because Windows PowerShell is built on top of the .NET Framework, it's no surprise that when you use regular expressions in Windows PowerShell, you're actually using the `Regex` .NET class. This means that if you see any documentation using regular expressions in .NET, you can use the same information and apply it to Windows PowerShell.

The most direct way to use regular expressions is to use the `Regex` object's methods directly. You can see whether a string contains a particular character or substring by doing something like this:

```
[Regex]::IsMatch("This book is really interesting.","book")
```

This code snippet just looks to see whether the string `"This book is really interesting"` contains the string `"book"`. If so, it returns `true`; otherwise, it returns `false`. In this example, `"book"` is a very simple regular expression using what's called literal characters (which I get into in the next section). You can put any kind of regular expression you want in place of `"book"` to perform your desired search. Here's another quick example:

```
[RegEx]::IsMatch("I have 2 siblings.","[0-9]")
```

The regular expression I'm using here is just a bit more powerful. `"[0-9]"` means "match any digit from 0 to 9," which in this case will match the `2`. Imagine trying to do that with the string's `IndexOf` method. You'd have to have ten separate calls for `IndexOf` to look for each character separately.

The actual regular expressions are the second parameter in the `IsMatch` method; the first parameter is simply the string you want to search in. For the rest of the examples in this chapter, where I use `IsMatch` to demonstrate how a particular regular expression works, you need to pay attention only to the second parameter, because that's the actual regular expression.

People have written books longer than this one on regular expressions, which says a lot about how powerful they really are. Luckily for you, I don't spend the rest of this book teaching you regular expressions. Instead, I use the rest of this chapter to show you the most important regular expressions concepts you need to know.

Creating the simplest RegEx using literal characters

Probably the most fundamental and natural of all the regular expressions is a *literal character,* which is a single character match. If you have a string such as "`Regular expressions are powerful!`", and your regular expression is the character u, the code will find a match based on the first occurrence of u in that string. You can also combine characters to perform a match. So given the same string as before, if you have the regular expression "press", the code will match the first occurrence of the string "press", which in this case is the substring "press" in the word "expressions":

```
[Regex]::IsMatch("Regular expressions are powerful!","press")
```

In some ways, this method is very similar to the IndexOf method you use in the preceding section to find a position of a substring in another string. The difference is that by default, regular expressions are case sensitive. Searching for windows in Windows PowerShell won't return a match because the code is specifically looking for windows in all lowercase characters.

Although you can use any character you want for your literal character search, you have to watch out for *special characters,* which are characters that have special meaning in regular expressions. These special characters are

- ✔ **Backslash:** \
- ✔ **Dollar sign:** $
- ✔ **Dot:** .
- ✔ **Pipe:** |
- ✔ **Question mark:** ?
- ✔ **Star:** *
- ✔ **Plus sign:** +
- ✔ **Open square bracket:** [
- ✔ **Open parenthesis:** (
- ✔ **Close parenthesis:**)
- ✔ **Caret:** ^

If you want to use any of these characters as a literal character, you must first *escape* (mark to not treat as special) it by prefixing it with a backslash (\). In the following example, I'm looking for dummies.com in the given string. Because dummies.com contains a special character (namely, the dot) I have to write the expression as "dummies\.com" instead:

```
[RegEx]::IsMatch("Visit us at www.dummies.com.","dummies\.com")
```

The dot operator is a very powerful character because it matches any single character except for a new-line character (typically used if the string you're searching in consists of multiple lines). Take a look at this example:

```
[RegEx]::IsMatch("bell",".ell")
```

This example returns true because the RegEx ".ell" means any character followed by "ell". As a result, it also matches cell, tell, and well — and also "4ell" and "#ell". In other words, it matches anything followed by "ell". The dot is a single-character wildcard.

You really should use the dot as a single-character wild card sparingly. You have much better ways to describe string patterns, and these methods give you much more control of which values are actually valid. What I mean by this is that you should be as specific as possible when describing your pattern. For instance, if you know it's going to be a numeric value, then use the pattern [0-9] instead of just using the dot which will match any single character including non-numeric values.

Performing more dynamic searches using character sets

Often, you need to perform a match based on variations of characters. A very obvious example is looking for a digit from 0 to 9. Conducting a search like this one without using regular expressions is tedious at best, so being able to formulate a RegEx to describe this pattern is a godsend for lazy people like me. Consider this code snippet:

```
$username = "testuser1"
[RegEx]::IsMatch($username,"testuser[0-9]")
```

Here, you have a username variable that contains the value testuser1. If you want to check for a match of this string, you can just perform a literal match. But if you want to match any testuser string followed by a number, you must instead replace the digit at the end with [0-9] instead. This code matches anything that contains the string testuser followed by a single digit from 0 through 9. [0-9] is called a *character set* and is used to define a list or range of characters that you want to find in a given position.

A character set defines a list or range of characters to match exactly one character within a given search string.

You aren't limited to a range of characters such as [0-9] or [a-z]. You can also define a list of characters you want, as in this example:

```
$name = "Anna"
[RegEx]::IsMatch($name,"Ann[ae]")
```

Here, I want the name to match either Anna or Anne. I do this by making the last character a character set of [ae], which means that a match will occur whenever the string Ann is followed by either a lowercase a or a lowercase e.

If you want to exclude characters from a match, you can negate a character set by prefixing it with the caret (^) symbol. This example shows how you can look for a substring that ends in "ood" and starts with any character except for f or h:

```
[RegEx]::IsMatch("food","[^fh]ood")
```

By placing a caret symbol within the character set [^fh], you negate the statement and change its meaning to match any character except f or h. So this example returns a value of false, because "food" starts with the letter f.

As you might expect, writing regular expressions tends to get a bit tedious. Some character sets are so common that some shortcuts for using them have been defined. Table 9-1 lists the most common shortcuts.

Table 9-1	Most Common Shortcuts for Character Sets	
Character	**Description**	**Equivalent Character Set**
\d	Any digit from 0–9	[0-9]
\w	Any digit, uppercase and lowercase letter, and underscore	[A-Za-z0-9_]
\s	White-space characters (space, tab, new line, and carriage return)	[\b\t\n\r]
\D	Not a digit	[^0-9]
\W	Opposite of of \w. Any character that is not any digit, uppercase and lowercase letter or underscore.	[^A-Za-z0-9_]
\S	Negative of \s. Any character that is not a whitespace character.	[^ \b\t\n\r]

Using modifiers to define optional or repeating sequences

The character sets you've looked at so far in this chapter are useful for representing various character permutations for a given match, but you also need a way to define repeating characters or even optional characters. Suppose that you have a script that needs to find a match to the word `"favorite"`. You can use a literal character match (refer to "Creating the simplest RegEx using literal characters," earlier in this chapter), but what if the script also must work with either the American or British spelling of this word? You need to do something like this:

```
[RegEx]::IsMatch("favorite","favou?rite")
[RegEx]::IsMatch("favourite","favou?rite")
```

Both of these calls return `true`. The reason is that the character u is followed by a question mark (?). The question mark indicates that the preceding character can exist zero times or one time, making it effectively optional. Technically, the question mark indicates that previous token is optional. *Tokens* can be single characters, character sets, or even multiple characters enclosed in parentheses. In the following example, both statements return `true` because the `"day"` portion of the string `"Monday"` is enclosed in parentheses, making the entire substring a token, and followed by a question mark, which means that `"day"` is optional:

```
[RegEx]::IsMatch("Monday","Mon(day)?")
[RegEx]::IsMatch("Mon","Mon(day)?")
```

Repetition is another one of those patterns that you need to be able to describe. Here's a scenario in which repetition is useful. You work in an organization in which all the server names start with the string `"SRV"` and are followed by some other descriptive name and a number, such as "SRVWEB1" for your first Web server. You can't just use character sets, because you don't know how many characters may follow the string `"SRV"`. You can create a regular expression to define this pattern by using this statement:

```
[RegEx]::IsMatch("SRVWEB1","SRV[A-Z0-9]+")
[RegEx]::IsMatch("SRVDC1","SRV[A-Z0-9]+")
[RegEx]::IsMatch("SRVFILE1","SRV[A-Z0-9]+")
```

All three of these statements return `true`. The plus (+) operator is used to describe a pattern in which the previous token is repeated one or more times. `SRV[A-Z0-9]+` describes a sequence in which you have a substring that starts with `SRV` and is followed by one or more uppercase alphanumeric characters.

This solution isn't perfect, though, because SRV[A-Z0-9]+ also matches TESTSRV2323. In other words, the string doesn't have to start with SRV. Rather, a substring must contains the sequence SRV followed by any character one or more times, which can also include just numbers. To refine this code a little, you can change it to something like this:

```
[RegEx]::IsMatch("SRVFILE1","SRV[A-Z]+[0-9]")
```

This example is a little bit better because now you're saying to match a substring that starts with SRV followed by one or more capital letters and then a digit from 0—9. This code matches the naming convention better, but it still has the limitation of not enforcing the convention that the string itself must start with SRV. (I address this limitation in the next section, "Using anchors to maintain position.")

The plus operator is good at defining repetition, but what if the repetition is optional? Suppose that you want to perform a name search in which the string that defines the name starts with Ann but can have zero or more letters after it. The first thing that might come to your mind is

```
[RegEx]::IsMatch("Ann","Ann[a-z]+")
```

This example works in most cases and matches variations such as Anna, Anne, and Annie. The problem is that it won't match the name Ann because the plus operator requires the token (which in this case is the character set [a-z]) to exist at least once. How do you solve this problem?

The answer is the star (*) operator, which is similar to the plus operator but means that the preceding token must match zero or more times. Any time you see the description "zero or more times," it should automatically ring the "It's optional" bell. So the correct solution to the name-search problem is

```
[RegEx]::IsMatch("Ann","Ann[a-z]*")
```

This statement returns true because the remaining characters after "Ann" are optional.

The plus (+) operator means that the preceding token is repeated one or more times, whereas the star (*) operator means that the preceding token is repeated zero or more times, making it optional.

Another problem with a repeating pattern is you have to be able to set limits. If you have to define a pattern of characters that fits the format of a U.S. zip code (which is five digits in sequence), you can do this by using character sets:

```
[RegEx]::IsMatch("90210","[0-9][0-9][0-9][0-9][0-9]")
```

This example works because you use a sequence of five character sets, each of which restricts each character to a digit from 0–9. The code is a bit inefficient, however, and — dare I say it? — tedious. The way to correct this is to define repetition limits using curly braces. You can define a sequence of exactly five numeric characters like this instead:

```
[RegEx]::IsMatch("90210","[0-9]{5}")
```

The number inside the curly braces indicates exactly how many times the preceding token must repeat to represent a match. You can also use the curly braces to define a range of repetition counts. If you want to describe a string that starts with "USER" and ends in a sequence of two to five uppercase letters, you can use

```
[RegEx]::IsMatch("USERA","USER[A-Z]{2,5}")
[RegEx]::IsMatch("USERABC","USER[A-Z]{2,5}")
```

Only the second statement returns true because the first statement has only one character after the string "USER". The first value in the curly braces is the minimum repeat count, whereas the second value is the maximum repeat count.

Using anchors to maintain position

The regular expressions you've created so far in this chapter are wonderful, but something is lacking: defining the position of the search string within the string being searched. This factor is important, as you see in the server-list example in the preceding section. To go back to that example briefly, you know that a server name starts with SRV followed by some characters that represent its function and then a number, such as SRVWEB1. The best you can do with what you know so far is

```
[RegEx]::IsMatch("SRVFILE1","SRV[A-Z]+[0-9]")
```

The problem, of course, is that this code also matches TESTSRVFILE1, because a RegEx match looks for only the first occurrence of the given RegEx pattern in the string. To fix this problem, you have to have a way to indicate that this match must occur at the beginning of the string. You do this by using the caret (^) symbol:

```
[RegEx]::IsMatch("SRVFILE1","^SRV[A-Z]+[0-9]")
[RegEx]::IsMatch("TESTSRVFILE1","^SRV[A-Z]+[0-9]")
```

By adding the caret symbol to the beginning of your RegEx, you're saying that this pattern must occur at the beginning of the string. Now the first statement continues to return `true`, but the second statement returns `false`.

The caret symbol has two faces. When you use it at the beginning of a RegEx as in the preceding example, you're using it as an anchor. When you use it inside a character set, it acts as a negation operator, excluding the characters defined in the set.

The opposite of the caret symbol is the dollar sign (`$`), which is used to perform a match at the end of a string, as shown here:

```
[RegEx]::IsMatch("SRVFILE1","SRV[A-Z]+[0-9]$")
[RegEx]::IsMatch("TESTSRVFILE1","SRV[A-Z]+[0-9]$")
[RegEx]::IsMatch("SRVFILE1TEST","SRV[A-Z]+[0-9]$")
```

By removing the caret symbol and putting a dollar sign at the end of the RegEx, you're telling it to look for the pattern at the end of the string. The first two statements return `true`, but the last statement returns `false` because SRVFILE1 (which matches the pattern) doesn't occur at the end of the string.

Coming up with alternatives

Sometimes, the pattern you're trying to describe by using RegEx has a finite number of variations. If you want to perform a simple domain-name check using a RegEx to look for a string that contains any number of alphanumeric characters followed by a dot and then ending in com, edu, or net, you'd do this:

```
[RegEx]::IsMatch("dummies.com","[A-Za-z0-9]+\.(com|edu|net)")
```

Examine the RegEx a little closer. The first part is `[A-Za-z0-9]+`, which defines a sequence of one or more alphanumeric characters. The next element is `\.`, which is a literal dot (remember that you have to use the backslash to escape the special character). The last part is the most interesting. You use the pipe (`|`) symbol to define various alternative matches. Because you're restricting this check to domain names that end in .com, .edu, or .net, this method is the most efficient way to define those variations.

Making use of RegEx in Windows PowerShell

So far, I've used `[RegEx]::IsMatch` to help demonstrate the different regular expressions because it's very simple and returns a `true/false` value so that you can easily check to see whether an expression matches a given string. An even easier way exists, however, to perform string comparisons using regular expressions without having to use `[RegEx]::IsMatch`. You already know that you can perform an exact string match by using the `-eq` operator. You can also use `-match` and `-notmatch` operators to compare strings with a regular expression. Here's how you can use `-match` to perform a RegEx match on a given string:

```
$email = "somebody@dummies.com"
if ($email -match "[A-Za-z0-9]+@dummies.com") {
    Write-Host "$email is a dummies.com email address"
}
```

You can actually find many more uses for regular expressions. You can use them to replace substrings by using the `-replace` switch, for example. Here's an example in which you want to replace a Web site's name with the string `"WEBSITE NAME KEPT SECRET"`:

```
$str = "Visit us at www.dummies.com"
$newstr = $str -replace "www\.[A-Za-z0-9]+\.(com|edu|net)","WEBSITE NAME KEPT
          SECRET"
Write-Host $newstr
```

The first parameter of `-replace` is the RegEx that describes the pattern you want to find, and the second parameter is the string you want to replace it with. Think of this switch as being a very powerful search-and-replace feature.

Don't confuse the `-replace` switch with the string's `replace` method, which performs a literal search and replace. The `-replace` switch allows you to define regular expressions to describe the matching text that needs to be replaced.

Chapter 10

I'll Take Numbers for $100, Please

Computers big and small have one thing in common: They're excellent number crunchers. Next to strings, numbers probably encompass one the most widely used data types in any programming or scripting language. It's highly unlikely that you're going to use Windows PowerShell to perform massive calculations to conduct weather simulations, but no matter how hard you try, you just won't be able to escape the need to deal with numbers. The need can be something as simple as incrementing a value to control a for loop or something a bit more complex, such as calculating the probability of winning the lottery.

In this chapter, you use Windows PowerShell to perform many common mathematical operations. Computer are just big calculators after all, so knowing how to take advantage of PSH to make these calculations for you can leave your brain cells to do more productive things, like reading the rest of this book.

Putting Numeric Data Types under a Microscope

I touch on data types in Chapter 5, but now I want to focus on just the numeric data types in Windows PowerShell (which, not surprisingly, are the same as .NET numeric data types). All the numeric data types in Windows PowerShell can be classified in either of two categories: integral and nonintegral data types.

Having a look at integral data types

Integral data types are *whole numbers* (numbers that don't have decimal values at the end). The only real difference among the four integral data types is that each one supports a different range of values controlled by the number of bits that composes it. The four integral data types are

- ✔ **Byte:** A *byte* (`System.Byte` in .NET) is an 8-bit unsigned data type that has a range of values from 0 through 255. This data type is the only numeric data type that can't contain negative numbers. One use of this data type is to represent the *octets* (another way to say "8-bit values") of a typical IP address. Because IP addresses consist of four octets, each representing an unsigned value from 0 through 255, the byte data type naturally is the ideal data type to represent these values. (For more info on bytes, see the sidebar "Knowing your bits and bytes," later in this chapter.)

- ✔ **Short:** A *short* (`System.Int16` in .NET) is a 16-bit signed data type that has a range of values from –32,768 through 32,767. Short is the smallest of the signed integral data types. Typically, you use a short only if you want to store lots of small signed values while minimizing the memory footprint. In the real world, however, you rarely see the short data type being used except maybe to hold a short value retrieved from a data store such as a SQL database.

- ✔ **Integer:** An *integer* (`System.Int32` in .NET) is a 32-bit signed data type that has a range of values from –2,147,483,648 through 2,147,483,647. Integer is the basic data type of 32-bit processors because they process 32-bit chunks of data at a time, which means that using integer data types is optimal on these processors and results in the best performance. This data type is also very convenient to use because it can store a whole number within a range that's more than 4 billion values wide. That scenario covers 90 percent of the cases in which you need to use whole numbers.

  Integer is the default data type that Windows PowerShell uses when you define an integral number, such as 28, without specifying the data type.

- ✔ **Long:** A *long* (`System.Int64` in .NET) is a 64-bit signed data type that has a range of values from –9,223,327,036,854,775,808 through 9,223,372,036,854,775,807. Obviously, it's designed to store awfully large numbers. You're going to need a long if you run out of values in an integer to represent the value you're trying to store. Realistically, though, you'll probably use this data type sparingly because in most cases, the range is bigger than you'll need and takes up twice as much memory. The only upside to a long is that it's a natural data type for use with 64-bit processors, which calculate 64-bit values faster than other –bit values. Otherwise, unless you plan to add large values (to calculate the national debt or count the days until you can afford that red Ferrari), you probably won't use this data type much.

Getting precise using nonintegral data types

Nonintegral data types are data types that aren't integral. (Ha! I bet you didn't expect that lame definition, did you?) Actually, this definition is mostly true no matter how blatantly obvious and third-gradeish (is that even a word?) it looks. Nonintegral data types are simply values that can contain *fractional* (decimal) values. You use them when you want to get really precise, as in storing the value of pi (3.14159265 . . .). The nonintegral data types are:

- **Decimal:** When you perform calculations involving incredibly large numbers that must be super-precise, such as calculating financial data or measuring distances to satellites in space, the decimal data type is what you want by your side. A *decimal* (`System.Decimal` in .NET) is a 96-bit signed value that can represent values up to 7.9228×10^{28}. I could write out the exact value, but I think it's sufficient to say that it can represent enormously large numbers and, likewise, ridiculously small fractions of a value.

- **Single:** A *single* is a single-precision IEEE 32-bit floating-point value from -3.402823×10^{38} to -3.402823×10^{38}. It's also the smallest of the nonintegral data types, but in most cases, its range of values is wide enough to cover most instances in which you need to calculate fractional data.

   IEEE (pronounced "Eye-triple-E") originally was an acronym for *Institute of Electrical and Electronics Engineers,* a nonprofit organization comprised of industry associations that focus on the advancement of technology. Today, however, *IEEE* is a word of its own. The scope of IEEE has grown so much over the past few decades that it's now much larger than that covered by its original meaning.

- **Double:** A *double* is a double-precision IEEE 64-bit floating-point value from $-1.79769313486231 \times 10^{308}$ to $1.79769313486232 \times 10^{308}$. Because it contains double the number of bits to represent a fractional value, it's much more precise than a single (but still not as precise as a decimal). What does this mean in plain English? If you're representing a value that has a fractional component and want it to be more precise than a single, but the value doesn't have to be as precise as a decimal, use this data type.

   Double is the default data type that Windows PowerShell uses for nonintegral data types unless you specify otherwise.

Doing Some Calculations

At some point you'll use numbers to perform various calculations, no matter how simple or complex those calculations may be. The four most important operations are addition, subtraction, division, and multiplication.

Adding things up

The most commonly used mathematical operation is probably addition. You add things up all the time, such as the cost of all the items in your shopping cart or the number of tiles you'll need for that bathroom makeover. You add two numbers in PowerShell by using the plus (+) operator, as shown here:

```
$sum = 2 + 2
Write-Host $sum
```

This example contains nothing really earth-shattering. A number plus another number equals some value. You can add only values that have the same data type. Luckily for you, Windows PowerShell also converts different data types for you automatically so that it can add the values correctly without requiring you to do any extra work. Adding an integer to a double, for example, works without any problems because Windows PowerShell automatically converts the integer to a double, and the resulting data type is added to the other value to return a double as well:

```
$sum = 4 + 9.321
Write-Host $sum.gettype().Name
Write-Host $sum
```

I output the type of $sum to show that it is indeed a double and that the value of sum will be 13.321, as expected. Sometimes, you just want to change a variable by adding a value to it, as in this example:

```
$children = 2
Write-Host ("My friend has " + $children + " children!")
$children = $children + 2
Write-Host ("His wife just had twins so now they have " + $children)
```

You change the value of $children by adding 2 to it and then reassigning this value back to itself. Although this code works fine, it's much better to take advantage of the += operator. The following code snippet is equivalent to the preceding one:

```
$children = 2
Write-Host ("My friend has " + $children + " children!")
$children += 2
Write-Host ("His wife just had twins so now they have " + $children)
```

Adding a value to itself is as simple as using the variable name += the value you want to add. This code not only looks cleaner, but also saves you some typing — which is always a huge plus.

Within the realm of addition, a common procedure performed on integral values is incrementing those values. Typically, for example, you increment a value by 1 when running through loops to keep track of how many times the loop has run. To increment a value by 1, you could do something like this:

```
$i = 0
$i = $i + 1
Write-Host $i
```

Needless to say, the output is 1 because you start off with $i having the value 0 and then adding 1 to it, effectively incrementing its value. This operation is so common that you can perform it in an even easier way. You can increment a value by 1 simply by putting two consecutive plus signs together:

```
$i = 0
$i++
Write-Host $i
```

This code snippet is exactly the same as the preceding one, because $i++ by itself is the same thing as $i = $i + 1. You're a smart person, so you're probably thinking that you can simplify this code even further by changing it to

```
$i = 0
Write-Host ($i++)
```

Oddly enough, the output is 0. What happened? Well, the ++ operator is actually a two-faced creature (know anyone like that?). It can operate as either a *preincrement* or *postincrement* operator, which means that where you put the ++ determines when the value is incremented. To get a better understanding, look at this slight variation on the preceding code snippet:

```
$i = 0
Write-Host ($i++)
Write-Host $i
```

The only thing I do differently here is output the value of $i one more time at the end. If you run this code, you'll find that the first call to Write-Host displays 0, whereas the second call displays 1. The reason? In the first call, you use the ++ operator after the variable name, signifying a postincrement operation.

When you postincrement by placing the ++ operator after the variable name, the value of the variable is incremented only ***after*** the value has been used.

So in the first call to Write-Host, PSH first reads the value of $i (which is 0), and only after the value is read does it actually increment its value to 1. This explains why the first call displays 0 (that's the value it read before incrementing it) and why the second call displays 1 (the value has already been incremented).

To get the behavior you really want in the first place, you can use this code instead to display the value 1 correctly using Write-Host:

```
$i = 0
Write-Host (++$i)
```

When you preincrement by placing the ++ operator before the variable name, the value of the variable is incremented **before** the value is used.

Reducing values with subtraction

The opposite of addition is subtraction, and the great thing is that everything I just showed you about addition applies to subtraction. You only need to replace the plus sign with the minus (–) sign:

```
$difference = 10 - 5
Write-Host $difference
```

Similarly, you can use the -= operator if you want to decrease a variable by a certain amount:

```
$hairOnHead = 10000
Write-Host ("When I was 16 I had " + $hairOnHead + " strands of hair on my
            head.")
$hairOnHead -= 7000
Write-Host ("...now I only have " + $hairOnHead + " :-( ")
```

Just as incrementing is in the realm of addition, decrementing is in the realm of subtraction. Decrementing is just as useful as incrementing, and you can find many good reasons for decrementing values, such as going through array indices in reverse or writing a Windows PowerShell script to count down the seconds to a space-shuttle launch. You can use the -- operator to *predecrement* or *postdecrement* a value. The same rules apply to predecrementing and postdecrementing and to preincrementing and postincrementing, so make sure that you pay attention to where you place the -- operator in relation to your variables. Here's an example:

```
$a = 10
Write-Host ($a--)
Write-Host $a
Write-Host (--$a)
```

The resulting output is

```
10
9
8
```

Expanding through multiplication

When you want to multiply values, you use the star (*) operator, as in this example:

```
$area = 4 * 7
Write-Host $area
```

You can also use the *= operator when you want to multiply a variable by a value and then assign the result back to itself, like this:

```
$x = 5
$x *= 10
Write-Host $x
```

This code results in an output of 50 on the screen.

Reducing through division

If you can multiply, you also need to be able to divide. You can divide a number by using the forward slash (/) operator:

```
$memoryInMB = 4096
$memoryInGB = $memoryInMB / 1024
Write-Host $memoryInGB
```

Knowing your bits and bytes

A *bit* is a single value that can have the value 0 or 1. A group of 8 bits is called an *octet,* whereas a group of 4 bits (half an octet) is called *a nibble.* In general, you may think of bytes as having 8 bits as well, but this isn't always so, because a *byte* is actually the smallest number of memory that a CPU can address. In today's computing environment, a byte is almost always 8 bits wide, so usually you can safely assume that a byte equals an octet.

Most people refer to a *kilobyte* (KB) as 1000 bytes, but technically, it's 1024 bytes (2^{10}). Likewise, a *megabyte* (MB) is 1024 KB, a *gigabyte* (GB) is 1024 MB, and a *terabyte* (TB) is 1024 GB. The distinctions are important when you perform value-conversion calculations among these different units, because if you use 1000 instead of 1024, the result will be incorrect.

Consider the value 325454832107489 bits. If you want to convert this value to terabytes, you first have to divide it by 8 to get bytes, divide that result by 1024 to get kilobytes, divide that result by 1024 to get megabytes, divide that result by 1024 to get gigabytes, and (finally) divide that result by 1024 to get terabytes. The final value you get is 36.99 TB. If you use the value 1000 instead of 1024, you get 40.68 TB. The difference may seem small at first glance, but it's actually a difference of around 3700 GB, which is big.

You guessed what's next. The /= operator can be used to divide a variable by a value and assign the result back to itself, like this:

```
$val = 8
$val /= 4
Write-Host $val
```

That's not the end of the story, though. Whenever you divide anything, there's a high probability that the resulting value will be a fraction. When the resulting value contains a fraction, the result is automatically converted to a double, as in this example:

```
$val = 15 / 4
Write-Host $val
Write-Host $val.GetType().Name
```

The output of this example is 3.75, and the resulting data type is a double even though you're dividing integers.

Sometimes, you don't care about the entire result of a division operation — only about the remainder (otherwise known as the *modulus*). You do this using the modulus (%) operator, as shown here:

```
$x = 54
$remainder = $x % 10
Write-Host $remainder
```

The output of this command is 4, because 10 can go into 54 only 5 times, leaving a remainder of 4.

Rounding Off Values

Oftentimes, when you're multiplying or dividing, you get a result that contains far more decimal places than you really care for. Consider this code snippet, which calculates the sales tax on an item that costs $49.99, assuming that the sales tax is 8.375 percent (.08375):

```
$price = 49.99
$taxRate = 0.08375
$tax = $price * $taxrate
Write-Host $tax
```

Although this code produces an accurate result of 4.1866625, what you really want is to return a value in dollars and cents, so you have to round this value off to contain only two decimal places. You can do this by using the [Math]::round method:

```
Write-Host [Math]::round($tax, 2)
```

Now the code returns the result you want, which is 4.19.

The [Math]::round method takes two parameters. The first parameter is the value you want to round off; the second parameter is the number of decimal places you want to keep. If you want to leave out the last parameter, it defaults to zero decimal places. So if you want to return the value in whole numbers, you can run this code instead:

```
Write-Host [Math]::round($tax)
```

Creating Random Numbers

At times, you need to generate a *random number* (a number that is selected for no particular reason). The uses can vary from creating a Windows PowerShell–based number game to generating random filenames. This task is very simple in Windows PowerShell because all you need to do is create an instance of the Random object and use its Next method to generate the value, as in this example:

```
$objRandom = New-Object Random
$rnd = $objRandom.Next(1,1000)
```

The Random object's Next method takes two parameters, which represent the lowest and highest values you want it to return. In this case, $rnd contains a random value from 1 to 1000.

Converting Numbers

As I say in "Adding things up," earlier in this chapter, Windows PowerShell automatically converts numbers to whatever data type is necessary to perform the requested operation successfully — usually, by converting to a data type that can represent both values without losing any precision. You can force a number to be a different data type, but you have to watch out for data loss. You convert from one data type to another by *casting* it into that data type. (I talk about casting in Chapter 5, if you need a refresher.)

When Windows PowerShell converts to a data type that has more bits (which means that it can also store a larger range of values), no data loss occurs, which means that converting from an integer to a long is always successful and the precision of the value is preserved. If you try to convert a value to a data type that has a lower range, a few things can happen.

If the value you're trying to convert is too large or too small for that data type, Windows PowerShell returns an error, as in this example:

```
$val = 256
$newval = [byte]$val
Write-Host $newval
```

Windows PowerShell automatically treats the value 256 like an integer because it's an integral value that doesn't have the data type explicitly defined. The next line, which tries to convert this value to a byte, fails because a byte can contain only values from 0 through 255, and 256 is outside that range.

Converting from a nonintegral data type to an integral data type will succeed as long as the integral data type has a range that can accommodate the value of the nonintegral value. This operation results in data loss if the nonintegral value contains any fractional portion, because Windows PowerShell automatically rounds off the number to make it a whole number. Take a look at this code snippet:

```
$val = 365.58
$newval = [int]$val
Write-Host $newval
```

This code results in the output 366, because for 365.58 (which, by default, has the data type of double) to be converted to an integer, it first must be rounded of to the nearest whole number.

Watching Out for Overflow

Overflow is another common problem. *Overflow* is what happens when performing any of the mathematic operations results in a value beyond the range supported by that data type. Windows PowerShell solves this problem for you whenever possible by automatically converting the overflowed value to a data type that supports the larger value, as in this example:

```
$x = [byte]255
$y = [byte]3
$sum = $x + $y
Write-Host $sum
Write-Host $sum.GetType().Name
```

Here, I define two values of the byte data type, add them, and store the result in $sum. As you recall, a byte can store only values from 0 through 255. Adding these two variables results in the value 258, which is greater than the range of values that a byte can hold. Oddly enough, Windows PowerShell doesn't complain and displays the value 258 in the first Write-Host statement. What's interesting is that in the next Write-Host statement, you' see that $sum is no longer a byte data type but has been converted to an integer data type (Int32). PowerShell does all this work in the background, so you don't even have to think about it.

Chapter 11

Grouping Data Using Arrays and Hash Tables

*P*eople naturally try to group similar things, whether those things are shapes, patterns, objects, or even abstract thoughts. Perhaps grouping is our way of creating order in a world that naturally wants to fall apart. To take off my philosopher's hat for a second, grouping things makes sense for some very obvious reasons. For one thing, groups allow you to organize a large number of items in manageable units. An additional benefit is that you can refer to a group of items by a single name rather than having to know the name of each individual item. Arrays are one way you can group data elements in Windows PowerShell, and hash tables provide an efficient way to store data elements by using name/value pairs.

In this chapter, you use arrays and hash tables to group data elements together into a manageable structure rather than just having a variable for each value you want to store. Arrays and hash tables are some of the most effective and widely-used ways for organizing large groups of related data, and you'll see these concepts used repeatedly within this book and in many of the scripts you'll find out there.

Taking an In-Depth Look at Arrays

An *array* is a structure for organizing data sequentially in which each element is accessed via an index value. In practice, you use arrays whenever you have several items and want to use a single name to access them. Suppose that you want to store a list of 100 computer names. Without arrays (or other data structures), you have to define 100 variables. This process is not only inefficient, but also highly impractical. Suppose that you have 10,000 computer names instead. Do you want to create and manage 10,000 variables?

Arrays solve this problem. First, you create a block of data containing as many elements as you want to reference by using just one name; then you use a combination of the variable name and an index to access each data element. To understand this concept better, see Figure 11-1, which shows what an array might look like in memory. This array contains nine elements, all of which are random integers. The array is called `Array1`. The first element of an array is always index 0. The second element is index 1, the third element is index 2, and so on.

Figure 11-1:
An array as it might look in memory.

Array1

35	72	23	61	83	42	86	57	43
0	1	2	3	4	5	6	7	8

In other words, to get to any position you want in the array, you can find the corresponding index value by subtracting 1 from the position you're interested in. So if you want to find the fifth element in the array, you reference it by using the array name and the index value of 4 (5–1).

Creating and Using Arrays

Arrays are very easy to define in Windows PowerShell. If you already know the values of all the elements you want to include in the array, you can create the array by using the comma operator. If you want to create an array like the one depicted in Figure 11-1, earlier in this chapter, do this:

```
$Array1 = 35,72,23,61,83,42,86,57,43
```

The only tricky thing about using the comma operator is creating an array with only one element. To do this, you have to put a comma *before* the value. Here's how you'd create an array with only one element (in this example, the number 12):

```
$SingleValArray = ,12
```

You can also explicitly cast values into an array (see Chapter 5 for more information on casting) by doing this:

```
$Array1 = [array](35,72,23,61,83,42,86,57,43)
```

Windows PowerShell treats arrays no differently from collections. A *collection* in Windows PowerShell is just what the name implies: a collection or grouping of any number of objects. You create a collection by using the @() method, so you can also use this method for creating an array, like this:

```
$Array1 = @(35,72,23,61,83,42,86,57,43)
```

You can create an array or collection with no elements by using the @() method by itself with nothing inside the parentheses, as in this example:

```
$BlankArray = @()
```

Accessing array elements

You can access any element in the array by using the array's name followed by open and close square brackets with the index for the element specified within the braces. To display the fourth and eighth elements (index 3 and 7, respectively), you just need to do this:

```
Write-Host $Array1[3]
Write-Host $Array1[7]
```

You can think of the array name/index format as being a kind of unique variable name. You can use it not only to read data, but to set it as well, as follows:

```
$Array1[5] = 83
```

You can access the last item of an array by using the index –1, as in $Array1[-1].

Looping through arrays

All arrays have a property called `length` that returns the number of elements in the array. Using this property, you can easily loop through all the elements in an array by using a simple `for` loop, such as this:

```
$names = "Steve","Bill","Jeff","Mark","Ryan"
for ($i = 0; $i -lt $names.length; $i++) {
    Write-Host $names[$i]
}
```

It's important to check that the loop's iterator (`$i`, in this case) is less than `$names.length`, because the highest index you can go to is the array's length minus 1.

Unlike other programming and scripting languages, Windows PowerShell doesn't complain if you specify an index of an array that doesn't exist. It simply returns a null value. This situation can be a source of bugs in your scripts if you don't pay attention to the indexes you're using, because the script will continue without complaining (or at least until you try to use an empty value for things that expect a value to exist).

Treating arrays like collections has another really interesting side effect. Sure, you can use the `for` loop as I just showed you to go through each item in the array, but because an array is no different from a collection, you can take advantage of the `foreach` loop to achieve the same result. The output of the following `foreach` loop is exactly the same as the `for` loop using iterator values (If you aren't sure what iterators are, you can flip back to Chapter 6 where I cover them in greater detail):

```
$names = "Steve","Bill","Jeff","Mark","Ryan"
foreach($item in $names) {
    Write-Host $item
}
```

The `foreach` loop way of doings is very useful if you plan to do something with all the items in the array; it saves you quite a few keystrokes, and you don't have to worry about indexes. The first method I showed you, however — using index values — makes much more sense if you want to go through the array in a different manner, such as going backward or processing every other item in the array, as in these examples:

```
$names = "Steve","Bill","Jeff","Mark","Ryan"
Write-Host "Showing every other name..."
for($i = 0; $i -lt $names.length; $i += 2) {
   Write-Host $names[$i]
}
Write-Host "Showing the names in reverse order"
for($i = $names.length - 1; $i -ge 0; $i--) {
   Write-Host $names[$i]
}
```

Growing Arrays Dynamically

In traditional programming languages, arrays are allocated as contiguous spaces in memory because their sizes are fixed based on how many elements you say they will contain when you create them. This arrangement makes arrays highly efficient data structures, especially for sequential read operations. Unfortunately, the downside is that if you want to *grow* the array so that it is capable of storing more elements than you created it to store, you typically have to create a new array and then copy each element of the old array into the new array, which has more space to grow. Some programming languages address this limitation by creating ways to grow arrays at will.

Adding more elements to an existing array in Windows PowerShell is so easy; you won't even have to think about it. You use the same += operator that you use to increment the value of a numerical data type by a certain amount (refer to Chapter 10). In the following code snippet, first I create an array with five values and use a for loop to display the values. Next, I use the += operator to add another five values to the array. Then I use a for loop again to display the values one more time, just to show that now the array truly contains these ten values.

```
$arr = 2,3,5,7,11
Write-Host "First time around..."
for ($i = 0; $i -lt $arr.length; $i++) {
   Write-Host $arr[$i]
}
$arr += 13,17,19,23,29
Write-Host "Second time around..."
for ($i = 0; $i -lt $arr.length; $i++) {
   Write-Host $arr[$i]
}
```

Creating Multidimensional Arrays

You can also think of an array as being a single row of data. By creating an array of arrays, however, you can create *multidimensional arrays.* A two-dimensional array, for example, is one array of multiple arrays. You can use this type of array to represent rows and columns of data, such as representing data in a table. The easiest way to create a multidimensional array is to use the comma operator, but you need to enclose each nested array in parentheses, as follows:

```
$array1 = (1,2,3),(4,5,6),(7,8,9)
```

Just so you can visualize this concept a bit better, Figure 11-2 shows what this multidimensional array might look like. Each of the value sets in parentheses represents an array of data. By using commas between these arrays, you create an array that combines these arrays, so you can think of each array as a row in a larger grid.

	0	1	2
0	1	2	3
1	4	5	6
2	7	8	9

Figure 11-2:
A two-dimensional array as it might look in memory.

You still use the square brackets and indexes to access the data, but now that you have two dimensions, you need to specify two indexes. The first index selects the array *(row)* you want, and the second index selects the data element in that array *(column)* you want to access.

To see this in practice, suppose that you want to get the third element of the second array (the number 6 in $array1). Going back to what I said about positions and indexes at the beginning of this chapter, you know that these positions represent index 2 and index 1, respectively. Now, which order do these values go in when you specify it with the index name? Well, the first index you need to specify is which array you want to retrieve. In this case, you want the second array (index 1). Then you want the third element (index 2) of this array, so to read this value, you have to do this:

```
Write-Host $array1[1][2]
```

If you look at Figure 11-2 again, you can see where I got this example from. In that figure, the number 6 is in row 1, column 2.

Finding Other Uses for Arrays

Probably one of the coolest features of Windows PowerShell is how easy it makes converting things to arrays. Suppose that you want to have an array that contains all the currently running processes. You know you can run the `Get-Process` Cmdlet to get this kind of information at any time, but you want to take a point-in-time snapshot of what processes are running (perhaps to compare with something later). You really have two options:

✔ Run `Get-Process` and write the output to a file for later reference

✔ Create an array; run `Get-Process`; and then, for each process, store the values in that array.

This very short script is one way to implement this functionality by using arrays:

```
$processes = @()
foreach($proc in Get-Process) {
    $processes += $proc
}
Write-Host ("Number of items: " + $processes.length)
for($i = 0; $i -lt $processes.length; $i++) {
    Write-Host $i.name
}
```

The script creates a blank array, loops through each item returned by Get-Process, and keeps adding these Process objects to the array by growing it dynamically via the += operator. The second half of the script simply displays the process names from the array on the screen to show that it does indeed have the correct information.

A script like this one has a few problems however. Although it works, it's tedious and not very efficient because you're constantly resizing the array. The great thing is that Windows PowerShell has an even better way to perform this operation for you. As it turns out, when you run a Cmdlet like Get-Process or even a pipeline of commands, the resulting data is automatically returned as a collection. Because collections and arrays are interchangeable, the preceding script can be converted to this one instead:

```
$processes = Get-Process
Write-Host ("Number of items: " + $processes.length)
for($i = 0; $i -lt $processes.length; $i++) {
    Write-Host $i.name
}
```

The array resizing and adding of elements is completely unnecessary; all you need to do is simply assign the result of the Cmdlet to a variable. You're not limited to the return value of just one Cmdlet; you can take the result of a pipeline of Cmdlets, as in this example:

```
$processNames = Get-Process | Select-Object Name | Sort-Object Name
for($i = 0; $i -lt $processNames.length; $i++) {
    Write-Host $processNames[$i]
}
```

Using for loops to display the contents of everything in an array is the traditional way of doing things. Windows PowerShell is truly the scripting language made for lazy people like me, because it lets you achieve the same thing just by entering the name of the array. In other words, the whole for loop thing I've been using to display each item in the $processNames array can be reduced to this:

```
$processNames
```

Yes, that's right — just "running" the array name automatically displays its contents in the same way that you've been using the for loop method. Don't believe me? Try it out for yourself. Now wipe that grin off your face.

Working with Hash Tables: The Array's Useful Cousin

A *hash table* is another data structure that allows you to group data under a common name. Hash tables are similar to arrays in that they too have an index that's used to access data elements, but unlike arrays, hash tables don't use sequential numbers for these indexes. Instead, hash tables store data by using name/value pairs. The name is the index you use to get to the value. The good thing about hash tables is that those names can be anything. You can create a hash table that uses a user's logon ID as the name and the user's password as the value, for example.

If you're familiar with VBScript, a hash table is similar to a `Dictionary` object.

Creating and using hash tables

The most straightforward way to create a hash table in Windows PowerShell is to use the `@{}` method. It works almost the same way as the `@()` method that you use to create collections (refer to "Creating and Using Arrays," earlier in this chapter), except that hash tables require you to explicitly define the name *(index)* for each value and that you separate name/value pairs with semicolons instead of commas. Here's a hash table that implements a simple username/password lookup:

```
$userpwdhash = @{jimmy = "n3uTR0n"; optimus = "Pr!m3"; pinky = "8R@!n"; bob =
        "B1L03r"}
Write-Host ("Pinky's password: " + $userpwdhash["pinky"])
Write-Host ("Jimmy's password: " + $userpwdhash["jimmy"])
```

You can create a blank hash table by using `@{}` with nothing inside the curly braces, as follows:

```
$emptyhash = @{}
```

You can think of a hash table as being a simple table with two columns and as may rows as you have items in the hash table. The first column contains the name, and the second column contains the value. To see the entire contents of the `$userpwdhash` hash table, all you need to do is type `$userpwdhash` and then press Enter to get this output:

```
PS C:\TEMP> $userpwdhash

Name                    Value
----                    -----
pinky                   8R@!n
optimus                 Pr!m3
bob                     B1L03r
jimmy                   n3uTR0n
```

When you want to retrieve the value of any name, you simply use the same syntax that you use to get the content of an array item, except with hash tables, the index is the name portion of the name/value pair, as in this example:

```
$userpwdhash["pinky"]
```

You can also access the value directly by using the dot operator:

```
$userpwdhash.pinky
```

The names you use in a hash table must be unique because they're indexes into the data structure.

When I create the $userpwdhash hash table and initialize it with these four name/value pairs, I don't put double quotes around the names. Although I can do that (and the table would still behave the same way), I've purposely not done it to demonstrate an assumption that Windows PowerShell makes:

When you specify name/value pairs during the creation of a hash table, Windows PowerShell always assumes that the names are strings.

This assumption is why the hash-table creation and initialization processes work just fine even though I left out the double quotes. I explicitly put double quotes around the values, though, because technically, values can be anything. By using double quotes, I'm explicitly defining the values as strings.

A hash table returns $null whenever you try to retrieve a value for a name that doesn't exist. If you want to check whether a given name is already defined in a hash table, you simply query for the value for that name and see whether the value equals $null, like this:

```
if ($userpwdhash["somebody"] -eq $null) {
    Write-Host ("The name somebody doesn't exist in the hash table!")
}
```

Hash table internals

Hash tables derive their name from the way they work and how the data is structured. You already know that you can present a hash table visually as a two-column table, but what's this whole *hash* thing? A *hash* is essentially a value derived by putting some piece of data through a hashing function. A *hashing function* is a complex mathematical algorithm used to generate a unique value based on the initial value you provide. The algorithm is also designed to give you the same unique hash value whenever you give it the same input.

Putting these concepts together, a hash table works by taking the index (name) you provide, generating a hash from it, and then using it internally to mark the location of the value for this given index. Later, when you try to retrieve or update the data, all you need to do is provide the same index. The hash function automatically generates the same hash value that it generated the first time you created that entry and gives you access to that value's location.

Because of all this, hash tables are highly efficient data structures. Retrieving data from a hash table that contains 100 items is just as fast as retrieving data from a hash table containing 10 million items, because the hash values generated from your given index are numeric and can be used to find an item quickly by means of very fast numbers-based searching algorithms. This high efficiency means that hash tables are often used in database indexes to create fast lookups, even on very large databases.

Modifying hash tables

Naturally, whenever you have a table structure (such as that of a hash table), you want to be able to perform two key operations: adding and removing entries. If you want to add another name/value pair to an existing hash table, you use the hash table's `add` method. The `add` method takes two parameters, which are (not surprisingly) the name and value, in that order. So if you want to add another user/password pair to the `$userpwdhash` hash table in the preceding section, you can do something like this:

```
$userpwdhash.add("tony","S7@rK")
```

It's important to enclose the name in double quotes if the name is a string, because unlike the initialization routine, the `add` method doesn't assume that the name you provide is a string.

You can remove an entry from the hash table by using the `remove` method. The `remove` method takes just one parameter, which is the name of the entry you want to remove. Here's an example:

```
$userpwdhash.remove("pinky")
```

Looping through hash tables

Because the indexes used in hash tables are pretty much anything you can come up with, you can't use a simple `for` loop to go through each item. One way to get around this limitation is to use your friend the array. You can grab the names (otherwise known as *keys*), convert them to an array, and then loop through the array to retrieve the values. I know that this process sounds confusing, but here's a nice little code snippet to show you how easy it is:

```
$names = @($userpwdhash.keys)
foreach($name in $names) {
   Write-Host ($name + " = " + $userpwdhash[$name])
}
```

See, that wasn't too hard, was it? You use the `@()` method to create a collection of names by giving it the `keys` property of the hash table. The `keys` property contains a list of all the names being used in the hash table. Now that you have the names in an array, you just use a `foreach` loop to go through each item in the collection and do what you want with it. In this case, I'm using it to display the name/value pairs onscreen in a different format.

Chapter 12

Readin' and Writin' Files

. . . .

In This Chapter

▶ Navigate through the file system

▶ Manage your files and folders

▶ Create your own data format using XML

▶ Make your output presentable using HTML

. . . .

Although it's great to perform calculations and do all kinds of fun stuff in the Windows PowerShell console, many times you need to store data somewhere such as in a file or database. The easiest and most direct place to store data for long-term use is a file. Windows PowerShell not only makes reading and writing simple text files easy, but also lets you create even more complex files, like XML and HTML files.

In this chapter, you exercise your ability to both act as a producer and consumer of files within your file system. Many files are created by people but even more are automatically created by computers through programs and scripts, so your ability to read, write, and even manage files within your file system becomes a necessary skill, just like being able to use a remote is to a couch potato.

Having Some Fun with the File System

One of the most fundamental skills you need to possess as a Windows PowerShell user is the ability to manipulate files within the file system. This manipulation includes creating, deleting, copying, moving, and renaming files and folders. Sure, you can go back to using Windows Explorer, but have you ever tried renaming 100 files by using the Windows GUI? Not much fun, was it? How about deleting files matching a certain pattern? I can think of quite a few scenarios in which managing the file system through the command line is far easier than doing it through a graphical user interface (GUI). As you can probably guess, Windows PowerShell includes many Cmdlets to help you do all these things.

Moving around the file system

There's a saying that you can't get anywhere without knowing where you are right now, and that's especially true when you're working in a command line environment. In the Windows PowerShell console, the most obvious way to find out which directory you're in is to look at the Windows PowerShell prompt directly. The current path is displayed there all the time, but if you want to get this value (perhaps to use it somewhere else in a script), you can use the `Get-Location` Cmdlet. This Cmdlet simply returns the full path to your current location as a string.

Moving around the file system is another important capability because files are spread throughout it. Being able to go from drive to drive and directory to directory is critical. You do this by using the `Set-Location` Cmdlet. You can go to a different directory, such as `C:\Windows\System32`, by running this code:

```
Set-Location C:\windows
```

`Set-Location` is also aliased as `CD`, which means that you can use the familiar CD (change directory) DOS command. You can just run `CD C:\Windows` to achieve the same results `Set-Location C:\Windows`.

As you see in upcoming chapters, Windows PowerShell uses `Set-Location` as the Cmdlet name rather than something like `Change-Directory` because `Set-Location` can also be used to change the current location to nontraditional "drives" that are now available in Windows PowerShell.

Managing directories

Directories (folders) offer a great way to organize your files in manageable units. To use them effectively, of course, you need to be able to create, delete, copy, move, and rename them.

Creating directories

When you want to create a directory, you use the `MKDIR` or `MD` command. No, I didn't make a mistake. Those aren't aliases to some fancy-looking Cmdlet. It's a bit odd to not have a Cmdlet for this task, because there's a Cmdlet for practically everything else, but yes, you just use the old `MD` or `MKDIR` command. So if you want to create a `temp` directory at the root of the C: drive, you run:

```
MD C:\temp
```

or

```
MKDIR C:\temp
```

Deleting directories

Deleting directories, on the other hand, requires the help of the `Remove-Item` Cmdlet (I know — not very consistent). If you want to delete `C:\temp`, you can just run

```
Remove-Item C:\temp
```

`Remove-Item` is aliased as `RMDIR`, so you can run `RMDIR C:\temp` to achieve the same effect.

If the directory that you're trying to delete isn't empty, Windows PowerShell prompts you to confirm the action. Alternatively, if you're sure that you want to get rid of that directory (including all subdirectories), you can use the `-Recurse` switch:

```
Remove-Item -Recurse C:\temp
```

Copying directories

If I say that your next task is making a copy of a folder, I'm sure that you'll guess that the Cmdlet is `Copy-Item` and its alias is `COPY`. If you did make those guesses, congratulations; you're correct!

You need to be aware of something interesting about `Copy-Item`, though. Take the simple case in which you want to copy `C:\temp` to `C:\temp2`. The command you run is

```
Copy-Item C:\temp C:\temp2
```

Excellent! Now suppose that `C:\temp` contains a bunch of files and possibly even subdirectories, so a recursive listing of the directory looks like this:

```
C:\temp
C:\temp\powershell.txt
C:\temp\temp2\testscript.ps1
C:\temp\temp2\testscript2.ps1
```

You want to do exactly what you did earlier: copy the entire directory structure of `C:\temp` to `C:\temp2`. You run the same `Copy-Item C:\temp C:\temp2` command, correct? No! If you run that command, a surprising thing happens. Yes, you do get a `C:\temp2` directory, but if you look inside the directory, you see that it's empty. You may think that there's a bug in Windows PowerShell. Well, there isn't, so don't bother contacting Microsoft about it.

`Copy-Item` literally makes a copy of the particular item you specify. If you tell it to copy a folder, it creates a copy of that specific folder and nothing else — not even its contents. You're clever, so you've probably guessed what the solution is: a `-Recurse` switch in the `Copy-Item` Cmdlet. With this knowledge in hand, you know that the correct way to make an exact copy of the directory structure is to do something like this:

```
Copy-Item -Recurse C:\temp C:\temp2
```

That's it! Now if you check the contents of C:\temp2, you see that it contains a copy of all the contents of C:\temp.

Moving directories

If you decide to reorganize things and have to move directories around, you use the Move-Item Cmdlet to get the job done. Here, I'm moving C:\temp to E:\temp:

```
Move-Item C:\temp E:\temp
```

Yes, you guessed it: Move-Item is aliased as MOVE, so you achieve the same thing by running MOVE C:\temp E:\temp.

Renaming directories

You can rename directories by using either of two methods:

✔ Rename-Item: The first method is to use the Rename-Item Cmdlet. (Give yourself a pat on the back if you guessed the Cmdlet's name before seeing it here.) Suppose that you want to rename E:\temp to E:\temp.bak. You can do that by running

```
Rename-Item E:\temp E:\temp.bak
```

The Rename-Item Cmdlet is aliased as REN.

✔ Move-Item: With Rename-Item out of the way, what could the other method be? Notice the similarities between Move-Item and Rename-Item. Both Cmdlets take two parameters, one being the old name and the other being the new name. Not surprisingly, you can effectively rename a directory by moving it. If you want to rename E:\temp to E:\temp.bak, you can also do this:

```
Move-Item E:\temp E:\temp.bak
```

Manipulating files in the file system

File systems consist of files and directories. You can practically treat files and directories like the same thing, however, when it comes to manipulating files within the file system. You use exactly the same Cmdlets to create, delete, copy, move, and rename files that you use for directories. The same cast of characters — New-Item, Remove-Item, Copy-Item, Move-Item, and Rename-Item — is valid for files as well.

Reading Text Files

You may often need to read some information from a file, usually because you need to take in data generated by the operating system or other applications for your own consumption. An example is reading a log file to determine whether last night's backups were successful before performing some action based on the information you gather from that file.

You read text files in Windows PowerShell by using the Get-Content Cmdlet. In its simplest form, Get-Content takes one parameter, which is the name of the file you want to read. It automatically opens the file, reads in each line, and then stores these lines as an object array. Because Get-Content returns an array, you can store the data it retrieves in a variable, as in this example:

```
$data = Get-Content C:\Windows\setuplog.txt
```

Now that you have the contents of the file in a variable (or, more specifically, in an array), you can treat the data as an array of strings, and all array functions and techniques apply. You also may want to use text files to store information to be used as input parameters for a script — the names of computers on which you want to perform some action, for example, or perhaps a comma-delimited file of user attributes you want to use to update user account metadata in Active Directory. Suppose that you have a text file that contains a bunch of computer names, like this:

```
labdc1
labdc2
filesrv1
printsrv1
mailsrv1
```

You want to query the computer manufacturer and model for each of these computers. You can use a combination of techniques that I cover earlier in this book, such as reading from a text file, looping through an array (Chapter 11), and using Windows Management Instrumentation (WMI) (Chapter 8) to query remote computers.

Take a look at this script, which does exactly what you want:

```
$computernames = Get-Content c:\temp\computers.txt
foreach($name in $computernames)
{
    $compinfo = Get-WmiObject -class Win32_ComputerSystem -computername $name
    Write-Host ($compinfo.name + " - " + $compinfo.manufacturer + " - " +
            $compinfo.model)
}
```

If you forget how to use `Get-WmiObject`, you can flip back to Chapter 8 for a refresher.

The best part is that other than using `Get-Content` to read the computer names from the text file, the rest of the script is just a standard way of working with a collection.

You can also use `Get-Content` in a pipeline to achieve a similar effect. This command pipeline performs essentially the same thing:

```
Get-Content c:\temp\computers.txt | foreach{Get-WmiObject -class Win32_
    ComputerSystem -computername $_ | select-object name,
    manufacturer, model}
```

You can control how many lines are retrieved, and when you use `Get-Content` in a pipeline, you can also control how many lines to send through at a time. To do this, you use the `-totalCount` and `-readCount` switches for the `Get-Content` Cmdlet. If you want to read only the first 100 lines of a file, for example, you run this command:

```
Get-Content c:\temp\readme.txt -totalCount 100
```

Similarly, to read two lines at a time, you run this command:

```
Get-Content C:\temp\computers.txt -readCount 2 | Write-Host
```

`Get-Content` can read the contents of any file, not just text files. It can even read binary files (although, of course, none of it will make sense unless you know how to interpret the binary format). You can read file contents by using the `-Encoding` switch of `Get-Content` and specifying whatever data type you expect the data to be in (such as `Byte`) to read the raw data as bytes.

Writing Files

You have three ways to write to a file. The first method is probably familiar to you already: redirecting the output to a file by using the *redirection operator* (a fancy name for the greater-than sign). This command sequence lists the contents of `C:\windows\System32` and writes this output to `C:\temp\system32_contents.txt`:

```
Get-ChildItem C:\windows\system32 > C:\temp\system32_contents.txt
```

The next method uses aCmdlet. The Cmdlet version of the redirection operator is the `Out-File` Cmdlet. This command sequence is functionality equivalent to the preceding one:

```
Get-ChildItem C:\windows\system32 | Out-File C:\temp\system32_contents.txt
```

On the surface, Out-File may seem to be a redundant addition to Windows PowerShell, but in fact, it's capable of doing much more than just simple redirection. With redirection, all you get is the equivalent of a file dump of what you see onscreen, which is exactly what you get from the default use of Out-File. The difference is that Out-File gives you a few options in addition to performing a quick dump of what would have been displayed onscreen. You can take advantage of these options by specifying the appropriate Out-File Cmdlet switch listed in Table 12-1.

Table 12-1	Out-File Cmdlet Switches	
Switch	*Description*	*Example*
-encoding	Specifies the character encoding used in the file. This encoding can be one of the following values: Unicode, UTF7, UTF8, UTF32, ASCII, BigEndianUnicode, Default, or OEM. Unicode is the default encoding type.	Out-File c:\ test.txt -encoding ASCII
-append	Appends to the file rather than overwriting its contents.	Out-File c:\ test.txt -append
-width	Defines the maximum number of characters on each line. If the line being written contains more than this value, it is simply truncated. By default, this switch follows the value used by the current Windows PowerShell console settings.	Out-File c:\ test.txt -width 150
-force	Tries to overcome any restrictions for writing to the output file, such as overriding the read-only attribute of the file.	Out-File c:\ test.txt -force
-noClobber	Prevents Out-File from trying to write to the output file if it already exists.	Out-File c:\ test.txt -noclobber
-Confirm	Prompts for confirmation before continuing with the command.	Out-File c:\ test.txt -confirm

The final way to write to a file is to use the `Set-Content` Cmdlet. Because so many options are already built into `Out-File`, it may seem a bit strange to have yet another Cmdlet to write to a file, but some differences exist between `Set-Content` and `Out-File`. The biggest difference is that by default, `Out-File` formats the data in the same way that it's displayed onscreen before writing that data to a file, whereas `Set-Content` writes the data without any modifications.

Use `Out-File` to perform a straightforward file dump of what you would see onscreen, but use `Set-Content` to write a file if the data is already formatted a certain way and you don't want it going through any kind of conversion.

For completeness, here's how the preceding output examples look with `Set-Content`:

```
Get-ChildItem C:\windows\system32 | Set-Content C:\temp\system32_contents.txt
```

If you run `Get-Help` on `Set-Content`, you notice that it doesn't have an append switch like `Out-File` that appends to an existing file. That's because `Set-Content` can't append to a file; you have to use the `Add-Content` Cmdlet instead.

Working with XML

Extensible Markup Language (XML) is document format that allows you to define your own markup within the document. A typical document format such as a Microsoft Word document or a HTML Web page has a very specific formatting structure, with specific tags defining how various elements should be rendered onscreen (such as bold and underlined text). XML is different in that you can create the format that suits you best; however, you want to define the data it contains. In general, XML describes and defines data, not how the data should appear onscreen. XML doesn't care about how the document will eventually look; its only concern is to give meaning to the data that it contains. Here's an example of a very simple XML file:

```
<?xml version="1.0" encoding="ISO-8859-1"?>
<desert name="Sahara">
<animal type="camel">Joe</animal>
<animal type="snake">Mark</animal>
<animal type="elephant">Allan</animal>
</desert>
```

The first line declares what this file is: an XML Version 1.0 file encoded with the Latin-1 character set (ISO-8859-1). *Note:* This first tag is optional, but it's always a good idea to start an XML file with this tag so that anyone looking at it knows that it is in fact an XML file and not some random jumble of text.

Next comes the root element. You can think of XML elements as having a tree structure (see Figure 12-1). The *root element* is the common point that glues all the other elements together. In this example, I define a root element of a type that I call `desert`. This element has one attribute, called `name`, which has the value `Sahara`. The `desert` root element contains three child elements (nodes) of a type I call `animal`. Each `animal` element has an attribute called `type` that defines what kind of animal it is. The text outside the angle brackets is the data associated with that element. In this case, I'm giving each of these `animal` elements a `name` as its data. Then each element must be terminated by a closing tag, which is an angle bracket followed by a forward slash, the element `name` again, and a closing angle bracket (see Figure 12-2).

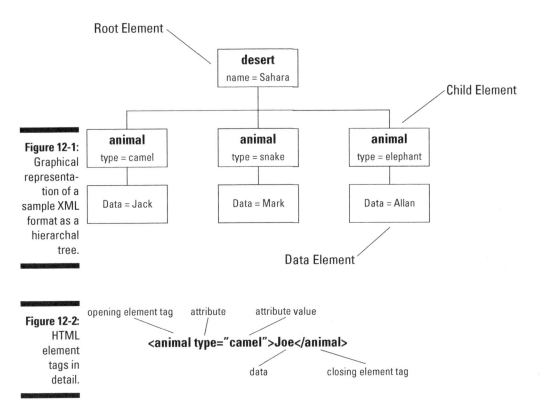

Figure 12-1: Graphical representation of a sample XML format as a hierarchal tree.

Figure 12-2: HTML element tags in detail.

Because XML files are really nothing more than flat text files, they offer the ultimate flexibility and portability when it comes to defining your own data structures. If you can create an XML file and read an XML file, you can most certainly talk to any other program that can read and write XML files.

Reading and writing XML files

One of my favorite things about Windows PowerShell is how reusable everything is. Reading an XML file in Windows PowerShell, for example, is no different from reading a regular text file; you just use the Get-Content Cmdlet. Get-Content by itself returns just the contents of the file, so to tell Windows PowerShell that you want the file to be treated like an XML file, you have to cast the variable with the [xml] tag. This example, which assumes that the sample XML file in the preceding section was saved as sample.xml, reads the contents of sample.xml into $myXMLFile:

```
[xml]$myXMLfile = Get-Content C:\temp\sample.xml
```

I've said that you can think of an XML file as having a tree structure. Well, now that you have the contents of the XML file stored in the $myXMLfile variable, you can access the different elements of the XML file by using the dot operator to access each child element in the tree. If you want to retrieve the desert name, you can run

```
$myXMLfile.desert.name
```

You can list all the animal elements within desert like this:

```
$myXMLfile.desert.animal
```

The output will be

```
type                              #text
----                              -----
camel                             Joe
snake                             Mark
elephant                          Allan
```

Because the contents of the file are now in memory, you can add more child nodes, if you want. Suppose that you want to add another animal node in which the type equals vulture and the data (#text) equals George. You can do this by running this sequence of commands:

```
$newanimal = $myXMLfile.CreateElement("animal")
$newanimal.SetAttribute("type","vulture")
$newanimal.psbase.innertext = "George"
$myXMLfile.desert.AppendChild($newanimal)
```

The first line creates a new element using the existing XML object. The element is called animal and is stored in the $newanimal variable. Right now it's not part of the hierarchy because you're just creating an element that you'll insert later. Then you use the SetAttribute method to set the type attribute to vulture and finally to set the data attribute to George. You set the text data of an element by assigning the value to the psbase.inner-text property of the element.

Now that your new element contains all the attributes and data you want it to possess, you can insert it into the tree. In this case, because you want the new element to be at the same level as all the other animal elements, you call the AppendChild method on the desert element and give it the newly created animal element as a parameter. Now if you run $myXMLfile. desert.animal, you get this output:

```
type                          #text
----                          -----
camel                         Joe
snake                         Mark
elephant                      Allan
vulture                       George
```

With the data updated, you may want to go ahead and save the changes. You save XML data to a file by calling the save method of the XML object. In this case, if you want to save your changes back to the sample.xml file, you can run

```
$myXMLfile.save("C:\temp\sample.xml")
```

If you open the sample.xml file in a text editor, it now contains the new child node you just created and looks like this:

```
<?xml version="1.0" encoding="ISO-8859-1"?>
<desert name="Sahara">
   <animal type="camel">Joe</animal>
   <animal type="snake">Mark</animal>
   <animal type="elephant">Allan</animal>
   <animal type="vulture">George</animal>
</desert>
```

Saving objects in XML files

XML is a highly extensible format, and you can use it to save and represent practically anything you can imagine. Sometimes, for example, you want to save objects to a file so that you can retrieve them later. Objects can contain any number of properties and values, and without XML, your only other option is to store the objects in a binary format. Windows PowerShell gives you the ability to export and import objects to and from XML files just as easily.

Consider a scenario in which you want to keep a record of running processes. You know that you can get this information by running Get-Process and storing it in a variable. The problem is that you want to save this information to a file so you can analyze it later. One simple way is to run Get-Process and redirect the information to a simple text file. If you open the simple text file in Notepad, you see that it's neatly formatted and easy to read, but you can't manipulate it easily in Windows PowerShell without having to perform some string parsing. This method is the old way of doing things; Windows PowerShell offers a much better option.

Remember that Windows PowerShell is object-oriented. If you save objects to a file, you want to be able to load the contents of that file later and continue to treat the objects as objects without having to figure out string patterns and parse the file to re-create the objects. Windows PowerShell solves this problem by providing two very useful Cmdlets: `Export-CliXML` and `Import-CliXML`. `Export-CliXML` exports objects to an XML file, and `Import-CliXML` imports XML files into objects.

Going back to the process-tracking problem in the preceding section, you can persist the process information by running

```
Get-Process | Export-CliXML C:\temp\process.xml
```

If you're curious what the processes look like now that they've been saved in an XML file, go ahead and open `process.xml` in a text editor. You get something very messy-looking, like this:

```
<Objs Version="1.1" xmlns="http://schemas.microsoft.com/powershell/2004/04"><Obj
        RefId="RefId-0"><TN RefId="RefId-0"><T>System.Diagnostics.
        Process</T><T>System.ComponentModel.Component</T><T>System.
        MarshalByRefObject</T><T>System.Object</T></TN><ToString>System.
        Diagnostics.Process (alg)</ToString><Props><I32
        N="BasePriority">8</I32><B N="HasExited">false</
        B><S N="Handle">4000</S><I32 N="HandleCount">105</
        I32><I32 N="Id">2012</I32><S N="MachineName">.</S><S
        N="MainWindowHandle">0</S><S N="MainWindowTitle" /><S
        N="MainModule">System.Diagnostics.ProcessModule (alg.exe)</S><S
        N="MaxWorkingSet">1413120</S><S N="MinWorkingSet">204800</S><Obj
        N="Modules" RefId="RefId-1"><TN RefId="RefId-1"><T>System.Diagnos
        tics.ProcessModule (UxTheme.dll)</S>
```

Okay, you caught me — that's just a small excerpt of what the file actually looks like. All the data is spelled out in clear text but of course tagged appropriately with XML elements to define what each data element is supposed to represent. This result is a big difference from the simplistic output you get from just redirecting the output of `Get-Process` to a plain-text file.

If you want to recover your data into PowerShell so that you can use it like any other object, you can run

```
$ProcHistory = Import-CliXML C:\temp\process.xml
```

You can see the processes you saved by running

```
$ProcHistory
```

Hmm . . . so what? You could have done that with a regular text file, right? Well, yes, the default output is the same — but now try to filter the objects so that only processes where the `Handle` value is greater than 100. Also, make sure that the output is sorted by the Handles column. That sorting would take more than a bit of clever manipulation if all this data were just raw text, but because you recover the objects themselves, you can run all your standard Windows PowerShell object manipulation tricks, as in this example:

```
$ProcHistory | Where-Object {$_.Handles -gt 100} | Sort-Object Handles
```

Sweet! In one line, you've accomplished what traditional textcentric script writers would have to write dozens of lines to do.

Working with HTML

When talking about Windows PowerShell, I sometimes feel like I'm selling knives on one of those infomercials — you know, the ones that keep saying, "But wait, there's more!" With Windows PowerShell, there's always more, and because you can manipulate regular text files and XML files, why shouldn't manipulation work with HTML files? This functionality never fails to bring a stupid grin to my face, because I don't know how many times in my career I've written scripts only to have someone not like the simplistic text output and demand something a bit fancier, like HTML.

To generate HTML pages from a traditional script, you have to write the HTML code output from scratch yourself, meaning that you also have to know how to create HTML files manually. Writing HTML files is a topic beyond the scope of this book, but it's the most awesome part about PowerShell's ability to generate HTML output: You don't need to know about writing HTML files (or at least don't need to know much). Windows PowerShell allows you to just do something like this to convert the output of `Get-Process` to a simple HTML page:

```
Get-Process | ConvertTo-HTML | Out-File C:\temp\processes.html
```

What you end up with is what you see in Figure 12-3.

Is it pretty? No! Will it get you that big raise you've been asking for? Highly doubtful! Was it easy? Yes! It's hard to really appreciate how big a leap generating HTML output using PowerShell is compared with, say, Windows Shell scripting or VBScript unless you've ever tried to code one of these routines yourself. Even without that appreciation, you have to admit that the ability to do all this with only one line of code is impressive.

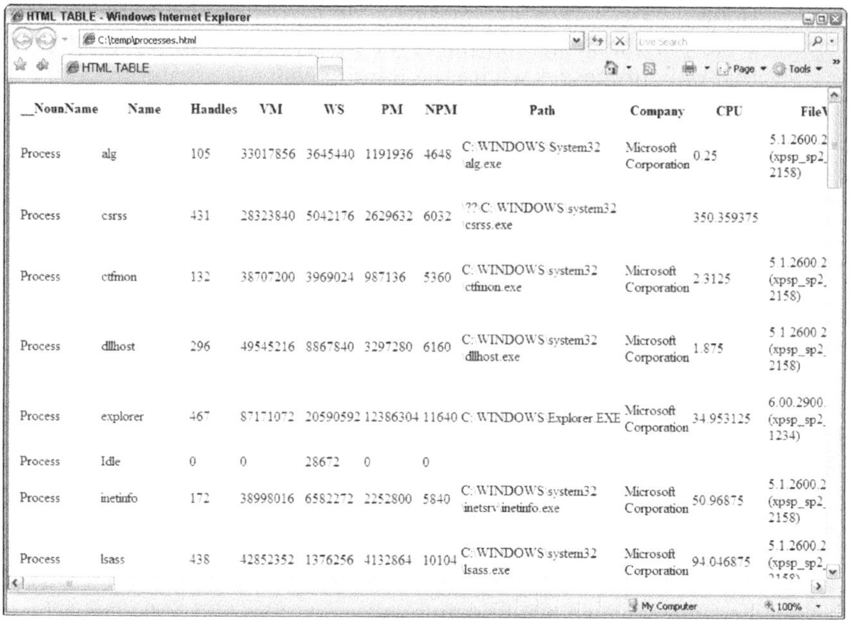

__NounName	Name	Handles	VM	WS	PM	NPM	Path	Company	CPU	File\
Process	alg	105	33017856	3645440	1191936	4648	C:\WINDOWS\System32\alg.exe	Microsoft Corporation	0.25	5.1.2600.2 (xpsp_sp2_ 2158)
Process	csrss	431	28323840	5042176	2629632	6032	\??\C:\WINDOWS\system32\csrss.exe		350.359375	
Process	ctfmon	132	38707200	3969024	987136	5360	C:\WINDOWS\system32\ctfmon.exe	Microsoft Corporation	2.3125	5.1.2600.2 (xpsp_sp2_ 2158)
Process	dllhost	296	49545216	8867840	3297280	6160	C:\WINDOWS\system32\dllhost.exe	Microsoft Corporation	1.875	5.1.2600.2 (xpsp_sp2_ 2158)
Process	explorer	467	87171072	20590592	12386304	11640	C:\WINDOWS\Explorer.EXE	Microsoft Corporation	34.953125	6.00.2900. (xpsp_sp2_ 1234)
Process	Idle	0	0	28672	0	0				
Process	inetinfo	172	38998016	6582272	2252800	5840	C:\WINDOWS\system32\inetsrv\inetinfo.exe	Microsoft Corporation	50.96875	5.1.2600.2 (xpsp_sp2_ 2158)
Process	lsass	438	42852352	1376256	4132864	10104	C:\WINDOWS\system32\lsass.exe	Microsoft Corporation	94.046875	5.1.2600.2 (xpsp_sp2_

Figure 12-3: Get-Process output converted to HTML.

Face it, though — the vast majority of people don't enjoy sitting down looking at plain text all day long unless they're . . . umm . . . Unix admins. Wouldn't it be great if you could somehow change the way `ConvertTo-HTML` works so that the output can be a bit more dressed up? Of course you can!

You can format HTML in either of two ways. The most straightforward way is to add formatting tags directly to the document. If you want to display bold red text, for example, you can have something like this in your HTML file:

```
<FONT color="red"><B>My Bold Red Text</B></FONT>
```

That's a quick and easy way to change the presentation of any particular part of your HTML document.

Another (and often better) method is to use style tags, which are defined globally in the document. Instead of setting the formatting of an individual element, as in the preceding example, you can say something like "all table headers will have a blue background, and all table cells will have a red background."

`ConvertTo-HTML` has three switches that you can use to customize the way that the resulting HTML file is rendered, as shown in Table 12-2.

Table 12-2	ConvertTo-HTML Switches	
Switch name	**Description**	**Example**
-title	Sets the title of the HTML page.	-title "Process List"
-head	Adds whatever you want to the <HEAD> section of the HTML page.	-head "<META name="Author" content="Steve Seguis"
-body	Adds whatever you want to the <BODY> section of the HTML page.	-body "<CENTER><H1>PowerShell FTW!</H1></CENTER>"

Armed with this knowledge, you can create a Windows PowerShell script to enhance the look and feel of the Get-Process HTML output:

```
$format = "<TITLE>My Processes</TITLE>"
$format += "<style>"
$format += "TABLE{border-width:2px;border-style:solid;background-color:yellow}"
$format += "TH{color:blue}"
$format += "TD{color:red}"
$format += "</style>"

$body = "<CENTER><H1>Process List</H1></CENTER>"

Get-Process | ConvertTo-HTML -head $format -body $body | Out-File c:\temp\
            processes.html
```

In this example, I use the $format variable to store the text that will be inserted into the <HEAD> tags of the HTML file. I create a title for the HTML page and then define a style that sets the TABLE tag to apply a 2-pixel solid border and a background color of yellow. All table headers (TH) will have blue text, and all table cells (TD) have red text. I also add a heading, centered on the page, by adding something to the <BODY> section. The resulting output is a tad bit prettier (okay, maybe not prettier, but more colorful) than the first attempt, as you can see in Figure 12-4.

Figure 12-4:
A colorful
version of
the Get-
Process
HTML
output.

NounName	Name	Handles	VM	WS	PM	NPM	Path	Company	CPU	File
Process	alg	105	33017856	3645440	1191936	4648	C:\WINDOWS\System32\alg.exe	Microsoft Corporation	0.296875	5.1.2600.2 (xpsp_sp2 2158)
Process	csrss	389	27480064	4988928	2617344	5432	\??\C:\WINDOWS\system32\csrss.exe		356.453125	
Process	ctfmon	123	38670336	3969024	995328	5000	C:\WINDOWS\system32\ctfmon.exe	Microsoft Corporation	2.71875	5.1.2600.2 (xpsp_sp2 2158)
Process	dllhost	296	49545216	8867840	3297280	6160	C:\WINDOWS\system32\dllhost.exe	Microsoft Corporation	2.078125	5.1.2600.2 (xpsp_sp2 2158)
Process	explorer	493	88182784	21196800	12836864	12080	C:\WINDOWS\Explorer.EXE	Microsoft Corporation	39.4375	6.00.2900 (xpsp_sp2 1234)
Process	Idle	0	0	28672	0	0				
Process	iexplore	363	86245376	21946368	14311424	10680	C:\Program Files\Internet Explorer\IEXPLORE.EXE	Microsoft Corporation	5.921875	7.00.6000 (vista_gdr. 1500)

You may be wondering why I explicitly defined "`<TITLE>My Processes</TITLE>`" in the head when I could just as easily have used the `-title` switch. Unfortunately, that's not how things work. Yes, the `-title` switch sets the contents of the `<TITLE>` tags when it's used, but if you also have `-head` defined, anything that you specify for `-head` overwrites everything in the `<HEAD>` tag.

REMEMBER

Whenever you use `-head` to manipulate the resulting HTML document by using `ConvertTo-HTML`, you need to define the `<TITLE>` tags explicitly to set the title of the page because the `-title` parameter is ignored.

It doesn't seem like much right now, but `ConvertTo-HTML` opens a world of potential for you as a script writer, because it lets you create output files that have a much richer look and feel than just plain text. Also, because the files are formatted in HTML, you can post them quickly on an intranet page to share with your colleagues. Imagine having a Web page where people can find up-to-date HTML pages containing the latest information about your servers retrieved through Window PowerShell. The possibilities are endless.

Chapter 13

Going On a Date with PowerShell

. . . .

. . . .

*W*hether you're scheduling an automated task, generating time stamp–based log file names, or trying to deal with date-related problems such as the infamous Y2K bug or the change in daylight saving time, dates are an important part of many computing tasks. Windows PowerShell builds on top of the rich `Date` and `Time` support provided by the .NET Framework and adds a few features such as the capability to use Unix-style formatters to modify how the dates are presented.

In this chapter, you define dates and times and use them in different scenarios such as calculating elapsed time or figuring out daylight savings time. You might not use dates and times as much as you use other data types, but they're very important because they're very relevant to our day-to-day life. Even if you don't need it just now, make a note of this chapter because soon enough you're bound to need it, even if it's something as simple as trying to display the current date and time to screen.

Going On Your First Date

To work with dates and times in Windows PowerShell, you use the `Get-Date` Cmdlet. It's the Swiss Army Knife of Windows PowerShell dates and times; you use it to find out the current date and time as well as to create date objects to define any arbitrary date. To find out the current date and time, you run `Get-Date` by itself without any parameters, like this:

```
Get-Date
```

When you run this Cmdlet by itself, it returns the current date and time and displays it in a string format, as in this example:

```
Tuesday, March 18, 2008 10:14:42 PM
```

You can change how the date and time are displayed by using the `-displayhint`, `-format`, and `-uFormat` switches. You use the `-displayhint` switch when you want to obtain just the date or time portions of a given date and time, as follows:

```
Get-Date -displayhint date
Get-Date -displayhint time
```

Getting the date and time in a specific format

The `-format` and `-uFormat` switches let you format the date and time in a very specific way. Although these switches are similar in functionality, the difference is that `-format` uses .NET-based format specifiers, whereas `-uFormat` uses Unix-style formatters.

One common use for dates is to generate unique filenames. Suppose you want to generate a string that represents the current date in the format YYYYMMDD, where YYYY is the four-digit year, MM is the two-digit month, and DD is the two-digit date. This is how you do it using both format methods:

```
Get-Date -format yyyyMMdd
Get-Date -uFormat %Y%m%d
```

Both methods yield the same result, which is something like this:

```
20080318
```

Which one you choose boils down to convenience. Windows PowerShell attempts to appeal to both existing Windows administrators and other administrators who have a Unix background and seek to apply much of their existing scripting knowledge to Windows. If you're already familiar with Unix-style date modifiers, simply using `-uFormat` to take advantage of that skill set may make sense; otherwise, I feel that the .NET format is more consistent with its definition (which makes me more inclined to use it). No one expects you to know all the possible date modifiers, so I put together Table 13-1 to list the most common ones.

Modifiers are case-sensitive. If you're not getting the output you want, double-check to make sure that you used the right case when specifying your modifier.

Table 13-1		Get-Date Format Modifiers
.NET (-format)	*Unix (-uFormat)*	*Description*
d, %d	%e	Day of the month (1, 2 . . . 31). Not zero padded.
Dd	%d	Day of the month (01, 02 . . . 310). Zero padded.
Ddd	%a	Abbreviated day of the week (Mon, Tue . . . Sun).
Dddd	%A	Full name of the day of the week (Monday, Tuesday . . . Sunday).
%h	%l	Hour of the day based on 12-hour clock without leading zeros (1, 2 . . . 12).
Hh	%I	Hour of the day based on 12-hour clock with leading zeros (01, 02 . . . 12).
H, %H	%k	Hour of the day based on 24-hour clock without leading zeros (0, 1, 2 . . . 23).
HH	%H	Hour of the day based on 24-hour clock with leading zeros (00, 01, 02 . . . 23).
%m	<none>	Minute without leading zeros (0, 1, 2 . . . 59).
Mm	%M	Minute with leading zeros (00, 01, 02 . . . 59).
M, %M	<none>	Numeric month without leading zeros (1,2 . . . 12).
MM	%m	Numeric month with leading zeros (01, 02 . . . 12).
MMM	%b	Abbreviated month name (Jan, Feb . . . Dec).
MMMM	%B	Full name of the month (January, February . . . December).
s, %s	<none>	Seconds without leading zeros (0, 1, 2 . . . 59).
Ss	%S	Seconds with leading zeros (00, 01, 02 . . . 59).
Tt	%p	AM/PM in capital letters.
Yy	%y	Two-digit year (98, 99, 00 . . . 10).
Yyyy	%Y	Four-digit year (1998, 1999, 2000, 2010).

Many more modifiers are available, of course. All the .NET date and time format modifiers are based on the `System.Globalization.DateTime` `FormatInfo` class. You can find more information about this class on the MSDN Web site (`http://msdn2.microsoft.com/en-us/library/` `system.globalization.datetimeformatinfo.aspx`). To find more Unix-format modifiers, you can take a look at the `Get-Date` detailed help text (`Get-Help Get-Date -detailed`). A notes section at the end of that help text lists all the Unix date and time modifiers.

Creating your own dates

`Get-Date` always returns the current date and time by default. Many times, though, you need to define a date or time other than "right now." `Get-Date` gives you several ways to accomplish this task. The most straightforward of all these methods is to define the date literally in string format, as in this example:

```
$mydate = Get-Date "03/29/2008"
```

Notice that I define the date only. That's fine! If you leave out any portion of a date or time, Windows PowerShell fills in the rest for you. If you leave out a time, Windows PowerShell uses midnight (12:00:00AM) as the time. Similarly, if you define just the time, Windows PowerShell uses the current date as the date.

The other way to define your own dates is to use the date and time switches of the `Get-Date` Cmdlet. You can define a very exact date and time down to the second by doing something like this:

```
Get-Date -year 2008 -month 3 -day 29 -hour 14 -minute 23 -second 15
```

All these switches are optional, and if you omit any one of them, Windows PowerShell assumes certain default values. When exact values aren't specified, the year, month, and day default to the current year, month, and day, and the hour, minute, and second default to `0`.

The hour is based on a 24-hour clock, so 1pm is `13`, 2pm is `14`, and so on.

Using Date Math (It's Not Just for Nerds)

Although being able to find out the current date and time or to define dates and times in general is useful, more often than not, the reason you need to do these things is to calculate duration or elapsed time. Calculating the time difference between two dates gets complicated, because sometimes the calculation isn't as trivial as just subtracting one number from another. Do you know how many days elapsed between February 3, 1983, and July 14, 2008, for example? This operation isn't exactly something that you can easily do in your head.

Calculating time differences

You can calculate the difference between two dates very easily in Windows PowerShell. All you need to do is subtract the two dates. Going back to the problem I presented in the preceding section, you can perform the date calculation by defining the two dates and subtracting one from the other to get your answer:

```
$date1 = Get-Date -year 1983 -month 2 -day 3
$date2 = Get-Date -year 2008 -month 7 -day 14
$diff = $date2 - $date1
```

Now you have some value in $diff that represents the difference between the two dates, but exactly what is this value? When you subtract two DateTime objects, what you end up with is a Timespan object. If you output the value of $diff, you see these values:

```
Days              : 9293
Hours             : 0
Minutes           : 0
Seconds           : 14
Milliseconds      : 808
Ticks             : 8029152148086132
TotalDays         : 9293.00017139599
TotalHours        : 223032.004113504
TotalMinutes      : 233253.972977117
TotalSeconds      : 802915214.808613
TotalMilliseconds : 802915214808.613
```

The best part of the `Timespan` object is that it already contains the value of the time span in different units that you may care about. If you want to know the number of days, you can just read the `Days` parameter by running this code:

```
$diff.Days
```

If you want to know the number of milliseconds, you read the value of the `Milliseconds` parameter. Hmm . . . wait. If you look at the values in the `$diff` variable, something doesn't seem quite right. Surely, more than 808 milliseconds elapsed between 1983 and 2008.

The days, hours, minutes, seconds, and milliseconds are actually part of one value. In other words, Windows PowerShell (well, actually, the .NET Framework) determined that 9,293 days, 0 hours, 0 minutes, 14 seconds, and 808 milliseconds elapsed between those two dates. If you want to know just the total number of days, hours, minutes, seconds, or millisec-onds, use `TotalDays`, `TotalHours`, `TotalMinutes`, `TotalSeconds`, or `TotalMilliseconds` instead.

Then there's that other strange value. What are ticks, and why are there so many of them? No, this value isn't the number of tiny bloodsucking insects that existed between those dates. A *tick* is equal to 100 nanoseconds and is the smallest unit of time defined in the .NET Framework. The term isn't used often to describe time, but if you have to come up with time differences with a granularity smaller than a millisecond, you have to use the tick count instead.

Looking into the future

Sometimes, you need to find what the date or time will be based on a known date and a given period. This scenario is actually fairly common. Suppose that you're creating a scheduler that runs a task every 15 days for a period of 60 days. To figure out when these tasks will run, first you have to have a reference date (in this case, the first time when the task is scheduled to run); then you add 15 days to that date to get a new date. Do this a total of four times, and you've got all the future dates when this task will run. In Windows PowerShell, this function is implemented as follows:

```
$startDate = Get-Date "8/13/2008 11:00pm"
Write-Host ("Task runs on: ")
Write-Host $startDate
for($i = 15; $i -le 60; $i += 15) {
    Write-Host $startDate.AddDays($i)
}
```

The first thing that the script does is establish a start date and time. Then it uses a `for` loop to generate all other times when the task will run. The most important part of this code is the `date` object's `AddDays` method, which adds whatever number of days you specify to the `date` object and returns a date object representing the new date after all those days have elapsed.

You're not limited to adding just days. Variations of the `Add` method that allow you to add practically any date or time value you want. The plain `Add` method, which takes a `Timespan` object as a parameter and adds whatever duration you want, is specified in the `timespan` object. All the other `Add` methods have very intuitive names:

- ✔ `Add` (adds a `Timespan` value)
- ✔ `AddDays`
- ✔ `AddHours`
- ✔ `AddMilliseconds`
- ✔ `AddMinutes`
- ✔ `AddMonths`
- ✔ `AddSeconds`
- ✔ `AddTicks`
- ✔ `AddYears`

You're not limited to getting future dates. You can give the different `Add` methods a negative value so that PowerShell will calculate dates in the reverse direction. If you want to know what date it was 8,723 hours ago, you can run

```
$now = Get-Date
$now.AddHours(-8723)
```

Checking whether it's daylight saving time

Daylight saving time (DST) is a really practical concept, when you think about it, because it lets humans make better use of the available sunlight. Although the simple action of moving the clock forward or backward is relatively simple (even though trying to get up on time when you have to move forward an hour isn't), it introduces another layer of complexity to the already-complex concept of date math. When the United States decided to extend its daylight saving time period, it created yet another scramble to correct computer code that rely on dates akin to Y2K but with less media hype. Some applications have the DST logic built in; others rely on various programming libraries or the operating system itself to provide this information.

Well, having gone through that process once, I highly recommend that you don't try to get smart and implement DST code yourself. Take advantage of the built-in DST calculator in Windows PowerShell, which can perform all the math for you. In fact, all the date math I discuss earlier in this chapter is already DST–aware. If any new changes have to be made in the DST logic, you'll have to update Windows PowerShell only once; then all your other programs will be aware of the new dates.

One other piece of information you may want to know is whether a date occurs during DST. Windows PowerShell has that task covered as well. You can use the `IsDaylightSavingTime` method of the `date` object, which returns `true` if that date occurs during DST. This code snippet results in the output `false` followed by `true`:

```
$date1 = Get-Date "1/3/2008"
$date2 = Get-Date "4/23/2008"
$date1.IsDaylightSavingTime
$date2.IsDaylightSavingTime
```

Dealing with Time Zones

If DST and leap years aren't enough, add time zones to the mix, and you've got yourself a really exciting date. Unless you work for a global company or design your Windows PowerShell scripts to connect to various resources in different time zones, you probably aren't too concerned about time zones. After all, if you care about dates and times only in the context of the current time zone, the standard `date` class already gives you this information for free.

Suppose that you have a script that's designed to run on several computers, and one computer may be in a different time zone from the others. You want to make sure that the date and time aren't based on local times but on the date and time at your headquarters in New York. Unfortunately, the `date` class can't help you with this operation. Instead, you must use the `Timezone` class to access this kind of information.

Standardizing with Coordinated Universal Time

The best way to deal with times and time zones is to base local times on a standard clock known as Coordinated Universal Time (UTC), which used to be called Greenwich Mean Time (GMT). This standard clock is based on the concept of time's being defined in relation to the local time at the Greenwich, England (prime meridian, 0 degrees longitude). As you move west from this location, the local time shifts by a negative amount; moving east shifts time by a positive value.

New York, for example, is –5 hours from UTC, which means that whatever time it is in Greenwich, England, the local time in New York is Greenwich time minus 5 hours. Tokyo, on the other hand, is +12 hours from UTC, which means that it's ahead of Greenwich time by 12 hours. These offsets are fixed, determined by the longitude of a location in relation to the prime meridian. As you and I know, however, time isn't fixed because you also have to factor in things like DST. Because different countries define the beginning and end of DST differently (if at all), DST acts as an adjustment factor when you're trying to work out the time differences between two geographic locations.

To see how this process works, consider New York, which is UTC –5:00, and Stockholm, Sweden, which is UTC +1:00. The time difference between New York and Stockholm is 6 hours — most of the time. Because New York starts DST earlier than Stockholm does and ends it later, for several weeks of the year, New York is on DST but Stockholm isn't. During these weeks, the time difference isn't 6 hours but 5 hours, because New York time jumps ahead by 1 hour before Stockholm does.

If you can determine the UTC offsets of any two locations and also determine whether those locations are observing DST, you can compare the two times by following these steps:

1. Get the UTC offset of the first location (–5 for New York, for example).

2. Add to the offset a DST adjustment factor (+1 if it's DST in this location and 0 otherwise).

3. Get the UTC offset of the second location (+1 for Stockholm, for example).

4. Add to this offset a DST adjustment factor (+1 if it's DST in this location and 0 otherwise).

5. Subtract the value you got in Step 2 from the value you got in Step 4.

   What you end up with is the true time difference between the two locations.

Using the TimeZone class

The `TimeZone` class gives you access to the world of using time zones in Windows PowerShell. This class has plenty of very useful methods that, when used in conjunction with date objects, can give you all that you need to calculate time-zone differences. You can find out what time zone you're in by using this code snippet:

```
$tz = [timezone]::CurrentTimeZone
```

The `$tz` variable now contains a `timezone` object that reflects the current time zone. You can see the name of this `timezone` object by running

```
$tz.StandardName
$tz.DaylightName
```

Notice that a `timezone` object has two names: one for use during standard time (Eastern Standard Time, for example) and one for DST (Eastern Daylight Time, for example). The display names are fine, but what you're really interested in is the UTC offset, because it's a numerical value that you can use to compare time zones. This is how you get the current UTC offset:

```
$tz = [timezone]::CurrentTimeZone
$d = Get-Date
$tz.GetUTCOffset($d).Hours
```

If you're in New York when you run this command sequence, you' get the value –5 because New York is in the UTC –5:00 time zone. If the current date or the date you give to the `GetUTCOffset` method occurs during DST, this code returns –4 instead. But wait — aren't UTC values constant? Yes, they are on paper, but what's happening is that Windows PowerShell (actually, .NET) is saving you some legwork. Rather than forcing you to calculate UTC offset and factoring in DST, it does all the work for you.

When you get the UTC offset of a time zone by using the `GetUTCOffset` method, this value already includes the DST adjustment factor, so it changes dynamically based on whether the time zone is observing DST.

Unfortunately, Windows PowerShell isn't capable yet of determining the time-zone information in a time zone other than its own. As a result, you have to use some other method to determine the UTC offset of the other location (such as looking it up online). When you have the two values, you can calculate the time difference between them.

Part IV
Controlling Where and How You Operate PowerShell

The 5th Wave   By Rich Tennant

@RICHTENNANT

"You know how cats love to play with strings? Well, Mittens would rather write them."

Part IV
Controlling Where
and How You
Operate

In this part . . .

It's now time to start really harnessing the power of Windows PowerShell 2. This part covers some really cool new features in Windows PowerShell. Chapter 15 gives you the ability to run commands on a remote computer and even run multiple commands or scripts simultaneously in the background. I like to call these features force multipliers because they really let you do more things simultaneously, which means getting things done faster with very little additional effort. If you like utilizing your computer to free up more of your time, you'll love these features. I show you how to make your scripts work within an international setting in Chapter 16. Trying to debug a script is usually a real pain, but Chapter 17 makes finding and squashing those bugs much easier.

Chapter 14

Using Functions to Divide and Conquer

. . . .

. . . .

*I*t's very rare for any of us to do something only once, especially when it has anything to do with computers. When writing your Windows PowerShell scripts, you'll eventually find that you repeat code over and over. Although that's good exercise for your fingers, it really is counterproductive. Modularizing your code into functions not only saves you tons of time, but also makes your code more robust by making sure that tried-and-tested code is reused so that you don't have to rewrite everything from scratch every time and possibly introduce unnecessary errors.

In this chapter, you harness the real power of scripting by creating reusable code blocks called functions (and their slightly upgraded version, Advanced Functions). *Functions* allow you to accomplish a lot without writing lots of repetitive code, and often functions makes troubleshooting or making changes to existing scripts a lot easier. So if you're looking for ways to save you more time in the future, keep reading!

Reusing Code Using Functions

Imagine a simple task such as displaying the words *I want a nice juicy steak right now* on the screen. You already know that you use `Write-Host` to display text. If your task is to display that text 100 times in a row, you also know that you can put the text in a loop. This method works great when you need to repeat something many times in sequence, but it doesn't work so well if you need to repeat a section of code more than once but not necessarily repeat it immediately.

When you want to have a piece of code that you'll reuse again and again, it often makes sense to put that code in a function. A *function* is like a black box with inputs and outputs. When you write a function, you generally design it in such a way that the user of the function doesn't need to know how it works. You just define what the inputs should be and what the function does, along with any values it might return.

Consider the remote control for your TV set. When you press the On button, you usually don't want to know the intricate details of how the infrared signal is sent to the TV, how the TV then activates a relay to power on its circuitry, and so on. You just want the TV to turn on. In effect, the On button is like a function. You press the button, and it does some magic and performs some action — in this case, turning on the TV.

Creating your first function

Functions consist of four parts: the function's name, input parameters, body, and return values. Only the function name and its body are required. Here's a function called MyUselessFunction that does nothing useful (actually, it does nothing at all):

```
function MyUselessFunction{
    #Here's the body that contains nothing if you want.
}
```

 When entering commands in the command line that span multiple lines, Windows PowerShell goes into a multiline prompt with each subsequent line preceded by >>. You can keep entering commands as you would in a script, and when you're ready to run the multiline command, just press Enter one more time.

You create a function by using the function keyword followed by the name of the function. The stuff between the curly braces is the body of the function, which defines what the function does. The body can contain whatever you want, even if it's nothing like the example in MyUselessFunction.

A useless function is about as helpful as being stuck in a desert with nothing but a million dollars. Sure, it's great to see, but it won't help you survive. Here's a more useful function that uses Windows Management Instrumentation (WMI) to query for, and then display, the computer's operating system details:

```
function GetOSInfo{
    $osinfo = Get-WmiObject Win32_OperatingSystem
    Write-Host ($osinfo.caption + " " + $osinfo.version + " Service Pack
            " + $osinfo.ServicepackMajorVersion + "." + $osinfo.
            ServicePackMinorVersion)
}
```

If you enter this code in the Windows PowerShell command line or put it inside a Windows PowerShell script by itself, you'll find that it doesn't do anything or display anything at all. This is okay, because all you've done is define the function. *Defining* this function simply tells Windows PowerShell about the function you want to create and what it's supposed to do. When you actually want to use the function, you just need to run

```
GetOSInfo
```

On a typical Windows Vista computer running Service Pack 1, this function displays

```
Microsoftr Windows VistaT Ultimate  6.0.6001 Service Pack 1.0
```

Note: The extra r and T after `Microsoft` and `Vista` are for the copyright and trademark symbols, respectively, which can't be displayed properly in a command shell.

Before you can use a function in Windows PowerShell, you must define it. If you want to define a function in a script, the definition (code) for the function must come before you use it the first time. This rule is especially important to keep in mind if you have some experience with VBScript, because unlike Windows PowerShell, VBScript allows you to define functions anywhere you want within the script.

Defining parameters

Most of the time, you create functions after you realize that you keep repeating a section of code with the only difference being some changes in a few variables. In the case of querying for operating system information, you may want to query different computers at different times. You can change the GetOSInfo function to accept a parameter that represents the name of the computer you want to query, as in this example:

```
function GetOSInfo($computername){
   $osinfo = Get-WmiObject Win32_OperatingSystem -computer $computername
   Write-Host ($osinfo.caption + " " + $osinfo.version + " Service Pack
           " + $osinfo.ServicepackMajorVersion + "." + $osinfo.
           ServicePackMinorVersion)
}
```

If you want to query the operating system name and version of another computer on your network (such as `mail01`), you can run

```
GetOSInfo mail01
```

Unlike other programming or scripting languages, Windows PowerShell requires you to put a space before each parameter when you pass parameters to a function. You don't enclose the parameter in parentheses, as in GetOsInfo(mail01). If your function takes more than one parameter, you separate the values with spaces, as in Myfunction param1 param2 param3.

The new GetOSInfo function just has a few changes. The most obvious one is in the main function definition:

```
function GetOSInfo($computername)
```

This code tells Windows PowerShell that the GetOSInfo function takes one parameter and that within the function, the value will be referred to as $computername. Now that GetOSInfo has the name of the computer you want to query, the other change in the function makes use of this newly defined parameter:

```
$osinfo = Get-WmiObject Win32_OperatingSystem -computer $computername
```

I added the -computer $computername parameter to Get-WmiObject and successfully converted this function to support querying other computers.

Defining more than one parameter

You can define more than one parameter, if you want. You just need to separate the parameters with commas, like this:

```
function FullName($firstname, $lastname) {
   Write-Host ($firstname + " " + $lastname)
}
```

You can also define your parameters in a different way. Instead of putting the parameter list between the function name and the first curly brace, you can define the parameter list inside the body of the function, like this:

```
function FullName{
   param($firstname, $lastname)
   Write-Host ($firstname + " " + $lastname)
}
```

So far, I've been using variable names in the parameter list. Windows PowerShell treats these variables as *variants* (variables that don't have a data type) so you can give them any values you want. This arrangement is useful but can cause bugs in your code if you suddenly get some data type that you didn't expect. The best solution is to define the type for each input parameter explicitly by prefixing each parameter name with the data type enclosed in square brackets. This version of the FullName function makes sure that both parameters given to it are of the type string (or at least can be converted to string) before the function proceeds:

```
function FullName{
    param([string]$firstname, [string]$lastname)
    Write-Host ($firstname + " " + $lastname)
}
```

Working with default parameters

The modifications I made in the GetOSInfo function in the "Defining Parameters" section, earlier in this chapter, allow users of the function to specify the computer name of whatever host they want to get the OS information from. The annoying thing about these modifications is that now, if I just want to query my own OS information, I either have to give the function my computer name explicitly or put in a dot (.), which in WMI means the local host. The good news is that you can define default values for each parameter so that if a value isn't specified, the default value is assigned automatically. Here's how GetOSInfo looks with a default value defined (making sure that a string is provided, of course):

```
function GetOSInfo([string]$computername = "."){
    $osinfo = Get-WmiObject Win32_OperatingSystem -computer $computername
    Write-Host ($osinfo.caption + " " + $osinfo.version + " Service Pack
            " + $osinfo.ServicepackMajorVersion + "." + $osinfo.
            ServicePackMinorVersion)
}
```

The key is the change in the main function definition:

```
function GetOSInfo([string]$computername = ".")
```

In addition to making sure that $computername is a string, PSH assigns the value "." to this variable. This value is used only if you run GetOSInfo without any parameters; otherwise, if you give the function a computer name, that value takes precedence and is assigned to $computername in lieu of the default value.

Returning values

So far, all the function examples in this chapter simply display some information onscreen. Most of the time, however, this result isn't what you want. Instead, you want to call a function with some parameters and get back a value that you'll either use or manipulate within your script.

You can return a value from a function by using the return keyword followed by the value you want to return. Here's a modified version of the FullName function that returns the full name string rather than just displaying it onscreen:

```
function FullName([string]$firstname, [string]$lastname) {
    return ($firstname + " " + $lastname)
}
```

Interestingly enough, if you call the `FullName` function by itself with the appropriate parameters, it still behaves the way it did before, displaying the full name onscreen. In other words, running

```
FullName "Steve" "Seguis"
```

results in this output:

```
Steve Seguis
```

You get this output because by default, when Windows PowerShell gets a value back from a function that you don't use by assigning it to some variable, that return value is simply displayed onscreen. It's really only a coincidence that the behavior of this new version of the `FullName` function is the same as that of the old one. The big difference is that now you can store the result in a variable for use later, as in this example:

```
$name = FullName "Steve" "Seguis"
Write-Host "I can do something now...then display"
Write-Host $name
```

This code outputs

```
I can do something now...then display
Steve Seguis
```

This version is different from the old version, which would have displayed the name immediately before continuing to the next line of code.

Sometimes, the value you want to return is a collection of values rather than a simple single value. If the value generated inside your function is already a collection, you can simply return that collection. Here's a simple function that does a directory listing of everything in the Windows directory and returns that result because the return value of Get-ChildItem in this case is already a collection:

```
function DirWin{
    return Get-ChildItem $env:windir
}
```

It's best to use environment variables when getting things like the path to the Windows directory, because you can't always assume that the result is going to be `C:\Windows`. To get any environment variable's value, just use `$env:<environment variable name>`.

If you're retrieving multiple values from within your function, and you want to return a collection of values, one easy way is to use the `Write-Output` method. Contrary to what you might think, `Write-Output` doesn't display the value onscreen when it's used within a function. Instead, it adds the item to an unnamed collection that is returned by the function when it completes. This new function uses `Write-Output` to create, and eventually return, a collection from the function that contains just the names of files and folders directly below the Windows folder:

```
function DirWinNames{
    $dir = Get-ChildItem $env:windir
    foreach($item in $dir) {
        Write-Output $item.name
    }
}
```

You can use the result of this function just as you would use any collection, such as looping through it with a `foreach` loop, like this:

```
$contents = DirWinNames
foreach($item in $contents) {
    Write-Host $item
}
```

Using Scope

Scope is a concept that often confuses new programmers because it's not entirely intuitive and sometimes is difficult to explain. For this reason, scope issues are among the top sources of bugs in scripts and are often frustrating to track down. Make sure that you pay attention to this section and reread it if things aren't clear the first time around.

Understanding scope rules

Scope defines the boundaries that control the visibility of variables from a given context. From the perspective of a function, Windows PowerShell has three scopes:

- **Global scope:** Visible throughout the entire shell
- **Script scope:** Visible only from within the script during its execution
- **Private scope:** Visible only from within the function

What exactly do I mean by *visible?* To get a better understanding of how scope works, take a look at Figure 14-1. Only the variables that are defined, either in your current scope or its parent (container), are visible to you.

Parents can't see the variables in any of their children. In other words, if you're in the Private scope, you can see and access the variables that exist in Script scope and Global scope, in addition to anything you define in the Private scope. If you're in the Script scope, however, you can see variables in the Global scope but not in the Private scope.

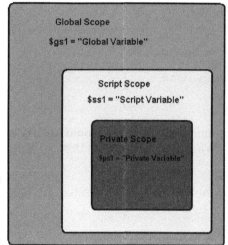

Figure 14-1:
The scope
diagram.

Have a look at the following script, which implements what Figure 14-1 shows. First, assume that $gs1 = "Global Variable" has been defined at the Windows PowerShell prompt, which immediately puts it into Global scope:

```
# testscript.ps1
# assumes $gs1 = "Global Variable" has been defined in the Windows PowerShell
               console.

function MyPrivFunction {
    Write-Host "Inside Function..."
    $ps1 = "Private Variable"
    Write-Host $ps1
    Write-Host $ss1
    Write-Host $gs1
    Write-Host "Function Done..."
}

Write-Host "Inside Script..."
$ss1 = "Script Variable"
Write-Host $ss1
Write-Host $ps1
Write-Host $gs1

MyPrivFunction

Write-Host "Script Done..."
```

Running this script results in the following output:

```
Inside Script...
Script Variable...

Global Variable...
Inside Function...
Private Variable...
Script Variable...
Global Variable...
Function Done...
Script Done...
```

As you can see, variables defined both within the script and globally are all accessible from within the `MyPrivFunction` function, and global variables are also accessible from within the script. Notice, though, that a line is missing between `Script Variable...` and `Global Variable...` in the output. This missing line is caused by the `Write-Host $ps1` line within the script. Scope rules prevent Private scope access from within Script scope, so in the main body of the script, you can't access variables within a function.

Some really technical facts explain this situation, but you can come up with the reason just by thinking. The script can't access variables in a function because those variables don't really exist until the function is called, and they exist only while the function is running. When the function is done, variables defined within the function are no longer needed and cease to exist.

The same holds true for variables defined in a script. Those variables don't exist until the script is running, so you shouldn't be able to access a variable in the Script scope from the Global scope.

Watching out for name overlap

The interesting aspect of scope is that it allows you to use the same variable name more than once, provided that the variable names are in different scopes. Consider this code snippet:

```
function scopetest{
    $myvar = "Jeremy"
    Write-Host $myvar
}

$myvar = "Royski"
Write-Host $myvar
scopetest
```

This code generates the following output:

```
Royski
Jeremy
```

Even though I used $myvar twice, there's no problem because of scope. Within the scopetest function, $myvar contains the string "Jeremy", but outside the function, $myvar contains the string "Royski". The variables have the same names, but internally, they're completely separate variables.

This behavior often leads to some confusion and in some cases to bugs. Here's some code that attempts to change the value of the variable $name from within a function:

```
function changename{
    $name = "Bradley"
}
$name = "Jason"
Write-Host $name
changename
Write-Host $name
```

Because functions can see variables in their parent scope (Script scope), you may think that simply assigning a new value to $name will change its value, but if you run this code snippet, you'll find that the output is "Jason" both times. Why hasn't the name changed? The reason is that although you can read the value of a variable in a parent's scope, you can't assign a value just by using the variable's name. In this case, instead of assigning the string "Bradley" to $name, the function simply creates a new Private scope variable called $name and gives it a value of "Bradley". Nothing is ever touched at the parent scope.

This mistake is a very common one; even experienced programmers and script writers sometimes make this mistake. If this code snippet were part of some much larger piece of code, it might be almost impossible to find and would result in some very unexpected behavior of the code. If you really want to change the value of a variable outside the current scope, you have to use a slightly different syntax. Here's a modified version of the preceding code snippet that changes the value of $name correctly at the script level:

```
function changename{
    $script:name = "Bradley"
}
$name = "Jason"
Write-Host $name
changename
Write-Host $name
```

Now the output is

```
Jason
Bradley
```

To change the value defined in the Script scope from a Private scope, use the format `$script:<variable_name>=<new_value>`. To change the value defined in the Global scope from either the Script or Private scope, use the format `$global:<variable_name>=<new_value>`.

Defining functions in Global scope

The best thing about functions is that they really help you modularize your code and allow you to reuse frequently used code. One way is to copy and paste the function code between scripts, but if you think you'll use the function often, it makes much more sense to define the function at Global scope level. Doing so makes the function available not only in the Windows PowerShell console, but also to any script you run from the console.

You have three options for defining a function at Global scope level:

- **Manually:** You type the function definition manually in the Windows PowerShell console.
- **Profile script:** You can put the code for your function in your profile script so that every time you open a new shell, the function will be defined automatically.
- **Dot-sourcing:** You put the code for the function in a script and dot-source it.

In *dot-sourcing*, you simply put the code in a script file such as `C:\scripts\myfunctions.ps1`. Then you run `. c:\scripts\myfunctions.ps1`, and the script runs in Global scope, which means that any variable or function you define in it will persist for the duration of the console.

Creating Your Own Cmdlets — Advanced Functions!

Cmdlets are typically written in the C# programming language but can also be written in VB.NET. Don't worry — I'm not going to ask that you become skilled in either of these programming languages. One of the coolest new features to be introduced with Windows PowerShell 2 is Advanced Functions.

Advanced Functions provide a way for you to write functions that behave like Cmdlets in the form of PowerShell scripts rather than the compiled C# or VB.NET methods. What this really means for you is that if you can write a Windows PowerShell script, you can most certainly write your own Advanced Functions. This feature has great possibilities because it allows you to create a library of Cmdlets that you can use yourself and also give to other people.

Understanding the structure of Advanced Functions

Advanced Functions have a very specific structure, one that's similar to the structure required by regular Cmdlets created in C# or VB.NET, because just like Cmdlets, Advanced Functions must define their behavior in a predictable format so that they can work seamlessly together. Look at the advanced function in Listing 14-1. It doesn't do much, but it demonstrates how the Advanced Functions concept works.

Listing 14-1:   Color-Coded Output Using Advanced Functions

```
#REQUIRES -Version 2.0
function Write-Yellow
{
   <#
   .Synopsis
       Writes some text in yellow foreground color
   .Description
       This function displays the text you provide to
       The screen using a yellow foreground color.
   .Parameter out
       String to display
   .Example
       PS>  Write-Yellow "Show this in yellow!"
   .Link
       about_functions
       about_functions_advanced
       about_functions_advanced_methods
       about_functions_advanced_parameters
   .Notes
       Author: Steve Seguis
   #>
   [CmdletBinding()]
   Param
   (
       [Parameter(mandatory=$true,ValueFromPipeline=$true)]
       [Alias("out")]
       [String]$OutString
   )
```

Listing 14-1:   Color-Coded Output Using Advanced Functions

```
Begin
{
    Write-Host "Hello, Write-Yellow starting up!"
}

Process
{
    Write-Host $OutString -foregroundcolor "Yellow"
}

End
{
    Write-Host "Bye bye!"
}
}
```

You should always start a script with #REQUIRES -Version 2.0 at the top, because this script doesn't work with version 1 of Windows PowerShell. The script defines a function called Write-Yellow in the typical verb–noun format, such as Get-Help. The first section, starting with <# and ending in #>, is a feature called AutoHelp. If you run Get-Help against this script, the AutoHelp feature displays the contents between those two delimiters in the window, which makes creating help for your scripts much easier.

Defining attributes

What differentiates a regular function from an advanced function is the use of the next piece, called the CmdletBinding attribute. You can define up to four distinct attributes for the CmdletBinding attribute:

- ✔ SupportsShouldProcess: When you specify the SupportsShouldProcess attribute, it enables the -confirm and -whatif parameters of the Cmdlet, which prompts the user before the script makes any changes to the system.

- ✔ DefaultParameterSet: You use the DefaultParameterSet attribute to define which parameter set the function should use if that set can't be determined automatically. This attribute is typically used if the function supports multiple syntaxes and the parameters aren't unique.

✔ ConfirmImpact: The ConfirmImpact attribute is used to determine when the action of the Cmdlet should be confirmed by a call to the ShouldProcess method. This setting is used in combination with the SupportsShouldProcess attribute and runs ShouldProcess only if this value is equal to or greater than the value of the shell's $ConfirmPreference variable.

✔ snapin: The last attribute you can define is snapin. Here, you define the name of the snap-in used to register the Cmdlet. Snap-ins provide a way for the custom Cmdlets to be loaded into a Windows PowerShell instance.

You can use a DefaultParameterSet called MyValues, for example, by defining it as follows:

```
[CmdletBinding(DefaultParameterSet='MyValues')]
```

You use commas to separate the property name and values, if you have more than one, like this:

```
[CmdletBinding(SupportsShouldProcess=$true,ConfirmImpact= "Medium")]
```

In practice, though, 99 percent of the time you're going to use this attribute with no parameters, as I show you in the Write-Yellow example in Listing 14-1:

```
[CmdletBinding()]
```

Defining parameters

Next, you must define the parameters that the function will accept. When you define a parameter, you can set several attributes for each parameter (see Table 14-1).

Table 14-1	**Parameter Metadata Attributes**	
Property Name	*Syntax*	*Purpose*
Mandatory	[Parameter (mandatory=$true)]	A value is required for this parameter.
Position	[Parameter (Position=<Int32>]	The position of this parameter on the command line.
Alias	[Alias(<String[]>)]	Another name that can be used to refer to this parameter.

Property Name	Syntax	Purpose
Parameter SetName	`[Parameter(Parameter SetName=<String>)]`	The name of the parameter set this belongs to. Use this attribute when you have multiple parameters with the same name to accommodate different syntaxes for the Cmdlet, depending on use.
ValueFrom Pipeline	`[Parameter(ValueFrom Pipeline=$true)]`	This Cmdlet can accept input from a pipeline.
ValueFrom Pipeline ByProperty Name	`[Parameter(ValueFrom PipeLineByProperty Name=$true)]`	This parameter can accept input from a property of a pipeline object. You use this attribute if you want to map the input property of the pipeline to a property of the Cmdlet with the same name. If the input has a `"name"` property, for example, and this Cmdlet also has a `"name"` parameter, these two values will be paired.
ValueFrom Remaining Arguments	`[Parameter(ValueFrom RemainingArguments= $true)]`	This parameter accepts any arguments that are not mapped to other parameters. Use this attribute if you want to take in an unknown number of values from the command line and store it as a list of items, such as a list of computer names.
HelpMessage	`[Parameter(Help Message=<String>)]`	The text to display as help for this parameter.

(continued)

Table 14-1 *(continued)*

Property Name	Syntax	Purpose
AllowNull	[AllowNull()]	This property can be null (have no value). You can use this attribute if you have a mandatory parameter in which null is a valid value.
AllowEmpty String	[AllowEmpty String()]	This property can have an empty string (blank text) assigned to it even though it's mandatory.
AllowEmpty Collection	[AllowEmpty Collection()]	This property can have an empty collection even though it's mandatory.
Validate Count	[ValidateCount(<Int32>,<Int32>)]	This property validates the minimum and maximum number of arguments supported by this parameter. The first number defines the minimum, and the second number defines the maximum.
Validate Length	[ValidateLength(<Int32>,<Int32>)]	This property validates the minimum and maximum length of the parameter value.
Validate Pattern	[ValidatePattern (<String>)]	This property compares the parameter value to the string pattern. You can use a regular expression to define the pattern that this property value must match. A *regular expression* is a sequence of characters describing a pattern, such as " [0-9] " to mean any digit from 0 through 9.

Property Name	Syntax	Purpose
Validate Range	`[ValidateRange (<Int32>,<Int32>)]`	This property validates the minimum and maximum values of the parameter.
Validate Script	`[ValidateScript (<ScriptBlock>)]`	This property specifies a script that'll be used to validate the parameter. Use this attribute to perform more complex validation of the parameter value.
Validate Set	`[ValidateSet (<String[]>]`	This property defines a set of values that's valid for this parameter.
Validate NotNull	`[Validate NotNull()]`	This parameter can't be null.
ValidateNot NullOrEmpty	`[Validate NotNullOr Empty()]`	This parameter can't be null, an empty string, or an empty array.

The table can be a bit confusing, but in practice, it's very straightforward. Suppose that you define a mandatory string parameter called `ServerName` that you also want to reference as `"SRVNAME"` or `"SRV"` and that has a minimum length of 3 characters and a maximum of 15:

```
Param
(
    [Parameter(mandatory=$true)]
    [Alias("SRVNAME","SRV")]
    [ValidateLength(3,15)]
    [String]$ServerName
)
```

All you need to do is enter each parameter property you want to define on a separate line, along with any necessary values, such as the minimum and maximum values in the case of `ValidateLength`. The exception is that some attributes (such as those specifying whether a parameter is mandatory) have to be specified with the `Parameter` function. You see which parameters need additional attributes if you look at the examples in Table 14-1. If you want to define more than one kind of attribute, you separate the attributes with a comma, like this:

```
[Parameter(mandatory=$true,position=0)]
```

Using methods

Each function can also define three *methods* (a collection of code that performs some function based on a given set of input) to define what it actually does. These methods are

- ✔ Begin{}: The Begin{} method is run once for each instance of this Advanced Function. It's typically used to facilitate initialization routines.

- ✔ Process{}: The Process{} method is called for each input of the Advanced Function. If the Advanced Function receives 100 lines of input (such as the output of a previous command in a pipeline), it is called 100 times (once for each line). This method is usually defined for Advanced Functions when you expect to receive input from a pipeline and need to define how to handle each of the inputs it receives. I talk more about pipelines in Chapter 7.

- ✔ End{}: The End{} method is called once, when the Advanced Function terminates. You use this method to define any postprocessing tasks you want the Advanced Function to do before quitting.

If you have some knowledge of object-oriented programming, you can loosely think of Begin{} and End{} as being the constructor and destructor of a class, respectively. The Process{} method is a single function that does the actual work on the data flowing into it.

I put some code in the Begin{} and End{} methods in Listing 14-1 only to demonstrate how they work. If you don't want to do anything specific when a Advanced Function starts or terminates, you can omit these methods.

Running Advanced Functions

Now that you have an advanced function to play with, follow these additional steps to start using it:

1. **Save the** Write-Yellow **Advanced Funtion code in a file called** myscriptcmdlet.ps1.

2. **Open Windows PowerShell, and run** . C:\scripts\myscriptcmd-let.ps1.

   This code assumes that you saved the script in a scripts directory at the root of the C: drive. Replace C:\scripts with the path to your script. Note that I use a dot followed by a space and then the path to the script.

3. **Test the script by typing** Write-Yellow -OutString "Does this work?" **at the PSH prompt and pressing Enter.**

Running the `Write-Yellow` command in Step 3 generates the following output:

```
Hello, Write-Yellow starting up!
Does this work?
Bye bye!
```

It works wonderfully. The code within the `Begin{}` method gets called first, followed by the code within the `Process{}` method, which displays the value you provided on the command line. The command finishes by executing the code in the `End{}` method.

You may be wondering about that strange Step 2, in which you have to use a dot followed by a space and then the script name. This process is called *dot-sourcing* the script; it makes any variable, function, or whatever else you define in your script globally available for that session.

If you don't dot-source a script that defines a Cmdlet and simply run the script as is, when you try to run your newly created Cmdlet, you'll get an error message saying that it's not a recognized command. This error occurs because the Cmdlet is defined only while the script is running. As soon as the script ends, that Cmdlet definition is removed. Dot-sourcing it tells Windows PowerShell that you want to make the Cmdlet available even after the script finishes executing.

Another way to make your advanced functions available is to put this code in your profile, because your profile script is automatically dot-sourced when you open a Windows PowerShell instance!

Because you defined an alias for the `OutString` parameter, you can also use the following command to display `"Does this work?"` onscreen:

```
Write-Yellow -out "Does this work?"
```

One of the most interesting parameter properties you set in Listing 14-1 for the `OutString` parameter is `ValueFromPipeline`. This property changes the behavior of the `Write-Yellow` Cmdlet a little bit by automatically taking the input and assigning it to the `OutString` parameter. The side effect of this property is that you can actually run `Write-Yellow` without having to specify the parameter name explicitly, as in this example:

```
Write-Yellow "Does this work?"
```

This feature really shines in a pipeline when it receives input from another command. Consider this command sequence:

```
Get-ChildItem C:\ | Write-Yellow
```

The first command, `Get-ChildItem`, lists the contents of the given path, which in this case is the root of the `C:\` drive. Then this result is piped to `Write-Yellow` via the pipe character (|). This command sequence generates the output in Figure 14-2.

Figure 14-2:
The result
of piping the
outputofGet-
ChildItem to
the Write-
Yellow
advanced
function.

This example really demonstrates how the three advanced function methods come into play. Because `Write-Yellow` appears only once on the command line, the code has only one instance of the `Write-Yellow` Cmdlet, and the `Begin{}` method is called once as usual. For each item returned by `Get-ChildItem C:\`, the `Process{}` method is called. Because the code uses the `ValueFromPipeline` property, each object returned by `Get-ChildItem` gets assigned to the `OutString` parameter, and for each object, the function displays this value to the console in yellow. When `Write-Yellow` finishes processing all the objects from `Get-ChildItem`, it runs the `End{}` method.

Out of curiosity, you can try piping the output of `Write-Yellow` to another instance of `Write-Yellow`, as follows:

```
Get-ChildItem C:\ | Write-Yellow | Write-Yellow
```

The output of this command sequence and the previous sequence where the output of `Get-ChildItem` was being passed to only one instance of `Write-Yellow` is that there is an additional `"Hello, Write-Yellow starting up!"` line at the beginning of the output and an additional `"Bye bye!"` line at the end of the output. This occurs because two instances of `Write-Yellow` appear on the line, and the `Begin{}` and `End{}` methods get called once for each instance.

Finding uses for Advanced Functions

As a script writer, you'll find that advanced functions are excellent ways to create reusable commands for yourself and even for other people. You can create a whole library of script Cmdlets and distribute them throughout your organization to build on custom business processes. You can create an advanced function to provision user accounts, for example, and call it `Create-MyCompanyUser`.

Another good use of advanced functions is creating a wrapper around an existing Cmdlet. The `Write-Yellow` advanced function is an example of creating a wrapper around what is essentially `Write-Host` to perform a specialized out routine. If you write a `Write-HostError` Advanced Function that takes some text and displays it onscreen in red, it'll be far easier to use that Advanced Function than using `Write-Host` with the `-foregroundcolor` parameter over and over again.

Chapter 15

PowerShell Ninjas: Running Jobs Remotely or in the Background

In This Chapter

▶ Multitasking with background jobs

▶ Managing background jobs

▶ Administering commands remotely

Most of what I've done (and continue to do on a daily basis) is geared to system automation. Whether you're managing tens of thousands of computers or managing a few of servers, one thing remains the same: To be efficient, you need to be able to manage all those systems easily from a central management point. Sure, you have plenty of ways to manage systems remotely, such as by using Windows Management Instrumentation (WMI), but sometimes even that method has drawbacks, such as reduced performance.

Now you can use Windows PowerShell 2 to run Cmdlets remotely. Another new feature you can take advantage of in Windows PowerShell 2 is the ability to run background jobs, which means that you can run Cmdlets and other things in the background while you do something else.

In this chapter, you explore one of the most compelling reasons for using Windows PowerShell 2, which is to run commands in the background as well as running commands on remote computers that are also running Windows PowerShell 2. This gives you the ability to run more things in parallel and take full advantage of all the PowerShell commands on remote computers just as if you were physically there.

Using Background Jobs

If you open Windows Task Manager, you'll see a bunch of running processes, most of which are processes that you don't use interactively and are running in the background (ideally, doing something useful). The traditional Windows command shell lets you run one command at a time unless, of course, the commands are piped together. Still, you're limited to running one series of commands at a time. One way around this limitation is to start a new command shell that in turn runs other commands. Although this method works, you really have little control after you get the process started. It's not easy to find out the status of the process after it gets going — which may be important if you need to make sure that the process has finished before moving on to something else.

You must be an administrator on the computer to take advantage of background jobs.

Enabling WinRM

You have to enable Windows Remote Shell (WinRM) before you can use any of the background job Cmdlets. As the name implies, WinRM is designed to allow commands to be run remotely on other computers as long as they have WinRM installed — even if you just want to create background jobs on the same computer where you're running the script because it uses the same WinRM features to create and run the jobs. Here's the easiest way to set up WinRM:

1. **Install WinRM 2, if it isn't already installed.**

   Currently available at `https://connect.microsoft.com/WSMAN/Downloads`.

2. **At a command or PowerShell prompt, run** `winrm quickconfig`.

3. **When prompted, press Y to make the configuration changes automatically.**

   When the configuration changes are made, the WinRM service starts.

Starting a new job

You create background jobs by using the `Start-Job` Cmdlet. Minimally, the only thing you need to do is give `Start-Job` the command you want it to run. This command can be as simple as getting a directory listing of everything at the root of the `C:` drive, like this:

```
Start-Job -scriptblock {"Get-ChildItem C:\"}
```

This code automatically starts the command sequence you specify in the background, and you immediately return to the Windows PowerShell prompt. You may notice, however, that in and of itself, running this command doesn't seem to do anything other than return some information about the job:

```
Id              Name        State    HasMoreData    Location     Command
--------        ----        -----    -----------    --------     -------
1               Job1        Running  True           localhost    Get-
                ChildItem C:\
```

You can see what each of the job properties is for in Table 15-1.

Table 15-1	Job Object Properties
Property	**Description**
ID	Displays a unique number assigned to the job while it's running.
Name	Shows the name you give the job, using the -name switch; otherwise, it'll contain a generic name such as Job1.
State	Shows the current state of the job.
HasMoreData	Lets you know whether you can retrieve more data from this job. (I talk about retrieving jobs in the next section.)
Location	Indicates where this job is running. If you're creating a job to run on the machine you're working on, this property will be localhost; otherwise, it'll be the name of the computer on which the job is running.
Command	Specifies the command that this job is running.

Start-Job returns a reference to the job so you can use this reference to access it later. You can save this reference in a variable, if you want, to make referring to that particular job easy, as in this example:

```
$myjob = Start-Job -scriptblock {"Get-ChildItem C:\"}
```

Getting results

If jobs that you create run in the background, how do you get the data returned by them? Here's probably one of the coolest features of Windows PowerShell background jobs: As the jobs run, any data they return is stored for you until you're ready for it. To retrieve the data from a job, you use the Receive-Job Cmdlet. Because it's possible to have many jobs running at the same time, you need to give PowerShell the job object from which you want it to retrieve the data. If you save the return value of `Start-Job` in a variable, you can use that variable to feed into `Receive-Job` because it acts as a reference to that job object, as in this example:

```
Receive-Job -job $myjob
```

Many times, you submit a job and don't keep track of the job object directly; instead, you store it in a variable. Don't worry — you can still get the data from the job as long as you have some other information that uniquely identifies the job you're interested in. One method is to run `Get-Job` to get a list of all the jobs on the system and then use the `ID` to let `Receive-Job` know which job you want to get data from. This example is how you get the result from the job with the `ID` value of 3:

```
Receive-Job -ID 3
```

You use `Get-Job` to see a list of all the jobs on the system.

If you look closely at the output of `Get-Job`, you'll notice a column called `HasMoreData`. This value stays true for as long as you can retrieve data from that particular job. When you run `Receive-Job`, it sets this property to `false` if the job is already complete and no more data is left to retrieve. If the job takes a long time to run (maybe you're doing a directory listing, using `Get-ChildItem` for your entire `C:` drive and all its subdirectories), and you run `Receive-Job` before the job finishes, the code returns the data it has for now, but `HasMoreData` continues to be `true`. If you run `Receive-Job` again, it gives you the rest of the data that's available until no more data is left to return.

The default behavior of `Receive-Job` seems reasonable. After all, after you get the data from the job, you probably don't care about the data anymore. Suppose, though, that the job is running `Get-ChildItem` against your entire `C:` drive and that the job takes 15 minutes to complete. At around the 8-minute mark, you want to use `Receive-Job` to take a peek at its progress, but you don't want to process the results just yet. The problem is that if you run `Receive-Job` before the job ends, you have to retrieve all the currently available data, which is subsequently cleared from the job. This means that if you run `Receive-Job` after it finally completes, you're getting only part of the results — the part that you didn't read the first time. To get around this limitation, run `Receive-Job` with the `-keep` parameter like so:

```
Receive-Job -ID 5 -keep
```

Running `Receive-Job` with the `-keep` parameter allows you to get all the currently available data from the job but doesn't clear the data. Subsequent calls to `Receive-Job` for the same job return all the data, not just the ones you haven't already read.

Waiting for a job

Background jobs are extremely useful because they allow you to run things in parallel by executing commands in the background, freeing your console for other things. If you write a script that takes advantage of background jobs, you'll undoubtedly find a scenario in which one of these jobs must complete before you can move on. With these jobs running in the background independently, what can you do? The easiest method is to wait for the job to finish before proceeding by using the `Wait-Job` Cmdlet like this:

```
$myjob = Start-Job -scriptblock {"Get-Service"}
#Do a bunch of stuff here...then...
Write-Host "Waiting for job to finish..."
Wait-Job $myjob
Write-Host "Finally done..."
Receive-Job $myjob
```

Granted, this example is a bit contrived, because `Get-Service` returns fairly quickly and I could've just waited for it to finish, but you can see how it works. You start a job that may take some time, and go off and do a few other things. Then, when you need the data, you can use `Wait-Job` to make sure that the job has completed before moving on.

Any kind of waiting process is basically a *blocking* process; the code is blocked from continuing until it reaches whatever condition you set for the waiting. The problem with this method is that the code could wait forever if something's wrong with the background job, causing it to hang. You can get around this problem by imposing a timeout on `Wait-Job`. A *timeout* is an ultimatum that says, "If you don't get done within this given time, I'm leaving without you." Here's how you can wait for a task for 60 seconds before moving on:

```
Wait-Job $myjob -timeout 60
```

The `-timeout` parameter is useful for averting an infinite wait condition. You have to be aware, however, that when the timeout has been reached, the code will just continue to the next statement without displaying any error messages. Whenever you use the `-timeout` parameter, you want to follow up with a check to see whether the job actually completed, as this code snippet does:

```
Wait-Job $myjob -timeout 60
if ($myjob.JobStateInfo.State -ne "Completed") {
   Write-Host "Job timed out!"
} else {
   $data = Receive-Job $myjob
}
```

Terminating a job

When a job completes, running `Get-Job` lists that job with a state of `Completed` and the `HasMoreData` property set to `true`. Interestingly enough, when you run `Receive-Job` on a completed job and retrieve all the available data, the job is still listed when you run `Get-Job`. The purpose of this list is to let you see what jobs have run on the computer. The obvious problem, of course, is that after you've created more than a few jobs, the list can get out of hand.

The solution is to delete the job when you're done using it. Most likely, you'll delete it after `Receive-Job` runs because the job won't have any more data to provide anyway. To accomplish this task, you use the `Remove-Job` Cmdlet. You identify the job you want to remove by providing a reference to that job object or by specifying some unique identifier, such as its session ID, as in this example:

```
Remove-Job $myjob
Remove-Job -ID 3
```

Bringing a job to a grinding halt

If you can start jobs, logically, you have to have a way to stop jobs. One of the most common occasions for stopping jobs is when you start a job that takes a very long time to finish and then decide that you don't want to run it anymore. Stopping a job is as easy as running the `Stop-Job` Cmdlet and giving it a reference to the job that you want to stop or the session ID (don't you just love how predictable Windows PowerShell is?), as in this example:

```
Stop-Job $myjob
Stop-Job -ID 3
```

Another reason for stopping a job is to respond to a timed-out `Wait-Job` command. Suppose that you're running a job that you expect to complete in less than a minute, but just to give it enough breathing room, you set its timeout to 3 minutes. If the job still times out after 3 minutes, it's safe to assume that something went wrong. You can go on doing something else and leave the job as it is so you can see what happened, but if you don't really care whether the process occasionally times out, deleting it is the way to go. Here's how you do it:

```
Wait-Job $myjob -timeout 180
if ($myjob.JobStateInfo.State -ne "Completed") {
    #something went wrong, stop this job.
    Stop-Job $myjob
}
```

Combining Wait-Job with Stop-Job is one way to make sure that a job isn't allowed to run more than a given amount of time. If you start a job that copies data from one computer to another, for example, and you want to make sure that it either finishes within the next two hours or stops immediately, first you create the job; then you immediately run Wait-Job and have it wait with a timeout of two hours. If the job isn't done within two hours, the timeout will cause PowerShell to go to the next statement in the script, which can be Stop-Job to stop the job from running immediately.

Running Commands Remotely

One of the things I love most about working in a networked environment is that there's very little you can't do right from your fingertips. You can access files, muck around with the registry, and do all kinds of fun stuff without leaving the comfort of your chair. With the power of Windows PowerShell at the ready, you can take advantage of the same powerful commands but run it against different computers.

Many of the built-in Cmdlets support a -computername parameter, which you can use to give the name of the remote computer on which you want to run the command. Most commands let you access common services such as querying WMI and getting process and service information. The great part is that for these commands, you don't even need Windows PowerShell to be installed on the remote host to get the data you're requesting. PowerShell simply relies on well-known Application Programming Interfaces (APIs) that are built into Windows.

Using Windows PowerShell everywhere

As great as all that is, sometimes (or, depending on what kind of work you do, all the time), you want to interact with a remote host by using Windows PowerShell Cmdlets as well as other Windows PowerShell features (such as variables), just as you do your own computer. You want to be able to enter command scripts or run Windows PowerShell scripts just as though you were physically on that computer.

You could cheat by using a remote-control program like Remote Desktop, connecting to the computer remotely, opening Windows PowerShell, and doing what you need to do. That method might work fine for connecting to a server, because Windows gives you your own environment to play in. If you try to use this method to manage workstations, however, your users will have to wait until you're done because you're taking over their desktops. This method may work well when you're troubleshooting something, but if you just want to make some changes or get some information remotely without interrupting users, remote control just isn't going to cut it.

What you really need is a remote shell — something that you can connect to from within Windows PowerShell and use to enter commands just as though that command shell were running on the remote host. This feature was lacking in Windows PowerShell 1 but is an integral part of Windows PowerShell 2.

Getting what you need for remote commands

Built-in Cmdlets like `Get-Service` just use the Windows API to retrieve data from remote hosts but for you to run commands remotely both the computer you are on and the computer you want to run commands on must have three essential components:

- ✔ Microsoft .NET Framework 2.0
- ✔ Windows PowerShell 2
- ✔ WinRM 2.0 service

You need to have Windows PowerShell installed on both computers to get remote commands to work.

WinRM is a Simple Object Access Protocol (SOAP)–based implementation of the WS-Management Protocol, which is an open specification designed to allow hardware and software from different vendors to interact. In the Windows operating systems, WinRM is implemented as a layer on top of WMI — another feature that allows cross-vendor interoperability.

Speaking PowerShell with a different computer

You can launch an interactive Windows PowerShell session that connects you with a remote computer and run commands on that computer just as though you were physically there by using the `Enter-PSSession` Cmdlet. You connect to the computer by giving `Enter-PSSession` the name of the computer to connect to, like this:

```
Enter-PSSession computer1
```

Windows Vista and Windows Server 2008 both require you to run the Windows PowerShell window as an administrator before running this command. Otherwise, the command will fail, even if you're logged in with administrative credentials.

Running a remote PowerShell session assumes, of course, that the remote computer (computer1) meets the requirements for running remote commands. You don't need to explicitly provide the credentials for logging into the remote computer because by default, PowerShell will automatically try to connect with the credentials you used to log in, so as long as you run this command with credentials that include administrative privileges on the remote computer, you'll be authenticated and logged in automatically.

By default, if you don't specify an authentication method or credential, PowerShell will try to use your Kerberos ticket to connect to the remote host.

If you want to connect by using alternative credentials, Enter-PSSessions has a -Credential parameter in which you can provide the username you want to use to log in, as in this example:

```
Enter-PSSession computer1 -Credential mydomain\admin
```

No parameter for providing the password exists; instead, you must key in the password when prompted.

If you connect successfully, the only difference you'll see at the Windows PowerShell prompt is that the usual PS <current_path> prompt is prefixed by the remote computer name in square brackets, like this:

```
[computer1]: PS C:\Windows\System32>
```

This prompt makes it very easy to see computer you're connected to and also serves as a reminder than any command you give at the Windows PowerShell prompt will be executed on the remote computer, not on your own.

When you're done doing whatever you need to do, you can get out of that computer and back to your own by issuing the Exit-PSSession Cmdlet (no parameter required).

Invoking commands remotely

Many times, you just want a quick session and don't need to open a whole interactive remote session with a computer; you want to issue your command and get out. Sure, you can accomplish this task by using Enter-PSSessions and Exit-PSSession, but those Cmdlets add two steps to the process. The quickest and most direct way to run a remote command is to use the Invoke-Command Cmdlet.

Just like `Enter-PSSession`, `Invoke-Command` takes the name of the computer you want to connect to. but it also has a bunch of other options. The most important of these options is the `-ScriptBlock` parameter, which you use to tell `Invoke-Command` which command or set of commands you want to run on the remote host. Here's how you would run `Get-Date` remotely on the computer called `CORPDC1`:

```
Invoke-Command -computername CORPDC1 -ScriptBlock {Get-Date}
```

Although I use a simple Cmdlet in the example, the script block can effectively contain any code that can be encapsulated within the curly braces — a whole sequence of commands or even the code for a small script.

You can run the same script block on more than one computer by giving `Invoke-Command` all the computer names at the same time. You do this by specifying the computers after the `-computername` parameter as a comma-separated list or as a collection of names. One way to get a collection of names is by running the `Get-Content` Cmdlet on a text file containing a list of computer names. Here's an example of both methods.

```
Invoke-Command -computername CORPDC1,CORPDC2 -scriptblock {Get-Date}
Invoke-Command -computername (Get-Content computers.txt) -scriptblock {Get-Date}
```

Creating a persistent connection

The method in the preceding section for using `Invoke-Command` is perfect for simple commands or command sequences in which you don't need to worry about maintaining state. If you just want to run `Get-Date` to get the current date and time on a remote computer, for example, using `Get-Date` in the script block is all you need to do. After the data is returned and displayed, you don't care about it anymore.

What happens, however, if you want to save the information retrieved in the script block for later use on the remote host? With the method I've shown you so far, this task isn't possible, because the next call to `Invoke-Command` has no information about the script block that you issued before. The solution is to have something that you can use to keep track of various connections and variables you define. This something is called a *session.*

A *session* is an object used to maintain a persistent connection between the local computer and one or more remote hosts. It allows state information such as variables and functions to be shared between the computers.

You create a session by using the `New-PSSession` Cmdlet and giving it the name of the computer with which you want to associate the session. `New-PSSession` returns an object that represents this session, so it makes sense to store this object in a variable (`$s`) so that you can use it for subsequent calls for `Invoke-Command`, like this:

```
$s = New-PSSession -computername CORPDC1
```

Normally, `Invoke-Command` sets up a temporary session, runs the script block, and then tears down the session so that all the variables and other pieces of information are removed from memory. `New-PSSession` establishes that connection, but rather than tearing it down, the Cmdlet keeps it going. Because you have an established connection with the remote host, you can maintain information between multiple calls to `Invoke-Command` as in this contrived example:

```
Invoke-Command -session $s -scriptblock {$start = Get-Date}
Invoke-Command -session $s -scriptblock {(Get-Date) - $start}
```

You may notice a couple of things in this example, starting with the use of the `-session` parameter. You provide `Invoke-Command` the session object that you created by using the `New-PSSession` Cmdlet. Because the session is an object that represents the connection between the local computer and other computers, you no longer have to give `Invoke-Command` the name of the computer you want it to connect to; that name is defined implicitly based on the computers participating in the session. The other noteworthy thing you may notice is that variables you use within the script block maintain their value even after `Invoke-Command` is done.

Because the session stays connected in the background, you want to make sure that you close the connection when you're done with the session. You can close it easily by using the `Remove-PSSession` Cmdlet like this:

```
Remove-PSSession $s
```

Run `Remove-PSSession` on any session you create when you're done using it to close the connection with the other computers and to free the memory consumed by maintaining the session's state.

Running remote background jobs

You can run a background job remotely by connecting to the computer with `Enter-PSSession` and then running the background job as you normally would with `Start-Job`. Because you're in a remote session, the background job will run on the remote computer you're connected to. This method generally is useful if you want to run background jobs on the remote computer on an ad-hoc basis.

Another way is to use the `Invoke-Command` Cmdlet to run `Start-Job` remotely. `Invoke-Command` establishes the connection with the remote host. Thereafter, anything that you tell the Cmdlet to run in the script block (such as `Start-Job`) runs on the remote machine. In practice, the code looks like this:

```
$mysession = New-PSSession -computername Computer1
Invoke-Command -session $mysession -scriptblock {$myjob = Start-Job -scriptblock
          {Get-Service}}
Invoke-Command -session $mysession -scriptblock {Receive-Job $myjob}
Invoke-Command -session $mysession -scriptblock {Remove-Job $myjob}
Remove-PSSession -$mysession
```

In both scenarios I describe above in the Invoking Command Remotely and the Running remote background jobs sections, the jobs are executed remotely, and so are the results. In some cases, you want to run background jobs remotely on a few computers but collect all those results on the machine you're running the command from, thereby centralizing the data. Windows PowerShell 2 solves this problem by adding the `-asjob` switch to Cmdlets that support this feature. The `-asjob` switch runs that command on the specified computer, but the job object itself is stored on the local computer. This arrangement means that although the job itself runs on the remote computer, you can check the status of the job as well as run any of the `*-Job` Cmdlets on this job object on the local computer as you would any background job you create.

Here's how you can run `Get-ChildItem C:\` on two computers as separate background jobs and manage these jobs locally:

```
Invoke-Command -ComputerName Computer1, Computer2 -scriptblock {Get-ChildItem
          C:\} -asjob
```

Now if you run `Get-Job` on your computer, you see two jobs running, just as would if you started two jobs locally by using the `Start-Job` Cmdlet. The difference is that the `Location` field displays the names of the computers on which these jobs are actually running, rather than just `localhost`. Then you can use the job ID or name to wait for the job, receive the data from the job, or even remove the job, just as you would with any background job.

Another really useful Cmdlet that supports the `-asjob` switch is `Get-WMIObject`. You can run `Get-WMIObject` on a bunch of computers by using the `-ComputerName` switch and then add the `-asjob` switch to create job objects automatically for each of these background jobs, which you can manage by using `*-Job` Cmdlets.

Understanding policies, profiles, and precedence

Now that you have a method for using Windows PowerShell locally on your computer as well as remotely, you have to worry about the issue of policies and profiles. The remote execution policy on your computer may be completely different from that of the other computer, for example. Also, because Windows PowerShell profiles are defined and loaded on a per-machine basis, how does Windows PowerShell behave when you're connecting to other computers remotely? Will the remote computer be able to run the aliases and other functions defined in your profile on the local computer?

The rule is actually very simple: When you're running commands locally, all local policies and profiles are in effect, but when you run commands remotely (whether you use `Invoke-Command` or `Enter-PSSession`), the remote computer's policies and profiles take precedence.

This rule may sound trivial, but if you have a complex set of aliases and other useful functions defined in your profile, none of these features will be available to you when you run Windows PowerShell commands remotely unless you copy your profile to the remote computer ahead of time.

Similarly, pay attention to remote execution policies. Commands that run perfectly fine on your computer may not run correctly on the remote host if it has stricter execution policies than your own computer does.

Although you have the convenience of running commands remotely in addition to taking advantage of sessions to keep information persistent, you mustn't forget that you're running these commands as though you're on that remote host. If you're referencing files or third-party Cmdlets, they must exist on the remote host for the command to work. This rule is easy to forget when you're trying to debug a remote command that isn't working the way it should.

Chapter 16

Making Your Script Speak Different Languages

. . . .

In This Chapter

▶ Understanding the purpose of internationalizing scripts

▶ Incorporating translated text into your scripts

▶ Sharing your scripts all over the world

. . . .

*I*f anything is undeniable, it's the fact that globalization is here to stay. Companies are becoming more global, and with the Internet being so prevalent in almost every part of the world, there's not a single place that you or your technology can't touch. This isn't some kind of political statement or shocking revelation: The truth is that if you work for any large organization, you're bound to be global now or are in the process of becoming globally present. Even if you don't work for a multinational company, you may have a great idea for a really useful Windows PowerShell script but need to collaborate with other script writers in other countries to make your script work in different languages. *Internationalizing* your scripts is the process of making them accessible to users who speak different languages.

In this chapter, you utilize techniques for making your scripts more accessible to users who communicate in a different language. While being able to internationalize your scripts is important if you work in a global company that speaks many languages, it's also very useful when you want to share your scripts with other Windows PowerShell users that use a language other than your own to communicate.

When I talk about languages in this chapter, I'm not talking about programming or scripting languages but rather languages as it refers to speech and dialects.

Seeing the Importance of Internationalizing Scripts

If you write a really useful script or advanced function in Windows PowerShell, you may want to share your brilliance with the rest of the world. Sometimes, however, your code isn't friendly for users in other parts of the globe; your code may create a lot of output in English, which may not be understood by people who don't use English as their primary language.

Or maybe it's the other way around. A Windows PowerShell programmer in Spain has written some code that's very useful, but the user prompts and help text are all written in Spanish. Unfortunately, you can't speak Spanish; therefore, you can't make use of this code.

When I talk about *internationalizing* a script, I'm referring to the process of making user-facing parts of the script (such as help text and output) available in different languages. It's impossible to make a script work for every language and dialect in the world, but internationalization allows you to incorporate different versions of your output text in different languages.

Giving Your Scripts Different Tongues

The easiest way to make your script display output in different languages is to have all these variations of output text in your code and to use some kind of if-then clause to control which language gets displayed. Here's some code that implements internationalization this way:

```
$lang = (Get-UICulture).Name
if ($lang -eq "en-US") {
    Write-Host "Hello!"
} elseif ($lang -eq "es-ES") {
    Write-Host "Hola!"
} elseif ($lang -eq "fr-FR") {
    Write-Host "Bonjour!"
}
```

Although this code works for a simple case, imagine a script that outputs dozens of kinds of text. That script would have to be riddled with messy code to handle each language you want to support. Even worse, if you decide to support yet another language later, you have to go back to your code (which is probably hundreds of lines long now, if not thousands of lines long) to add that language.

A more elegant solution — one that's used by most programs today — separates the text that gets displayed to users from the actual code. The different versions of the same text in different languages are stored separately; the code just outputs some text that's automatically substituted for the correct version based on the user's language. To do this in Windows PowerShell 2, query the user interface (UI) culture of the Windows PowerShell environment and then import the appropriately translated text and display it to the user. This feature is new in Windows PowerShell 2 and isn't backward-compatible with Windows PowerShell 1.0.

Using new internationalization features

Windows PowerShell 2 includes several new features that make internationalization possible. Table 16-1 highlights the different features that enable the detection of the computer's currently configured language (culture) as well as additional capabilities for introducing alternate text to support different languages.

Table 16-1	New Windows PowerShell Features That Support Internationalization
Feature	**Description**
`$Culture`	This new automatic variable stores the language used by the system (for date and time, for example).
`$UICulture`	This new automatic variable stores the language used by the user interface (for menu items, for example).
`DATA` section	Scripts can contain a `DATA` section that defines the default text to be used by the script.
`ConvertFrom-StringData`	This new Cmdlet converts a `strong` containing `name=value` pairs to a hash table.
`Import-LocalizedData`	This new Cmdlet imports the correct text for the specified language into a script at runtime.
`.psd1` files	These files contain translated text strings. You can think of them as being resource files that contain the appropriate translated text for a particular language. The files are used in conjunction with `Import-LocalizedData`.

Understanding cultures

Internationalization is synonymous with culture. The *culture* of the system defines the language that is used to represent system information, and a separate culture defines what is used in the UI. This difference is important because the system's culture doesn't necessarily have to match the UI's culture. This is usually found in shared computers used by more than one user that prefer different UI languages.

The culture is represented as one of three property values. The first property, LCID, is a numeric value representing that culture. The second property, Name, is a five-character code representing the culture. Finally, the last property, DisplayName, is just a more descriptive name for the culture. For the U.S. English culture, the property values are

- LCID: 1033
- Name: en-US
- DisplayName: English (United States)

To find the current culture or UI culture, you can run the Get-Culture and Get-UICulture Cmdlets, respectively.

Putting it all together

All these extra features are nice, but it's hard to see how everything fits together until you see what parts these features play. I'm going to start you off with a simple example. Suppose that you speak only one language — English — and you're writing a script that you know you'll eventually want to internationalize. Your first step is defining the different kinds of text that you want to display, and you define them in the form of a DATA section within your script. Then, when you want to output something in your code, rather than writing out the text as you normally would, you simply refer to the text that you defined in your DATA section. Here's a simple script that performs just that function:

```
DATA MyStrings {
ConvertFrom-StringData @'
Greeting = Hello!
str1 = I speak
str2 = English
str3 = The date and time is
Leaving = Good Bye!
'@
}
```

```
Write-Host $MyStrings.Greeting
Write-Host ($MyStrings.str1 + " " + $MyStrings.str2)
Write-Host ($MyStrings.str3 + " " + (Get-Date))
Write-Host $MyStrings.Leaving
```

All this script does is greet the user, say what language it speaks, give the date and time, and then say goodbye. In a real-world script that actually does something useful, any number of other Windows PowerShell commands would be sprinkled throughout, but the bottom line is that whenever you're ready to display the data, all the text you display should be pulled from your DATA section.

Okay, now you understand how to generalize the strings so that you can refer to them later in your code by using the DATA section. If I stopped here, you might conclude that to internationalize this script, all you need to do is make a copy of this script and replace the text defined in the DATA section. Sure, that method works. The problem is that rather than having one script that does everything, you have multiple copies of the same script in multiple places for different languages. This situation is a problem for a few reasons:

- ✔ You have to remember which script to run depending on the user's language.

- ✔ If you support ten languages, you need to have ten copies of the script.

- ✔ If you have to make changes in the script, you have to update the copy for each language that you support.

I'm sure that it didn't take you long to realize that this idea is a very bad one. It certainly doesn't make it easy to support as you add more languages or create more scripts. What you really want is to have a single script with different translations defined and have it choose the correct language automatically based on the current culture. This task is the job of Import-LocalizedData.

Import-LocalizedData looks at the UICulture that is in use when the script is executed (en-US, for example) and then looks for a subdirectory where the script is located that has the same name as that of the Culture. Next, it looks for a .psd1 file with the same name as the script and loads it, dynamically replacing the values of the predefined DATA section with the values from that file. If the Cmdlet can't locate the .psd1 file, the script continues to use the values from the DATA section you defined within the script.

The culture name consists of two elements separated by a hyphen. The first part is the general language abbreviation, and the second part indicates a specific variation of that language. If Import-LocalizedData can't find a folder matching the specific culture, such as en-US, it looks for a folder that matches just the first part, such as en. This default behavior allows you to create .psd1 files that apply to all specific forms of that language.

Here's what a `.psd1` file might look like for a Spanish (Spain) translation of the `DATA` section:

```
ConvertFrom-StringData @'
Greeting = Hola!
str1 = Yo hablo
str2 = Español
str3 = La fecha y hora es
Leaving = Adiós!
'@
```

If the script is called `CurrentTime.ps1`, you just create a subfolder containing `CurrentTime.ps1` and call it `es-ES`; then save this `.psd1` file in the `es-ES` subfolder as `CurrentTime.psd1`. The final step is adding the call to `Import-LocalizedData` to the `CurrentTime.ps1` script, like this:

```
DATA MyStrings {
ConvertFrom-StringData @'
Greeting = Hello!
str1 = I speak
str2 = English
str3 = The date and time is
Leaving = Good Bye!
'@
}

Import-LocalizedData MyStrings

Write-Host $MyStrings.Greeting
Write-Host ($MyStrings.str1 + " " + $MyStrings.str2)
Write-Host ($MyStrings.str3 + " " + (Get-Date))
Write-Host $MyStrings.Leaving
```

The only thing I added in the example is the call to `Import-LocalizedData` after the `DATA` section. You only have to give `Import-LocalizedData` the name of the `DATA` section that it's going to replace (if it finds that section, of course), and the Cmdlet automatically goes off and does its thing. Unless you happen to be using `es-ES` as your current UI culture, you're going to get a complaint that the Cmdlet can't find the `.psd1` file in the `en-US` folder, and the script will continue as normal.

You can test this script in two ways:

✔ Change your UI in whatever version of Windows you're running to `es-ES`, and run the script.

✔ Use the `-culture` parameter of `Import-LocalizedData` and specify `es-ES` as the culture. The Cmdlet finds and loads the `.psd1` file you created.

For testing, the latter method is a good way to see whether everything works as it should. Simply replace the existing Import-LocalizedData line with

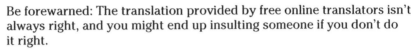
```
Import-LocalizedData MyStrings -culture "es-ES"
```

Now when you run the script, it executes happily, this time in Spanish. The best part is that if you want to support another language, all you need to do is follow these steps:

1. **Find someone who can translate your text into that language (or, if you're cheap, you can use many of the free online translators).**

   Be forewarned: The translation provided by free online translators isn't always right, and you might end up insulting someone if you don't do it right.

2. **Create a new** .psd1 **file with the translated text, and create a folder that matches the culture name for that language.**

   Save the new .psd1 file with the same name as the script, except with a .psd1 extension.

That's it! Now your script supports this new language, so if you run it from a computer that uses that UICulture, it'll pick up the new language automatically.

To find the culture names and identifiers for other languages, look up the CultureInfo class on MSDN (http://msdn.microsoft.com/en-us/library/system.globalization.cultureinfo.aspx).

Sharing Scripts with Others

One of the best aspects of scripting is that because all the code is wide open, it's open source by definition. Different companies have different policies about code sharing outside the organization, and of course, if you've written proprietary code that is critical to your business, you probably don't want to share it with the general public. If you think that you've developed a Windows PowerShell script that has universal appeal, however, it's probably good to share it with the rest of the Windows PowerShell community. In fact, the continued growth and acceptance of Windows PowerShell depend heavily on the contributions made to the community by people such as you.

Why am I mentioning all this? If you want to share your code with other people, you really should be cognizant of that fact that users in all parts of the world may want to use it and that their primary language may not be English. If you use DATA sections in your scripts for all your data output, other users can add more value to the scripts by contributing .psd1 files for their own cultures, thereby giving your scripts much better global appeal.

Chapter 17

Smashing Those Bugs

. . . .

In This Chapter

▶ Keeping bugs in check

▶ Examining bugs under a microscope

▶ Using the debugger for effective eradication

. . . .

*O*ne of the most frustrating things about writing any kind of code, such as a Windows PowerShell script, is that inevitably you'll run into a bug. A *bug* occurs when a piece of code does something that it's not supposed to do or acts a way that it wasn't designed to act. I'm not talking about bugs in Windows PowerShell itself, but bugs in Windows PowerShell scripts that you or someone else wrote. The nastiest kind of bug is one that's hard to reproduce. I like to call this type the *sneaky bug* (though you might refer to it as your in-laws). Whatever it is, when you do find a bug, you need to exterminate it quickly; otherwise, that bug will be staring right into your face someday at the most inopportune moment.

In this chapter, you make use of the new debugging features in Windows PowerShell 2 that'll make it much easier to track down errors in your code so you won't have to keep hitting your head on the wall in frustration the next time your script doesn't work as you expect.

Finding Out Where the Bugs Come From

Software bugs are never intentional. Instead, they usually occur when the script or program enters a state that it wasn't designed for. When you find a bug in a script, you'll usually find that it's caused by one of these situations:

- ✔ Unexpected input
- ✔ Incorrect logic
- ✔ System error

Guarding against unexpected input

Unexpected input occurs when some part of your code expects the data to be a certain type or format but instead gets something that it doesn't know how to deal with (or deals with incorrectly). A good example is when you're expecting a value that's supposed to represent a valid date but instead get some random text. Or, if you expect the data to be in MM/DD/YYYY format, you get YYYY-MM-DD instead. Bugs that come from unexpected input exist because the author of the script made assumptions that may not hold true.

The best way to protect yourself against unexpected errors is to be paranoid about any input that goes into your script that you don't have control of. Rather than assume that the input is in the correct format or data type, assume that it isn't going to be valid, and write code to handle each case where the input might be incorrect.

Watching out for incorrect logic

Incorrect logic can be caused by many things, but I've found that it's caused by predominantly incorrect assumptions, typos, or the programmer's simple failure to think through all the possible ways in which the script might run. Here's an example of incorrect logic in which I'm trying to find out whether $arr contains three or more items:

```
$arr = (1,2,3,4,5)
if ($arr.length -gt 3) {
    Write-Host "Array has 3 or more items!"
}
```

When I run this code, it displays "Array has 3 or more items!", as expected, because the array has five elements. But what if the code ended up looking like this instead?

```
$arr = (1,2,3)
if ($arr.length -gt 3) {
    Write-Host "Array has 3 or more items!"
}
```

Now the array has three elements, so you'd expect it to display the corresponding string . . . but it doesn't. The problem is that the logic is wrong. I'm supposed to use -ge (greater than or equal to), not -gt (just greater than). The correct code is

```
$arr = (1,2,3)
if ($arr.length -ge 3) {
    Write-Host "Array has 3 or more items!"
}
```

This example may seem to be very trivial and obvious, but that's easy to say when you have only four lines of code to look at. If this example were part of a script hundreds of lines long, tracking this problem would be hard, because it might never manifest itself except on those occasions when the array was exactly three elements long.

Expecting the unexpected: System errors

System errors are by far the most unpredictable of all the problems your script may encounter. System errors can introduce bugs that are nearly impossible to predict, account for, and (sometimes) troubleshoot. When I talk about *system errors,* I'm not referring just to hard drive crashes and the blue screen of death; I'm also referring to things like network drives not being available or running out of disk space. When writing your scripts, make sure that you pay close attention to pieces of your code that have a dependency and therefore might fail. If your scripts write lots of log files to disk, for example, you'll probably want to check periodically for disk free space to make sure that you don't fill the disk.

Understanding the Debugging Process

You have a few ways to debug your scripts. One way is to simply go over your script again and see whether you can spot the problem. When you get familiar with common mistakes, this method is usually good enough to catch bugs resulting from incorrect logic within your scripts. The invalid-input kind of bug is a bit harder to find, especially if it's hard to reproduce. Without any kind of debugging tools at your disposal, you're pretty much stuck with the old method of sticking a few `Write-Host` statements throughout your script and then watching the script run to see where the problem is coming from. Have a look at the code snippet in Listing 17-1.

Listing 17-1:   A Script with a Bug

```
$msg = "CODE 404"
if ($msg.substring(0,4) -eq "CODE") {
    $code = $msg.substring(4,3)
    switch($code)
    {
        200 { $outputMsg = "OK" }
        202 { $outputMsg = "Accepted" }
        401 { $outputMsg = "Unauthorized" }
        403 { $outputMsg = "Forbidden" }
        404 { $outputMsg = "Not Found" }
        500 { $outputMsg = "Internal Server Error" }
```

(continued)

Listing 17-1 *(continued)*

```
        503 { $outputMsg = "Service Unavailable" }


        default { $outputMsg = "Unknown Code" }
    }
    Write-Host $outputMsg
} else {
    Write-Host "No Code Received"
}
```

The script is fairly straightforward. Some string is stored in the $msg variable. The script looks at the first four characters and checks to see whether it equals the string "CODE". If so, it grabs the three-digit number that represents the code. Then, using a switch statement to decode what the message means, the script outputs the decoded message to the screen. So far, so good!

If you run this code, however, even though it's supposed to output "Not Found", it displays "Unknown Code" instead. Something is clearly wrong. The code listed in $msg clearly says 404, so it should map over to "Not Found". If you think about the situation for a second, you realize that "Unknown Code" would be displayed only if the value of $code didn't match any of the values defined in the switch statement.

Now look at how the script derives the value for $code. This value is taken as a substring of $msg starting with position four and continuing for three characters. To debug this code, you want to output the value of $code onscreen so that you know what the switch statement is comparing it with. You output the value of $code by adding a Write-Host statement immediately after you get assign its value so that the code looks like this:

```
$msg = "CODE 404"
if ($msg.substring(0,4) -eq "CODE") {
    $code = $msg.substring(4,3)

    #Added for debugging purposes
    Write-Host $code

    switch($code)
    {
        200 { $outputMsg = "OK" }
        202 { $outputMsg = "Accepted" }
        401 { $outputMsg = "Unauthorized" }
        403 { $outputMsg = "Forbidden" }
        404 { $outputMsg = "Not Found" }
        500 { $outputMsg = "Internal Server Error" }
        503 { $outputMsg = "Service Unavailable" }
        default { $outputMsg = "Unknown Code" }
    }
```

```
    Write-Host $outputMsg
} else {
    Write-Host "No Code Received"
}
```

Running the script this time results in this output:

```
40
Unknown Code
```

Instead of getting 404, as you want, the value of $code is 40. Looking back at the substring code, you can easily see why: The starting offset should be 5, not 4. You can fix this problem by replacing that code with this corrected version:

```
$code = $msg.substring(5,3)
```

This time when you run the script, the output is

```
404
Not Found
```

You have verified that $code contains the correct substring of $msg and that the message you want to show is displayed. Now that you're done debugging, you can delete the Write-Host $code line or simply comment it out in case you need to debug this code again in the future.

Working On Your Defense

There's a common saying that a good offense starts with a good defense. In any kind of programming, defense is very important. If you look back at the code in Listing 17-1 (see the preceding section) for manual debugging, you'll find many flaws in this script that could lead to bugs in the future. I chose to write the value of $msg explicitly in the example, but what if $msg contains some string that's returned dynamically whenever the script is run, such as by reading a line in a file?

The first problem is that $msg may not start with the word "CODE". Okay, this situation isn't a problem, because the script checks for it, and when msg doesn't start with "CODE", the script simply displays "No Code Received". The second problem is that the script assumes that $msg will contain at least four characters, because it uses the substring method to grab the first four characters of the string. What if, for some reason, $msg contains a string that has fewer than four characters? The script would throw an exception immediately and then quit.

To guard against this problem, you need to perform a sanity check on the string before trying to take a substring. Rather than taking the substring right away, you have to check that the length of the string is greater than or equal to four by using something like this example:

```
if (($msg.length -ge 4) -and ($msg.substring(0,4) -eq "CODE")) {
   ... code here..
}
```

Now if $msg contains fewer than four characters, the first part of the -and statement evaluates to false, which makes the whole line false, and the code inside this if statement is skipped.

This solution leaves yet another assumption, however. Immediately after the script determines that the string does begin with "CODE", it uses the sub-string method again to pull out the three characters, starting with offset 5. This piece of code assumes that if the string starts with "CODE", it must be at least eight characters long.

You know what to do. You simply modify that section of code so that it looks something like this:

```
if ($msg.length -ge 8) {
   $code = $msg.substring(4,3)
   ...and so on...
} else {
   Write-Host "Sorry, not enough characters!"
}
```

Now the code is a bit more robust, because it does away with assumptions; instead, it contains simple yet effective checks to validate the input before taking actions that could cause the script to quit unexpectedly.

I'm not happy with the code just yet, though. It seems a bit inefficient, don't you think? First, the script checks to see whether $msg has at least four characters; then it compares the first four characters with the word "CODE". If the result is true, the script immediately does another length check to see whether $msg is at least eight characters long. In reality, even if the first four characters match "CODE", whatever comes after it still depends on $msg to be at least eight characters long.

To make the code simpler, all you need to do is check that $msg is eight characters long before checking whether it matches "CODE". Then you can get rid of the extra $msg length check within the code block. The final, fixed script looks like this:

```
$msg = "CODE 404"
if (($msg.length -ge 8) -and ($msg.substring(0,4) -eq "CODE")) {
   $code = $msg.substring(5,3)
```

```
   switch($code)
   {
     200 { $outputMsg = "OK" }
     202 { $outputMsg = "Accepted" }
     401 { $outputMsg = "Unauthorized" }
     403 { $outputMsg = "Forbidden" }
     404 { $outputMsg = "Not Found" }
     500 { $outputMsg = "Internal Server Error" }
     503 { $outputMsg = "Service Unavailable" }
     default { $outputMsg = "Unknown Code" }
   }
   Write-Host $outputMsg
} else {
   Write-Host "No Code Received"
}
```

Unfortunately, error checking is one thing that most people forget to do, and it's easy to overlook, especially when you're so focused on getting the code to work first. Even I'm guilty of this lapse occasionally. The bottom line is that if you're writing a script that you expect to run many more times, you want to put in as much defensive code as possible to eliminate as many sources of potential bugs as you can.

Working with Debugging Tools

In "Understanding the Debugging Process," earlier in this chapter, I use the method of inserting `Write-Host` statements within the script. This method is really a hack, because many scripting languages lack any native debugging tools that allow you to peek at what they're doing.

What do debugging tools give you? Debuggers hook into the execution of your program so that you can see what's happening on the inside as the program is running. They also allow you to set *breakpoints,* which tell Windows PowerShell to pause execution when it gets to these points. When the code reaches a breakpoint, you can check the values of the variables and step through your code one line at a time to see how it's running.

The best feature of debuggers is that they don't require you to make any changes in your code. You don't have to worry about going back and removing a bunch of `Write-Host` statements that you've sprinkled all over the place just to find the problem.

Working with breakpoints

When you run a script through a debugger, the script runs pretty much the same way that it did before, except maybe a tad slower because now the debugger is in there snooping around. That's not going to help you figure out what's wrong, however. The only way to get any value from a debugger is to set breakpoints. If you don't know where the problem is, you may want to set multiple breakpoints until you find the cause of the problem. Listing 17-2 provides a script that you can use to test some debugging techniques.

Listing 17-2:   A Script with a Misspelled Variable

```
$number1 = 1
$number2 = 2
$sum = $number1 + $numer2
if ($sum -gt 2) {
    Write-Host "Sum is greater than 2!"
} else {
    Write-Host "Sum is less than 2!"
}
```

When you run the script, the output is "Sum is less than 2!", which isn't what you'd expect, because 1 + 2 = 3, and 3 is certainly greater than 2. This script is so short that you can easily see what the problem is. I assigned the value 2 to the variable $number2, but when I used it to calculate the sum, I misspelled the variable name and instead added $number1 to a new variable called $numer2 that has no value.

To debug something like this code by using a debugger, first you must create a breakpoint. Because the output of the script depends on the value of $sum, you need to find out what that value is just before the script gets to the if statement.

You set breakpoints by using the Set-PSBreakpoint Cmdlet. To set a breakpoint within a script, you need to give Set-PSBreakpoint the name of the script and the line at which you want it to pause execution. Assuming that you saved this script as C:\scripts\debugtest.ps1, you can use this command sequence:

```
Set-PSBreakpoint -script c:\scripts\debugtest.ps1 -line 4
```

Breakpoints are set and remembered only on a per-session basis. Any breakpoints you set during a session disappear when you close the Windows PowerShell window.

Now when you run the script, it stops execution just before line 4 of the script and enters debug mode. Notice that the Windows PowerShell prompt is now prefixed with [DBG]:, which indicates that you're in debug mode. This is what you'll see on the screen when you hit the breakpoint:

```
Entering debug mode. Use h or ? for help.

Hit Line breakpoint on 'C:\scripts\debugtest.ps1:4'

debugtest.ps1:4   if ($sub -gt 2) {
[DBG]: PS C:\scripts>
```

Now that you're in debug mode, you're effectively at the point where the breakpoint is set within the script, and you can obtain values of the variables used within it. To debug the script, you can start writing the values of variables to the screen this way:

```
[DBG]: PS C:\scripts> Write-Host $sum
1
[DBG]: PS C:\scripts> Write-Host $number1
1
[DBG]: PS C:\scripts> Write-Host $number2
2
```

The variable $sum has a value of 1 even though $number1 has the correct value of 1 and $number2 has the correct value of 2. This result points to a problem with the line that's performing the addition, so you copy and paste this line of code from Listing 17-2 into the debug prompt and display the value of $sum again:

```
[DBG]: PS C:\scripts> $sum = $number1 + $numer2
[DBG]: PS C:\scripts> Write-Host $sum
1
```

Same problem. This time, you manually enter the command that you want to run:

```
[DBG]: PS C:\scripts> $sum = $number1 + $number2
[DBG]: PS C:\scripts> Write-Host $sum
3
```

Finally, the correct answer! You look back at the code and realize that your $number2 is misspelled. You fix the problem, and now the script works perfectly. But wait — you're still at the debug prompt.

To exit the debugger, press c; then press Enter. This action quits the debugger and runs the rest of the script as normal.

Setting fancier breakpoints

You're not limited to setting a breakpoint based on a given line in your script. You can also set a breakpoint whenever a certain command is reached or even when a certain variable is encountered. Here's how you can set a break point whenever the Get-WmiObject Cmdlet is encountered:

```
Set-PSBreakpoint -script myscript.ps1 -command "Get-WMIObject"
```

You can even specify multiple commands in which the breakpoints should be set. Just specify each command, separating the commands with commas, like this:

```
Set-PSBreakpoint -script myscript.ps1 -command "Get-WMIObject,Write-Host,Get-
          Service"
```

If you're interested in a particular variable, you can also use Set-PSBreakPoint to set a breakpoint every time that variable is found. Here's how you can set a breakpoint whenever the variable outstring is encountered in myscript.ps1:

```
Set-PSBreakpoint -script myscript.ps1 -variable "outstring"
```

Just as you do with commands, you can set breakpoints at multiple variables by separating variable names with commas.

Issuing debugger commands

Breakpoints only serve as control points to stop the execution of code so that you can see what it's doing. Other than simply querying for variable values while in debug mode, you also have a set of debugger commands you can use to control how you proceed from a breakpoint. These commands are listed in Table 17-1. To run a command, you can either type the command alias or the full name of the command and then press Enter.

Table 17-1		Debugger Commands
Command Alias	**Command Name**	**Description**
s	Step	Runs the next statement and stops. It runs the next statement, not the next lines, because the next statement may be several lines away if the current statement is a logic statement. If the next line is a function, the debugger goes into the function and runs the next statement in that function.
v	Step-Over	Runs the next statement and stops. If the command is a function, however, unlike the regular Step command, it runs the function and then stops. In other words, it treats the entire function as one statement.
o	Step-Out	Goes to the next statement after the function is done (if you're currently in a function). If you run this command in the main portion of the script, it goes to the end unless it's stopped by another breakpoint.
c	Continue	Continues with the script until it reaches the end or until another breakpoint is reached.
<Enter>	<Enter>	Repeats the preceding command, if it was a Step or Step-Over command.
?,h	?,h	Displays the debugger's help text.

Listing all breakpoints

Because breakpoints are defined and stored for only as long as the current Windows PowerShell window is active, any breakpoint that you set doesn't actually make any changes in the underlying code that you're trying to debug; it doesn't try to sneak in some hidden characters or modify your scripts in any way. Windows PowerShell stores breakpoints in memory, and any time you run a command or script that matches one of these breakpoints, Windows PowerShell calls on the debugger.

Because you can set as few or as many breakpoints as you want, you probably want to find out what breakpoints are defined in your current session.
You do this by using the Get-PSBreakpoint Cmdlet. This Cmdlet returns
each breakpoint that you've defined along with its various properties, such
as whether it's enabled (covered in the next section), its unique identifier
within the session, and the script to which it applies.

Disabling and enabling breakpoints

Breakpoints are great; they're like roadblocks to keep your code from getting
too far without being inspected. Often, you'll set up a bunch of breakpoints
for testing and make changes in the script as you find problems. When you
think that you've fixed all the bugs, you'll want to run the script without the
breakpoints getting in the way. One solution is to delete all the breakpoints,
but that may not be a good idea. You could find another problem and need to
use those same breakpoints, and if you've deleted them, you'll have to spend
time re-creating them.

Instead, you can simply disable some or even all of the breakpoints in your
script. Disabling leaves a breakpoint's definition intact but deactivates it
from use. The easiest way to disable a breakpoint starts with knowing what
its breakpoint ID is. You can get the ID of a breakpoint by running Get-
PSBreakpoint. When that you have the ID, you can disable it by running the
following command (assuming that the ID is 7):

```
Disable-PSBreakpoint -id 7
```

If you simply want to disable all breakpoints in your session, you can pipe
the output of Get-PSBreakpoint to Disable-PSBreakpoint directly, like
this:

```
Get-PSBreakpoint | Disable-PSBreakpoint
```

The reverse process, of course, is enabling disabled breakpoints. It doesn't
take too much creativity to guess what this command looks like. If you
guess that it's Enable-PSBreakpoint, you're already thinking like a true
Windows PowerShell user. Here's how you enable a disabled breakpoint
(again assuming that the breakpoint ID is 7):

```
Enable-PSBreakpoint -id 7
```

You use the same technique to enable all breakpoints that you use to disable all breakpoints: piping the output of Get-PSBreakpoint into the Enable-PSBreakpoint Cmdlet.

Removing breakpoints

All breakpoints in a session are cleared as soon as you close the Windows PowerShell window, so you don't need to remove them explicitly. At times, however, you want to remove breakpoints without closing the window, such as when you create a breakpoint with the wrong parameters (such as the wrong line in a script). Sure, you can disable the breakpoint if it's not needed, but it's probably best to remove it to prevent any confusion for yourself later.

Fortunately, removing breakpoints is just as easy as using the Remove-PSBreakpoint Cmdlet. Just like Enable-PSBreakpoint and Disable-PSBreakpoint, Remove-PSBreakpoint needs either a breakpoint ID or a breakpoint object; then it happily removes the breakpoint for you, as in this example:

```
Remove-PSBreakpoint -id 7
Get-PSBreakpoint | Remove-PSBreakpoint
```

You can't undo the deletion of a breakpoint. If you accidentally delete the wrong breakpoint, you have no magical Restore-PSBreakpoint command to rescue you. Instead, you have to re-create the breakpoint yourself.

Part V

Real-World Windows Administration Using PowerShell

The 5th Wave   By Rich Tennant

WANDA HAD THE DISTINCT FEELING HER HUSBAND'S NEW SOFTWARE PROGRAM WAS ABOUT TO BECOME INTERACTIVE.

In this part . . .

You've now seen all the bits and pieces that make up
Windows PowerShell, so it's time to apply these concepts to real-world scenarios. This part is a collection of
chapters that include scripts addressing the various
needs you're bound to face on a regular basis at work.
Chapter 18 shows you how to monitor Windows event
logs, drive space and services. Interacting with the
Windows registry is covered in Chapter 19. You discover
how to query and interact with Active Directory in
Chapter 20. Chapter 21 deals with system status and managing security, and Chapter 22 provides tips on converting your old Windows Shell or Windows Scripting Host to
Windows PowerShell.

Chapter 18

Mission Control: All Systems Go

. . . .

In This Chapter

▶ Making sure you have enough drive space

▶ Translating System.IO.DriveInfo to Windows Management Infrastructure

▶ Keeping track of Windows services

▶ Scanning your event logs for problems

▶ Using Windows Management Infrastructure to query event logs

. . . .

*A*lthough it's fun to gain knowledge of how to display stuff onscreen and do tricks like counting to 100 by using a `for` loop, in reality, you're probably reading this book for one of two reasons. The first one is that you're truly interested in discovering what Windows PowerShell is all about and know that the *For Dummies* series helps you get there faster. The other highly likely possibility is that your boss told you two days ago that he needs you to automate some task by using Windows PowerShell, and you're using this book as a crash course.

From this chapter forward, I focus on bringing together everything that I've talked about so far and applying it to real-world scenarios. (Hey, you never know; I might already have the script you're looking for.) In this chapter, I cover some scripts that you can use to make sure your systems are ready to go.

Monitoring Drive Space

Even with cheap storage readily available everywhere, your computer or your servers always run out of disk space at the worst time possible. What you need is a script that can query the amount of drive (disk) space you have and let you know when that amount passes a certain threshold. Your script can display a pop-up window or send you an e-mail when any of the drives on your system has less than 5 percent free space, for example. Listing 18-1 provides a script that performs just that task.

Listing 18-1: Monitor Free Disk Space

```
function WarningPopup([string]$message)
{
   $oShell = New-Object -comobject WScript.Shell
   $ret = $oShell.popup($message,0,"Warning",0 + 48)
}


$freespace_threshold = 5

Write-Host "Performing disk space check..."
Write-Host "Looking for disks with less than $freespace_threshold free space"

$drives = [System.IO.DriveInfo]::GetDrives()
foreach($drive in $drives)
{
   if (($drive.DriveType -eq "Fixed") -and ($drive.IsReady -eq $true))
   {
      $freespace = [Math]::Round(($drive.TotalFreeSpace / $drive.TotalSize) *
            100,2)

      if ($freespace -lt $freespace_threshold)
      {
         WarningPopup "$drive.Name - $freespace % free space"
      }
   }
}
```

This script first defines a function called WarningPopup that takes a string and then displays that string onscreen as a pop-up window. Because Windows PowerShell doesn't have a built-in method for displaying a pop-up window, you use the New-Object Cmdlet to create an instance of WScript.Shell (in other words, Windows Scripting Host). Then you can use the shell's popup method to display the message onscreen. The popup method takes four parameters:

- The string to display
- The number of seconds to display the message
- The title of the dialog box
- A final value that defines the dialog-box type

The first parameter is the only one that's required; the rest are optional.

The dialog-box type specifies what kind of buttons and icons should be used in the dialog box. The buttons that can be used are defined as numeric values, as are the icon types. To select what you want, just add the button-type value of your choice to the icon type that you want to display. Listing 18-1 uses the value 0 + 48 to say that you want to display an OK button and a warning icon (a yellow triangle with an exclamation mark). Table 18-1 lists the possible values.

TIP

The WScript.Shell popup method returns a value that tells you which button was clicked. In this script, you simply store the value in a variable but don't use it. If you don't assign this value to a variable, the script displays the value on the console instead, which isn't what you want. Table 18-2 lists the possible return values of the popup method.

Table 18-1	Dialog-Box-Type Values for popup Method
Value	*Description*
0	OK button
1	OK and Cancel buttons
2	Abort, Retry, and Ignore buttons
3	Yes, No, and, Cancel buttons
4	Yes and No buttons
5	Retry and Cancel buttons
16	Error icon (stop sign)
32	Question-mark icon
48	Warning icon (exclamation point)
64	Information icon

Table 18-2	Return Values for popup Method
Value	*Description*
-1	A timeout value was specified and reached before a button was clicked.
0	The dialog box was closed without a button click.
1	OK button
2	Cancel button
3	Abort button
4	Retry button
5	Ignore button
6	Yes button
7	No button

Next, the script defines a variable called $freespace_threshold that sets the percentage of free space on each drive before generating a warning. Most of the time, you'll want to set this variable between 5 percent and 10 percent, which should give you ample time to react and clean up space if you can or increase the amount of storage.

Then the script contains this peculiar-looking line:

```
$drives = [System.IO.DriveInfo]::GetDrives()
```

Remember that because Windows PowerShell is built on top of the Microsoft .NET Framework, you can use any of the .NET classes within your code. This example script uses the System.IO.DriveInfo class because it conveniently has a GetDrives method that returns a collection of objects representing the drives on your system.

The next section of code takes advantage of the foreach loop construct to go through each drive in the system and check the space. An if statement checks the type of each drive and whether it's ready before making any calculations, as follows:

```
if (($drive.DriveType -eq "Fixed") -and ($drive.IsReady -eq $true))
```

This line of code is important for a few reasons. First, GetDrives returns all your drives, including removable drives such as CD-ROMs and USB memory sticks, as well as mapped network drives. In general, you're going to be interested only in the *fixed drives* (hard drives) on your system, and as a sanity check, you'll want to make sure that those drives are ready and accessible.

Now, to figure out the percentage of free space, you simply divide the total amount of free space by the total amount of disk space. This value may end up looking something like this: 0.3542413. To make things a bit easier to work with, multiply this value by 100 to get the percentage. This value is still more precise than you may care for, so use the [Math]::Round method to round off the value. The second parameter of the Round method indicates the number of decimal places to which you want to round the value. This example uses 2 as a value, because this value is about as precise as you may want to be:

```
$freespace = [Math]::Round(($drive.TotalFreeSpace / $drive.TotalSize) * 100,2)
```

Now that you have this value, which looks like 35.42, you can perform a straightforward "less than" comparison between this value and the $freespace_threshold value to see whether this particular drive's free space is below the given threshold. If it is, PowerShell displays the warning pop-up message onscreen.

Converting to Windows Management Infrastructure from System.IO.DriveInfo

I use the `System.IO.DriveInfo` class in the previous section to get all the drive information because it's very straightforward to use. What it lacks is the ability to query the drive information of remote computers, and this lack is one advantage of using Windows Management Infrastructure (WMI) over some of the built-in `System` classes. The code remains logically the same except that you have to replace the method for getting the drive information, and the drive property names change as well. Listing 18-2 shows a script that uses that WMI to monitor free disk space.

Listing 18-2: Monitor Free Disk Space Using WMI

```
function WarningPopup([string]$message)
{
    $oShell = New-Object -comobject WScript.Shell
    $ret = $oShell.popup($message,0,"Warning",0 + 48)
}

$freespace_threshold = 100
$compname = "."

Write-Host "Performing disk space check..."
Write-Host "Looking for disks with less than $freespace_threshold free space"

$drives = Get-WMIObject Win32_Volume -ComputerName $compname | Select-Object Dri
            veLetter,Capacity,FreeSpace,DriveType
foreach($drive in $drives)
{
    if ($drive.DriveType -eq 3)
    {
        $freespace = [Math]::Round((([Int64]$drive.FreeSpace / [Int64]$drive.
            Capacity) * 100,2)

        if ($freespace -lt $freespace_threshold)
        {
            WarningPopup (($drive.DriveLetter) + " - $freespace % free space")
        }
    }
}
Write-Host "Script Complete!"
```

In this section, I focus on the few things that change between Listing 18-1 and Listing 18-2.

First, Listing 18-2 adds a variable called $compname. You can use WMI to change $compname to whatever computer you want to query. (***Note:*** A period by itself means the local machine.) Next is the most important change, which is using Get-WMIObject rather than System.IO.DriveInfo, as shown here:

```
$drives = Get-WMIObject Win32_Volume -ComputerName $compname | Select-Object Dri
          veLetter,Capacity,FreeSpace,DriveType
```

You use Get-WMIObject to query the Win32_Volume WMI class, which is a WMI class that represents storage on a computer. This example uses the -Computername parameter to specify the computer that the script will query for the information. Get-WMIObject returns all the data associated with a given WMI class. You can reduce the results of Get-WMIObject to only the parameters you want by passing the Cmdlet through Select-Object and then using it to pull just the DriveLetter, Capacity (total disk space), FreeSpace, and DriveType properties. The resulting property values all maps out directly with the properties returned by System.IO.DriveInfo, so you simply replace the references to each property name in the script with these new property names.

You may have noticed a few gotchas. For starters, Win32_Volume doesn't have an IsReady flag (which is an indicator to show that the volume is ready for access), so you'll have to do without it for now. Also, the code gives the DriveType as an integer value, not as plain text that's easy to understand. The Local Disk (otherwise known as Fixed) drive type is the same as the value of 3, so the code compares the drive type with this value instead. Table 18-3 lists all the drive-type values.

Table 18-3   Win32_Volume WMI Class DriveType Property

Value	Definition
0	Unknown
1	No root directory
2	Removable disk
3	Local disk
4	Network drive
5	Compact disk
6	RAM disk

Something else peculiar about this version of the script is that it explicitly casts (see Chapter 5 for more on casting) the Capacity and FreeSpace values into Int64 (64-bit integer) before dividing them. The data type returned by WMI for FreeSpace and Capacity is UInt64 (unsigned 64-bit integer).

The problem is that Windows PowerShell currently doesn't support division of UInt64 values, so you have to convert these values to a data type that PowerShell does support. This example uses Int64 because it's the next-best thing.

Converting from UInt64 to Int64 can cause problems if the drive capacity (in bytes) is greater than the maximum value of an Int64. The good thing is that Int64 can store a value up to 9,223,372,036,854,775,807, which is roughly equivalent to 8.4 million terabytes.

Managing Windows Services

When it comes to checking for system status, finding out whether key Windows services are running comprises most of what you need to keep track of. If the server is simply acting as a print server, this task can be as simple as making sure that the spooler service is up and running. If the server hosts much more complex services, such as Microsoft Exchange or SQL Server, you may need to keep track of a long list of services and dependent processes.

Managing Windows services effectively involves monitoring for service state and taking some action based on that state. In this section, I focus on checking for service state. This script is designed to check a set of services you're interested in and then display the names and states of the services that aren't running:

```
$arrServices = ("spooler","winmgmt")
$strCompname = "."

$colServices = Get-Service $arrServices -Computername $strCompname
foreach($objService in $colServices)
{
   if ($objService.Status -ne "Running")
   {
      Write-Host ($objService.Displayname + " is " + $objService.Status)
   }
}
```

You have to define the list of services you want to monitor in the $arrServices variable, and you have to define this list of services as an array. To do that, just comma-separate the service names and enclose the whole thing in parentheses. In this example, you're interested in only the Print Spooler and Windows Management Instrumentation services for now. This code also adds the ever-powerful capability for querying services on a remote machine by defining a $strCompname variable. Just like in Get-WMIObject, a single period means "this machine."

This information is passed to `Get-Service`, which happily goes out and fetches the information about the services you specified. The resulting collection is stored in `$colServices`. Then you use a `foreach` loop to go through the services and find out whether a service is running by querying its `Status` property. If a service isn't running, the script displays the service's name and its status.

A big difference exists between service names and service display name. A *service display name* is the name you see when you go into the Services management console in Windows; it's usually very descriptive and often contains spaces. The *service name* is much shorter (typically, a single word with no spaces); Windows uses this name internally to name the service. By default, you have to use this internal short name when you use `Get-Service` to refer to services. You can use the display name if you want, but you need to specify the name by using the `-DisplayName` parameter of `Get-Service`.

If your task is to monitor your services, this script usually is enough. The only enhancement that you might want to make is to send an e-mail or something letting you know that the service on a particular computer is not running rather than just simply displaying it on the screen.

Sometimes, you might have a service that you know fails periodically. This situation is more common among poorly written services provided by third-party applications (otherwise known as *crapware*). The usual fix is restarting the service if it goes into a stopped state. Although you can configure this behavior directly by modifying the service properties so that it starts up automatically whenever the service stops, you may prefer to do this job yourself — especially if you need to do other things before restarting, such as deleting some temporary files that could prevent the service from starting up successfully.

Controlling services

Now that you can check for service status, it's time to change the script a bit so that it automatically starts the service when it detects that the service isn't running. You may think that because you have `Get-Service`, this task is as simple as running `Start-Service`. Well, that assumption is both right and wrong. Yes, you can use `Start-Service` to accomplish the task, but the caveat is that `Start-Service` doesn't have a `-ComputerName` parameter to run against a remote computer.

One solution is to use WinRM (Windows Remote Management, which I discuss in Chapter 15) and run `Start-Service` as a remote command. The other, more generic solution is to use WMI to start the service.

Although WMI is generally used for querying information, you can also use it to enact certain actions. With this knowledge in hand, you can rewrite the script so that it attempts to bring the service up when it detects that the service isn't running. Listing 18-3 shows how you can use WMI to query the state of a service and start it if it isn't running.

Listing 18-3: Using WMI to Make Sure a Service Is Always Running

```
$arrServices = ("spooler","winmgmt")
$strCompname = "."

$colServices = Get-Service $arrServices -Computername $strCompname
foreach($objService in $colServices)
{
   if ($objService.Status -ne "Running")
   {
      Write-Host ($objService.Displayname + " is " + $objService.Status)
      Write-Host ("Starting " + $objService.Displayname)
      $result = (Get-WMIObject -computer $strCompname Win32_Service -Filter
            ("Name='" + $objService.Name + "'")).StartService()
      do
      {
         Start-Sleep -s 1
         $currentState = (Get-WMIObject -computer $strCompname Win32_Service
               -Filter ("Name='" + $objService.Name + "'")).State
      } while ($currentState -eq "Start Pending")

      if ($currentState -eq "Running")
      {
         Write-Host -foregroundcolor Green ("Successfully started " +
               $objService.DisplayName)
      }
      else
      {
         Write-Host -foregroundcolor Red ("Failed to start " + $objService.
               DisplayName)
      }
   }
}
```

To access Windows services with WMI, you use the Win32_Service WMI class. Objects of the Win32_Service class contain a method called StartService that can be called to start a service. To do this, first you must get an object representing that service. Because you already have the service name and computer name, you simply need to pass this information to the Get-WMI Object Cmdlet. The important part is the use of the -Filter parameter to specify the exact name of the service you're interested in. When you have the object, you call the StartService method to start the service. You store the return value of this call in a variable only to suppress the default behavior of displaying the result in the console, like this:

```
$result = (Get-WMIObject -computer $strCompname Win32_Service -Filter ("Name='"
            + $objService.Name + "'")).StartService()
```

Just because you start a service doesn't mean that it's actually started. Depending on the service you're trying to start, actual start-up can be as quick as a second or two or as long as a few minutes if the service is very complicated (the Microsoft Exchange Information Store starting up with many large data stores to bring online, for example). From the time you start the service until the service enters `Started` state (or even `Stopped` state, if it can't start for some reason), it goes into a `Start Pending` state.

To enable the script to handle this scenario, you use a `do/while` loop to query for the state of the service. The loop continues to query until the state is no longer `Start Pending`, after which it checks to see whether the service is running. If it's running, the service has successfully started; otherwise, start-up has failed, and you probably have to look into the service yourself. (Perhaps a service logon failure occurred due to a password change, for example.)

Notice that Listing 18-3 uses the `Start-Sleep` Cmdlet. This Cmdlet pauses the script for a certain amount of time before continuing. It's perfect for something like polling a service, because you don't want to keep doing this over and over; instead, you want to pause the script for a while and then check again. `Start-Sleep` allows you to give the pause time in seconds (the default interval, also used with the –s parameter) or milliseconds (with the –m parameter).

Use the `Start-Sleep` Cmdlet whenever you want your script to pause for a specific amount of time.

Configuring services

If you use a script to automate service recovery, one thing you might encounter is a service that is having problems starting up. In some cases, you might want to automatically change the startup type of the service so that is doesn't run at startup. You do this by setting the start-up type of the service to `Manual` or `Disabled`. For the purpose of this example, assume that all the services you're monitoring in Listing 18-3 are set to start automatically whenever the system starts. Suppose that you change the script one last time. This time, instead of having the script display a message that the service failed to start, it sets the service to the `Manual` start-up type as soon as it encounters the error. Here's the section of code that changes:

```
if ($currentState -eq "Running")
{
   Write-Host -foregroundcolor Green ("Successfully started " + $objService.
           DisplayName)
}
else
{
   Write-Host -foregroundcolor Red ("Failed to start " + $objService.DisplayName)
   Set-Service $objService.Name -startupType Manual
   Write-Host ("Set the startup type of " + $objService.DisplayName + " to
           manual")
}
```

You can use the `Set-Service` Cmdlet to change the display name, description, and start-up type for a given service.

Checking Your Event Logs

Combing your event logs can be highly useful, but it can also result in information overload. Depending on how intense your logging is, you could have anywhere from a few to several hundred log entries being written in any given hour. Checking your event logs for errors is a good way of making sure that your system is running as it should, however. In particular, you should pay attention to any errors being generated in the System Log, as they could indicate a current problem or warn that something smelly is about to hit the fan.

The most straightforward way to comb event logs is to use the `Get-Event Log` Cmdlet. Just specify the name of the log file and what you're interested in getting, and you're all done. Listing 18-4 shows a simple script that gets any `Error` event-log entries that have been generated in the System Log in the past hour.

Listing 18-4: **Using Get-EventLog to Check the Event Log**

```
$objEvents = Get-EventLog -logname System -EntryType Error | Where-Object
             {[DateTime]::Now.AddHours(-1) -le $_.TimeGenerated}
if ($objEvents.Count -gt 0)
{
   foreach($event in $objEvents)
   {
     Write-Host ("Time    : " + $event.TimeGenerated)
     Write-Host ("Event ID: " + $event.EventID)
     Write-Host ("Computer: " + $event.MachineName)
     Write-Host ("Source  : " + $event.Source)
     Write-Host ("Message : " + $event.Message + "`n")
   }
```

(continued)

Listing 18-4 *(continued)*

```
}
else
{
    Write-Host "No entries to report!"
}
```

The heart of this code is the `Get-EventLog` Cmdlet. You specify the log name and the entry type by using these respective parameters, but this code returns all the log entries matching this criteria. To filter the result to just those events that were generated in the past hour, you have to compare the `TimeGenerated` property of the event-log entry with the time one hour ago and use `Where-Object` to refine the results.

The best way to calculate a time period before and after the current time is to use the `[DateTime]::Now` method and then use one of its `Add` methods to add or subtract (by providing a negative value) the appropriate amount of time from now. Not only is this technique convenient, but also, the resulting value is already a `DateTime` data type, so you can use it directly to compare other `DateTime` objects, such as the event log's `TimeGenerated` property.

The rest of the code shows how you can extract the relevant bits of information about the problem that you may need. Listing 18-4 uses a simple `Write-Host` statement, but it could just as easily be a function that generates a Web-based report or an e-mail message. Most organizations I've worked with use just this kind of script to keep an eye on potential problems.

This script checks for events within the past hour, but if you want more immediate notification, you can set it to look for events in the past 15 minutes and use `Task Scheduler` to run the script every 15 minutes.

The main downside to `Get-Event` is that it doesn't have built-in capability to run against a remote host. Also, it works only in Windows Vista and Windows Server 2008 and later running Windows .NET Framework 3.5 or later. The reality is that plenty of Windows XP and Windows Server 2003 servers will be out there for some time, so you need a solution that scales to those machines.

Querying EventLogs Using WMI

The solution for querying event logs remotely probably won't be all that surprising to you: Just use WMI. WMI truly is the key to accessing most information about Windows in a very standardized and straightforward manner. All the Windows event logs are accessed through the `Win32_NTLogEvent` WMI class. This class is one of the oldest WMI classes, which you can tell simply by its NT reference (meaning Windows NT). Listing 18-5 shows how you can use WMI instead of Get-EventLog to query for Event Log entries.

Listing 18-5:   Using WMI to Query the Event Log

```
$compname = "."
$objEvents = get-wmiobject -ComputerName $compname -query "select * from Win32_
             NTLogEvent where LogFile='System' AND Type='Error'" | Where-Object
             {[DateTime]::Now.AddHours(-1) -le [System.Management.ManagementDate
             Timeconverter]::ToDateTime($_.TimeGenerated)}
if ($objEvents.Count -gt 0)
{
    foreach($event in $objEvents)
    {
      Write-Host ("Time    : " + [System.Management.ManagementDateTimeconverter]
             ::ToDateTime($event.TimeGenerated))
      Write-Host ("Event ID: " + $event.EventIdentifier)
      Write-Host ("Computer: " + $event.ComputerName)
      Write-Host ("Source  : " + $event.SourceName)
      Write-Host ("Message : " + $event.Message + "`n")
    }
}
else
{
    Write-Host "No entries to report!"
}
```

This code runs substantially more slowly than the version using Get-EventLog in Listing 18-4 (refer to "Checking Your Event Logs," earlier in this chapter), but it has the benefit of being able to query event logs remotely. Rather than specifying a bunch of discrete properties, you can opt to specify a query to Get-WMIObject to select exactly the information you're interested in. The other difference is that the TimeGenerated property returned by WMI isn't in a nice DateTime format. Instead, the date and time look something like 20080616054859.000000-000, which is a standard date-and-time format defined by the Distributed Management Task Force (DMTF) Common Information Model (CIM) specification. (Phew, that was a mouthful!) To convert the date and time value returned through WMI to a regular DateTime object, you use the [System.Management.ManagementDateTimeconver ter]::ToDateTime method. When you convert the TimeGenerated property to a standard DateTime object, you can work with it just as you do in the preceding script.

Chapter 19

Taming the Windows Registry

. . . .

In This Chapter

▶ Glancing over the registry structure

▶ Establishing a connection with the registry

▶ Interpreting keys and values

▶ Creating keys and values

▶ Managing the registry

. . . .

*T*he heart and soul of Windows is the *registry,* a centralized repository of configuration information ranging from hardware driver information to application preferences. If you manipulate the registry correctly, you can get Windows and most applications to obey your command, but get it wrong, and you could end up with a system that won't even boot. As long as you stay away from changing things that you don't understand fully, you should be set. Windows PowerShell offers a whole slew of ways you can access and manipulate the Windows registry, and the best part is that it's really easy.

In this chapter, you use both some built-in Cmdlets as well as a .NET class called `Microsoft.Win32.RegistryKey` to query and manipulate the Windows registry. It's often said that he who masters the Windows registry masters Windows, so having the ability to automate registry changes with a few keystrokes brings you one step closer to reaching that goal.

I haven't been using too many warnings in this book, but this warning is really necessary. Before making any major changes in the Windows registry, make sure that you have it backed up somewhere safe. Making a backup is especially important when you're using scripts to modify the registry, because a problem or flaw in your code could result in massive changes being made very quickly, and if you're unlucky enough to change the wrong thing, you may not be able to boot correctly.

Following the Registry Tree

The Windows registry is made up of the five registry *hives* (each of the main sections of the registry is called a hive) listed in Table 19-1. The registry is structured so that each hive organizes the way information is stored. Some hives exist to store settings specific to the machine; others are designed to manage user-based settings. Some hives are used for application settings; others store hardware settings. A *registry key* is merely a branch within the tree that can contain other keys or values. You can think of registry keys as being like folders in a file system and values as being like files. You can view and edit the registry using the Registry Editor as seen in Figure 19-1.

To access the registry editor, select Start➪Run, type in `regedit.exe`, and press OK.

Table 19-1	The Registry Hives
Name	*Purpose*
HKEY_CLASSES_ROOT	Contains information regarding file types as well as registration and configuration data for Component Object Model (COM) objects and other automation objects.
HKEY_CURRENT_USER	Contains user-specific application and system settings related to the currently logged-on user.
HKEY_LOCAL_MACHINE	Contains machine-specific application and system settings for the local machine.
HKEY_USERS	Contains user-specific application and system settings for all loaded user profiles.
HKEY_CURRENT_CONFIG	Contains the configuration data for the currently loaded hardware profile.

Every registry key contains a *default value,* which is the value returned when you query a registry and don't specify the value you're interested in. Registry values consist of a name, a type, and the data (which is really the value of the registry value, but because that sounds ridiculous, Microsoft decided to be creative and call it data).

Registry values can be any of a few data types. Table 19-2 lists the most common ones.

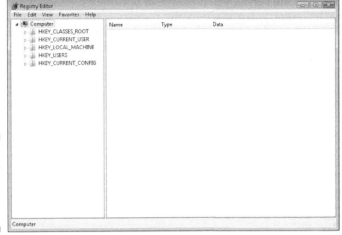

Figure 19-1:
The Registry
Editor and
the five reg-
istry hives.

Table 19-2	Registry Types
Data Type	*Description*
REG_SZ	Standard string data type
REG_BINARY	Any kind of binary data
REG_DWORD	32-bit number
REG_QWORD	64-bit number
REG_MULTI_SZ	Multivalued string
REG_EXPAND_SZ	String that contains unexpanded environment variables (such as %SYSTEMROOT% to dynamically indicate the path to the Windows directory)

Connecting to the Windows Registry

If you've worked with Windows for any amount of time, I'm sure that you already know (or at least have heard) that you can manage the Windows registry by using the Windows Registry Editor (regedit.exe). Unfortunately, this built-in Registry Editor isn't designed for automation other than the ability to import .reg (registry) files to make changes.

Windows PowerShell gives you a couple of options for connecting to and managing the registry. For starters, the registry is fully accessible as a PowerShell drive, which means that you can go into registry keys and *subkeys* (keys that are contained within other keys, just like subfolders are folders within other folders) just as though you were traversing your file system. The other option is using the `Microsoft.Win32.RegistryKey` class.

The main reason to use the `Microosft.Win32.RegistryKey` class instead of the virtual drive is to query or manipulate the registry of a remote host that's not running Windows PowerShell.

`HKEY_CURRENT_USER` is really just a shortcut to the subkey of `HKEY_USERS` containing the user's security identifier (SID). Also, a `.DEFAULT` subkey is used to generate the `HKEY_CURRENT_USER` tree for any new users who log on to the system.

Navigating the registry by using the PowerShell drives

The whole drive-letter concept dates back to the MS-DOS days, when each drive was assigned a unique drive letter. Each drive represents some logical partitioning of storage. Windows PowerShell takes this concept a step further by encapsulating the notion of a drive into a PowerShell drive. Extending the notion of a drive allows Windows PowerShell to access not only the usual drive letters through the console, but also some additional things that it knows it can represent in a hierarchal/tree structure. You can access aliases, certificates, environment variables, functions, regular variables, and even the registry in a manner similar to the way you access file systems. To see what drives you have available, run the `Get-PSDrive` Cmdlet. The output looks something like this:

```
PS C:\> get-psdrive

Name       Provider     Root                          CurrentLocation
----       --------     ----                          ---------------
A          FileSystem   A:\
Alias      Alias
C          FileSystem   C:\
cert       Certificate  \
D          FileSystem   D:\
Env        Environment
Function   Function
HKCU       Registry     HKEY_CURRENT_USER
HKLM       Registry     HKEY_LOCAL_MACHINE
Variable   Variable
```

The two drives you're interested in are the HKCU and HKLM drives. HKCU goes to the HKEY_CURRENT_USER registry hive; it represents the portion of the registry tied to your Windows profile and contains user-specific settings. HKLM goes to the HKEY_LOCAL_MACHINE registry hive and contains all the machine-specific settings. Only HKEY_CURRENT_USER and HKEY_LOCAL_MACHINE are accessible via a PowerShell drive; the other registry hives can't be accessed this way.

You can access the HKEY_CLASSES_ROOT registry hive indirectly by going through HKLM:\Software\Classes. It's really the same thing.

Getting into the registry drive is as easy as using the CD command to change directories (which is really just aliased to the Set-Location Cmdlet). Then you can use DIR (aliased to the Get-ChildItem Cmdlet) to list the contents of each key. The SKC property shows the number of subkeys that are below this key, and the VC property shows the number of values. The next command sequence shows how you can navigate through the registry just as if it was another drive within your filesystem:

```
PS C:\>cd HKLM:
PS HKLM:\>cd software
PS HKLM:\software>cd microsoft
PS HKLM:\software\microsoft>cd windows
PS HKLM:\software\microsoft\windows>dir
   Hive: Microsoft.PowerShell.Core\Registry::HKEY_LOCAL_MACHINE\software\
             microsoft\windows


SKC  VC Name                          Property
---  -- ----                          --------
 68   7 CurrentVersion                {SM_GamesName, SM_ConfigureProgramsName,
              CommonFilesDir, DevicePath...}
  0   2 HTML Help                     {IMTCTC.CHM, IMTCEN.CHM}
  1   0 ITStorage                     {}
  1   2 Tablet PC                     {IsTabletPC, DeviceKind}
  2   0 TabletPC                      {}
  3   1 Windows Error Reporting       {ErrorPort}
  1   0 Windows Search                {}
```

Using Microsoft.Win32.RegistryKey to access the registry

The Microsoft .NET Framework offers plenty of feature-rich classes that you can use to do a lot of things. Considering how important the registry is to the overall functionality of Windows, it's no surprise that the .NET Framework includes a whole cast of characters you can use to manipulate the registry. The most interesting of these classes is the `Microsoft.Win32.RegistryKey` class because it represents registry keys, and as you know by now, the registry key is literally the key to unlocking the power of the Windows registry.

To query a value from the registry by using the `Microsoft.Win32.RegistryKey` class, perform these steps:

1. **Use the** `OpenRemoteBaseKey` **method to connect to the desired registry hive.**

2. **Use to** `OpenSubKey` **method to open a specific subkey.**

3. **Use the** `GetValue` **method on the subkey to get the data for a given subkey value.**

Here's how you use these steps to query all the values in the `HKEY_LOCAL_MACHINE\Software\Microsoft\Windows\CurrentVersion\Run` key:

```
$computername = "workstation1"

$regHKLM = [Microsoft.Win32.RegistryKey]::OpenRemoteBaseKey("LocalMachine",$comp
            utername)
$regKey = $regHKLM.OpenSubKey("Software\Microsoft\Windows\CurrentVersion\Run")
foreach($valueName in $regKey.GetValueNames()) {
   Write-Host ($valueName + ": " + $regKey.GetValue($valueName))
}
```

The `OpenRemoteBaseKey` method takes two parameters. The first parameter defines the registry hive you want to connect to, and the second parameter contains the name of the computer to query. Yes, you can use this method to connect to the local machine or to any other machine to which you have remote registry access simply by providing the computer name here. You use `"LocalMachine"` to specify that you want to access the `HKEY_LOCAL_MACHINE` registry hive. Here's the list of the other values that you can use to access the other registry hives:

- `ClassesRoot`: HKEY_CLASSES_ROOT
- `CurrentUser`: HKEY_CURRENT_USER
- `LocalMachine`: HKEY_LOCAL_MACHINE
- `Users`: HKEY_USERS
- `CurrentConfig`: HKEY_CURRENT_CONFIG

`OpenSubKey` is straightforward. You can specify the full path to the registry key or even just put in the name of a subkey and loop through each subkey. To get the different values within that registry key, use the `GetValueNames` method. If you want to know the names of the subkeys, use `GetSubKeyNames` instead.

Reading Keys and Values

Going through registry keys and reading values account for probably 95 percent of all the operations done on the registry. After all, how often do you save new settings? You're far more likely to be querying for the value of a given setting to use within your script. Your query could be as simple as looking up Service Pack level to getting a list of installed software.

Using the PSDrive is a convenient way to get around, but it's not exactly the best for dynamically querying registry values. If you want to query the registry values in the HKEY_LOCAL_MACHINE\Software\Microsoft\ Windows\CurrentVersion\Run registry key, for example, you can use the Set-Location Cmdlet (alias CD) to navigate to it. Now, because it looks like you're browsing the file system, you'd assume that you can just run Get-ChildItem (alias DIR) to get a list of all the registry values. Unfortunately, that's not the case. Get-ChildItem only lists any registry subkeys, so in most cases, running Get-ChildItem again the Run key returns nothing.

In the PSDrive terminology, registry values aren't children of registry keys, but properties with name/value pairs. To get the actual registry values within a registry key, you have to use the Get-ItemProperty Cmdlet. This example shows how you'd use Get-ItemProperty to retrieve all values in the HKEY_LOCAL_MACHINE\Software\Microsoft\Windows\ CurrentVersion\Run registry key:

```
Get-ItemProperty HKLM:\Software\Microsoft\Windows\CurrentVersion\Run
```

What this command returns is completely dependent on what's installed on the machine where you run it. The bottom line is that it returns the registry values in that key. The biggest downside of this method of retrieving registry values is that it doesn't return these values in a very useful structure. You'd expect the values returned to be some kind of collection so that you can iterate through that collection, but that's not the case. Instead, to access the value (data) of each registry value, you have to use the value name explicitly.

The operating system, Service Pack level, and some other information about the operating system are stored in the HKEY_LOCAL_MACHINE\Software\ Microsoft\Windows NT\CurrentVersion registry key. The registry value storing the operating system name is called ProductName, and the value storing the Service Pack level is called CSDVersion. Here's how you obtain the operating system and Service Pack level (CSDVersion) by querying the value through the registry:

```
$regkey = Get-ItemProperty "HKLM:\Software\Microsoft\Windows NT\CurrentVersion"
$os = $regkey.ProductName
$servicePack = $regkey.CSDVersion
Write-Host ($os + " " + $servicePack)
```

You have to specify the registry value name directly to get its value. If you don't know the registry value name, you have no way to loop through it to get its value. If you already know what registry key and registry value you're interested in, however, using the PSDrive to get the information is perfect for the job; otherwise, you need to resort to using the Microsoft.Win32.RegistryKey class instead.

Writing Keys and Values

The most common method for making changes to the Windows registry is by using the Registry Editor. You double=click the value you want to change, enter in the new values, and press OK to save it. A more indirect way is to import .reg files using the Registry Editor. Because the registry is such an integral part of Windows, every scripting and programming language that runs on Windows has the ability to read and write to the registry. Windows PowerShell is no exception to this.

Writing keys and values using the PSDrive

Occasionally, you need to create registry keys and write registry values as well, most commonly to configure application settings. Creating registry keys is as easy as creating a new folder in your file system by using the New-Item Cmdlet. This is how you create a new registry key in HKEY_LOCAL_MACHINE\ Software called MyCompany:

```
New-Item HKLM:\Software\MyCompany
```

You create new registry values by using the New-ItemProperty Cmdlet. This Cmdlet takes the path of the registry key where the value will be created; the name of the registry value; the data type; and, of course, the value itself. Here's how you create a registry value called ConfigParams with the DWORD value 23 in the registry key you just created:

```
New-ItemProperty -path HKLM:\Software\MyCompany -name ConfigParams -PropertyType
          DWord -value 23
```

The New-ItemProperty Cmdlet supports all six property data types used within the registry. Look at Table 19-3 to find the PropertyType value you need to specify for each corresponding data type.

Table 19-3	New-Item Property PropertyType Values
PropertyType Value	*Data Type*
Binary	REG_BINARY
DWord	REG_DWORD
ExpandString	REG_EXPAND_SZ
MultiString	REG_MULTI_SZ
String	REG_SZ
QWord	REG_QWORD

If the registry value already exists, and you're merely updating its value, you use the Set-ItemProperty Cmdlet instead. Set-ItemProperty has the same syntax as New-ItemProperty except that you can't specify the PropertyType. Set-ItemProperty can only update a registry value — it can't change its data type. This is how you change the ConfigParams value to 25:

```
Set-ItemProperty -path HKLM:\Software\MyCompany -name ConfigParams -value 25
```

If you try to use Set-ItemProperty for a registry value that doesn't exist, the Cmdlet creates that value for you. The only caveat is that it creates the value as a REG_SZ data type, so if the value is supposed to be something other than REG_SZ, you should use New-ItemProperty instead.

Writing registry values using Microsoft. Win32.RegistryKey

Writing to a registry key by using Microsoft.Win32.RegistryKey class requires a few extra steps:

1. **Connect to the registry, using the** OpenRemoteBaseKey **method.**

2. **Open the subkey in writable mode.**

   This is done by using the OpenSubKey method and providing the value $true as the second parameter.

3. **Use the** SetValue **method to set the registry value.**

This method looks like a bit more work, but in practice, it's quite easy. Using the example from the preceding section, to create a REG_DWORD registry value called ConfigParams with a value of 23, you do something like this:

```
$computername = "workstation1"

$regHKLM = [Microsoft.Win32.RegistryKey]::OpenRemoteBaseKey("LocalMachine",$comp
          utername)
$regKey = $regHKLM.OpenSubKey("Software\MyCompany", $true)
$regKey.SetValue('ConfigParams',23,'dword')
```

It's really no different from reading from the registry value, except that the call to OpenSubKey now has an additional parameter that's set to $true. This second parameter defines whether the registry key will be opened in writable mode. By default, this parameter is set to $false, so leaving it off is fine for reading values. If you intend on making changes to any of its values later you have to set this parameter to $true.

The SetValue method takes three parameters: the name of the registry value, its value, and its data type. The acceptable values for the data type are the same as those used by the PSDrive, so all the possible PropertyType values listed in Table 19-3 can be used here as well.

Renaming and Deleting Registry Keys and Values

Sometimes, you need to rename a registry key or flat-out delete it. Because the registry contains settings for Windows and many of the applications installed on the system, this is typically done to clear these settings. As you might suspect, you can just use the Registry Editor to delete or rename registry keys and values. You can even create specially formatted .reg files that you can import to delete registry keys (but not for renaming).

This is what a .reg file to delete the iTunes calendar helper addin registry key would look like. You simply prefix the registry key path with a minus sign and that tells the Registry Editor to delete the key, like this:

```
Windows Registry Editor Version 5.00

[-HKEY_CURRENT_USER\Software\Microsoft\Office\Outlook\Addins\iTunesAddIn.
          CalendarHelper]
```

Renaming and deleting registry keys and Values using PSDrive

Because the `PSDrive` gives you the ability to treat the registry almost like a regular file system, you do this by using the `Rename-Item` (alias `ren`) and `Remove-Item` (alias `del`) Cmdlets, as in this example:

```
Rename-Item -Path HKLM:\Software\MyCompany -newname MyCorp
Remove-Item HKLM:\Software\MyCorp
```

If the registry key isn't empty, you'll be prompted to confirm the deletion. You can avoid this prompt by specifying the `-Recurse` parameter for `Remove-Item`, like this:

```
Remove-Item HKLM:\Software\MyCorp -Recurse
```

You rename and delete registry values by using the `Rename-ItemProperty` and `Remove-ItemProperty` Cmdlets, respectively. You simply need to provide the path to the registry value; the name of the value; and, in the case of `Rename-ItemProperty`, the new name for the value, as in this example:

```
Rename-ItemProperty -Path HKLM:\Software\MyCompany -Name ConfigParams -NewName
            ConfigParameters
Remove-ItemProperty -Path HKLM:\Software\MyCompany -Name ConfigParameters
```

Using Microsoft.Win32.RegistryKey to delete registry keys and values

Deleting registry values by using the `Microsoft.Win32.RegistryKey` class is very easy. Just use `OpenSubkey` to connect to the registry key that contains the registry value you want to delete and then call the `DeleteValue` method, giving it the name of the value, like this:

```
$computername = "workstation1"

$regHKLM = [Microsoft.Win32.RegistryKey]::OpenRemoteBaseKey("LocalMachine",$comp
            utername)
$regKey = $regHKLM.OpenSubKey("Software\MyCompany", $true)
$regKey.DeleteValue("MyCompany")
```

Deleting registry keys is just as easy, and you can use either of two methods, depending on what you're trying to achieve. The first option is to simply use the `DeleteSubKey` method, like this:

```
$regHKLM.DeleteSubKey("Software\MyCompany")
```

This method deletes the subkey but only if the registry key doesn't contain subkeys. (The DeleteSubKey method deletes the key if it just contains values, though.) This method is a good one to use when you don't think that the registry key you want to delete has any subkeys but don't want to inadvertently delete any subkeys that it may contain.

To delete a registry key and all its subkeys forcefully, you have to use the DeleteSubKeyTree method. This method works the same way as DeleteSubKey except that it deletes the key, including any subkeys and values it contains. This method is equivalent to using the -Recurse command with the Remove-Item Cmdlet, as follows:

```
$regHKLM.DeleteSubKeyTree("Software\MyCompany")
```

Currently, you have no way to rename a registry key or value by using the Microsoft.Win32.RegistryKey class.

Chapter 20

Reaching Out to Active Directory

C hances are that if you're running Windows servers in your network, you've already set up an Active Directory. It serves only as an account repository (allowing users to use a single credential to get authenticated and permissioned throughout your Windows network), but also as a central store for all kinds of user and computer account information. Needless to say, the importance of Active Directory within any Windows network is extremely high, and your ability to talk to and manage it effectively should be number-one on your priority list.

Windows PowerShell makes it very easy to talk to Active Directory (AD) because you can take advantage of the whole slew of .NET classes specifically designed for effective AD communications. In fact, if you like using Windows PowerShell for interacting with Windows Management Instrumentation (WMI), you'll find that interacting with AD is even easier. Let's face it — you're reading this book because you're a fan of finding easy ways to do things.

In this chapter, you find out just how easy it is to get information from Active Directory using the Active Directory Services Interface provider in addition to a handful of Microsoft .NET classes that help you refine your search criteria. You also use these same providers to modify attributes of objects within Active Directory.

A Really Brief Active Directory Primer

Active Directory is a directory service that stores information about a Windows domain, such as user and computer account information. The directory itself is managed by one or more domain controllers. If more than one domain controller is used, the Active Directory information is replicated among servers in a *multimaster configuration,* which means that when you change the information on any of the domain controllers, those changes propagate to the other servers whenever replication occurs.

I could go on and on, but I'm going to stop right here. The reality is that if you don't already know what Active Directory is or how it works, you really shouldn't be writing any scripts that touch it. For the rest of this chapter, I'm going to assume you know enough about Active Directory to understand how it works and that you have at least managed it manually.

If I've completely lost you, but you're still very much interested, you may want to read *Active Directory For Dummies,* 2nd Edition, by Steve Clines and Marcia Loughry (Wiley Publishing), before reading the rest of this chapter, as it might start sounding like gibberish otherwise.

Connecting to Active Directory

To connect to Active Directory by using Windows PowerShell, you connect using the Active Directory Services Interfaces (ADSI) and the Lightweight Directory Access Protocol (LDAP). Yikes — that sounds awfully complicated. Alas, it's not! You can find the username (sAMAccountName attribute) of all objects in your domain, for example, by running this code:

```
$objADSI = [adsi]""
$domain = $objADSI.distinguishedname
$userContainer = [adsi]("LDAP://cn=users," + $domain)
foreach($child in $userContainer) {
    Write-Host $child.samaccountname
}
```

The first line is a really simple way to define an ADSI connection. An empty string just tells the ADSI provider to connect to the default root directory entry. You use this code to dynamically obtain the distinguished name (DN) for the domain by accessing the distinguishedName property. This technique is really cool because you don't have to hard-code your domain's DN, which also means that you can hand off this script to someone else and he can run it on his domain without modification. In my test lab, this value looks something like DC=TESTLAB, DC=LOCAL.

You need the domain name's DN because it's part of every DN for every object in Active Directory. So in general, you want to have this information stored in a variable somewhere so that you can use it easily — which is exactly what you do in the next part. To establish a connection to the domain's user container, you run this bit of code:

```
$userContainer = [adsi]("LDAP://cn=users," + $domain)
```

This code connects to the object via LDAP and stores the reference to that object in `$userContainer`. This is where having that domain DN dynamically populated and stored as a variable comes in handy. If the container is well known, like the user container, a line like this works for everyone, regardless of what their domain names are. The users container contains any number of items, and you can loop through them by using a simple `foreach` statement. This statement loops through each item in the container and displays the value of the `sAMAccountName` attribute, as in this example:

```
foreach($child in $userContainer) {
    Write-Host $child.samaccountname
}
```

You use lowercase — `samaccountname` — when referencing the attribute in Windows PowerShell directly, even though the actual attribute contains a mix of character cases.

That's pretty easy, and it's certainly a lot easier than using VBScript.

Querying for Objects and Attributes

Querying Active Directory for various bits of information comprises the bulk of the operations done on it on a regular basis. After all, Active Directory is designed to be a central directory that stores all kinds of information. It's often used as an authoritative source for user information, especially if you use products that integrate heavily with it. Many Microsoft (and even third-party) products integrate with Active Directory to use it as a source of usernames, group information, and other important user information, and even as an authentication source.

To query Active Directory for object and attribute information, you need to follow a few steps:

1. **Get a reference to the** `DirectoryEntry` **where you want to start searching.**

    This reference can be the root of the domain or maybe even a particular Organization Unit (OU).

2. **Create a new** `System.DirectoryServices.DirectorySearcher` **object, using the** `DirectoryEntry` **object from the preceding step.**

3. **Define a query filter.**

   This filter defines the criteria for your search and is a bit tricky because you have to know a little bit about the syntax of a LDAP filter. (I talk about this topic in the next section.)

4. **Define a scope.**

   This scope controls whether the query is for just the objects in the search root or for the subtree as well.

5. **Execute the search, using the** `FindOne` **or** `FindAll` **method.**

   If the search returns results, extract the `DirectoryEntry` (in the case of `FindOne`) or loop through the results and get the `DirectoryEntry` (in the case of `FindAll`).

Here's a fairly simple script that queries Active Directory for the first and last name of all the user accounts that have values for these attributes:

```
$objADSI = [adsi]""
$domain = $objADSI.distinguishedname
$objDomain = [adsi]("LDAP://" + $domain)

$search = New-Object System.DirectoryServices.DirectorySearcher
$search.SearchRoot = $objDomain
$search.Filter = "(&(objectClass=user)(givenName=*)(sn=*))"
$search.SearchScope = "Subtree"


$results = $search.FindAll()
foreach($item in $results)
{
    $objUser = $item.GetDirectoryEntry()
    Write-Host ($objUser.displayname)
}
```

You've already seen the first part of this code, but I want you to take a close look at the section where the `DirectorySearcher` object is set up. The `New-Object` Cmdlet is used to create a new `System.DirectoryServices.DirectorySearcher` object. Now that you have a `DirectorySearcher` object, you can configure its various properties. The first is `SearchRoot`, which defines the `DirectoryEntry` where the `DirectorySearcher` will begin its search. In this case, you want to search the entire directory.

The next part is `Filter`. If you don't understand this part yet, don't worry — I explain it in the next section. In short, `Filter` looks for any object that has an `objectClass` of `user` and some value for both the `givenName` (first name) and `sn` (last name) attributes.

Finally, you set `SearchScope` to `"Subtree"`, which means that you want to search `SearchRoot` and any children it has (basically, perform a recursive search).

Now that `DirectorySearcher` is set up, you use the `FindAll` method to execute the search. All that's left is to loop through the results and get the display name.

The items returned by the search aren't `DirectoryEntry` objects. To actually get to them, you have to use the `GetDirectoryEntry` method.

If you have a lot of users in your domain, you may notice that not all the users are returned. For safety reasons, Microsoft defines a maximum result-set of 1,000 entries. This limit protects very large directories from errant queries that try to retrieve more values than expected (such as a faulty search filter that returns 100,000 results when you expected it to return only 5).

To get around the AD query limitation, you have to *page* the results, which means that you retrieve the results in chunks defined by the page size. This number should be no more than the maximum allowed by AD. This code snippet configures `PageSize` as `1,000`, which means that the query should try to retrieve no more than 1,000 results at a time:

```
$search.PageSize = 1000
```

Creating your LDAP filter

LDAP filters are very powerful because they give you the ability to define exactly what you're looking for when querying AD. The downside is that the syntax takes a little getting used to, so I'm going to take a moment to show you how to create your own LDAP filters.

Defining a simple filter

A *simple filter* consists of a condition you're checking to see whether a given attribute matches a specific value and is in this format:

```
(attribute=value)
```

The attribute name is case sensitive, so if you're trying to see whether the username (samaccountname) equals a specific username, you have to write out the attribute name in the same way that it appears in Active Directory, as in this example:

```
(sAMAccountName=sseguis)
```

I'm not using mixed case to make the code easier to read or because my Shift key has gone nuts. If you go into the Active Directory schema, you'll find this attribute defined exactly this way.

Using wildcards

Often, you want to match a specific pattern rather than a specific value. You can do this by using *wildcards.* The wildcard character, which is the asterisk character (*), can be used to match any pattern. If you use the asterisk by itself, it means to match any object that has a value for that attribute, such as any object in which the e-mail address isn't blank:

```
(mail=*)
```

Here's how you can match any object with a common name (cn) that starts with s:

```
(cn=s*)
```

You can also put the wildcard character at the beginning to find matches in which samaccountname ends in svc, like this:

```
(sAMAccountName=*svc)
```

You can even use the wildcard in the middle. Here's how you can look for any object with a display name that starts and ends with s:

```
(displayName=s*s)
```

Finally, if you're feeling a bit adventurous, you can sprinkle your wildcards anywhere. Here's a general wildcard search that finds objects in which the mail attribute contains a dot (.) and an @ symbol, but the dot has to come before the @ symbol:

```
(mail=*.*@*)
```

Negating the filter

Plenty of times, you want to find something that doesn't match a certain condition. You may have a naming convention requiring the usernames of all service accounts to end in srvc, for example. To exclude those usernames from a query, you have to create a filter that matches objects in which the samaccountname ends in `srvc` and then negates it. You negate a statement by using the exclamation point (`!`), as in this example:

```
(!(sAMAccountName=*srvc))
```

The negation happens outside the filter, so you define the matching filter, enclose it in parentheses, put an exclamation point in front of it, and then enclose the entire thing in parentheses.

Combining filter terms

In the real world, LDAP filters usually consist of multiple conditions, such as making sure that the `objectClass` is `user` and that the `mail` attribute has a value. You can use the Boolean `and` and `or` conditions when combining various filter terms. The symbol used for the Boolean `and` is the ampersand (`&`), whereas the symbol for the Boolean `or` is the pipe symbol (`|`).

Here's how you put together a filter that checks to see whether the `object-Class` is `user` and the `mail` attribute starts with the letter a:

```
(&(objectClass=user)(mail=a*))
```

Notice that all you have to do is define the two filter terms you want and then combine them by using the ampersand. What's interesting is that the ampersand isn't placed between the two terms, as you might expect, but at the very beginning, and then the entire combined filter is enclosed in parentheses. You must put the operator in front of the terms being combined. Using the Boolean `or` works in a similar fashion. Here, you're interested in users whose first name (`givenName`) starts with either a or s:

```
(|(givenName=a*)(givenName=s*))
```

That's easy enough, isn't it? Now, what if you have more than two terms to combine? All you have to do is add the extra terms. This code adds the condition that the last name (`sn`) start with s:

```
(&(objectClass=user)(mail=a*)(sn=s*))
```

You can even mix and match `and`, `or`, and even the negation operator. This code's going to look a little bit confusing, but bear with me for a second:

```
(|(&(objectClass=user)(!(mail=a*)))(&(objectClass=person)(sAMAccountName=a*)))
```

I know that it looks like I'm just trying to confuse you, but this code isn't very difficult to understand when you break it down. The important part is pairing the opening and closing parentheses so that you understand which terms are evaluated in relation to the others. The first thing you notice is that the first operator you encounter is the Boolean `or`. This means that you're checking for a condition that can match either of two terms. If you look closely at the matching parentheses, you find that the code is performing an or operation on these two terms:

```
(&(objectClass=user)(!(mail=a*)))
(&(objectClass=person)(sAMAccountName=a*))
```

Ah, okay, that's not too bad. The first term uses the Boolean and to make sure that both conditions are true. The first statement is simple, as it just makes sure that the objectClass is user. The second statement checks to see whether the mail attribute starts with a, but because it's enclosed with the negation operator, this *entire* statement means that the objectClass must be user and that the mail attribute must not start with a.

The second term is a simple Boolean and that makes sure that the object-Class is person and that the username starts with a.

The most important thing to get out of this example is that you shouldn't allow yourself to be daunted by long filter terms; you just need to break them into manageable chunks to figure them out. Likewise, if you're trying to create a very complex filter, it's best to break it into manageable filter terms and then combine those terms into the long, scary one that even you can barely make sense of.

If this stuff really interests you, and you want to get more details, you can read up on Request for Comment (RFC) 4515 (http://tools.ietf.org/html/rfc4515) and RFC 3687 (http://tools.ietf.org/html/rfc3687).

Looking up userAccountControl properties

One critical attribute for a user account is the userAccountControl attribute. This attribute is critical because it defines the kind of account the object is, along with any security restrictions and exclusions it has, such as whether the account is disabled or locked. Unlike simple attributes such as givenName, sn, and sAMAccountName, the userAccountControl attribute is actually a group of bits, with each bit representing a particular flag (true = 1 or false = 0, for example). A *flag* is the term given to a value that indicates whether something is set (value of 1) or not (value of 0). Table 20-1 contains a list of possible flags that you can set for this attribute.

Table 20-1	UserAccountControl Attribute Property Flags
Property Flag	*Value*
SCRIPT	1
ACCOUNTDISABLE	2
HOMEDIR_REQUIRED	8

Property Flag	Value
LOCKOUT	16
PASSWD_NOTREQD	32
PASSWD_CANT_CHANGE	64
ENCRYPTED_TEXT_PWD_ALLOWED	128
TEMP_DUPLICATE_ACCOUNT	256
NORMAL_ACCOUNT	512
INTERDOMAIN_TRUST_ACCOUNT	2048
WORKSTATION_TRUST_ACCOUNT	4096
SERVER_TRUST_ACCOUNT	8192
DONT_EXPIRE_PASSWORD	65536
MNS_LOGON_ACCOUNT	131072
SMARTCARD_REQUIRED	262144
TRUSTED_FOR_DELEGATION	524288
NOT_DELEGATED	1048576
USE_DES_KEY_ONLY	2097152
PASSWORD_EXPIRED	8388608
TRUSTED_TO_AUTH_FOR_DELEGATION	16777216

In practice, here's how all this works. If you look at the `UserAccountControl` attribute for most user accounts, the value is simply `512`, which means that it's a regular account. If the account is disabled, this value is `514`, because it's a normal account (`512`) that also has the `ACCOUNTDISABLE` flag (`2`) set, so you add the values to get the new value of `514`. Based on this table, it's easy to reach the conclusion that if a user account is locked, the value would be `528` (`NORMAL_ACCOUNT + LOCKOUT`), so you'd write an LDAP filter that looks something like this:

```
(&(objectClass=user)(userAccountControl=528))
```

This code works for this scenario, but the problem is that things always that simple. If other property flags are set, such as `SMARTCARD_REQUIRED`, this value could be `528 + 262144`, or `262672`. Given that a whole range of values may add up to a match, what you're really interested in is whether bit number 5 (value `16`) is set. You do this by performing a bitwise `AND` on the value of `user AccountControl` with the value you're interested in, such as `16`. The resulting value will be `true` if it's set; otherwise, the result will be `false`. This code sounds a whole lot more confusing than it really is, so I'm going to jump right to an example of a filter string that looks for locked-out accounts:

```
(&(objectClass=user)(userAccountControl:1.2.840.113556.1.4.803:=16))
```

The interesting part is this:

```
(userAccountControl:1.2.840.113556.1.4.803:=16)
```

This peculiar-looking value, 1.2.840.113556.1.4.803, is the LDAP version of the bitwise AND. What this entire string is saying is that you want to perform a bitwise AND operation on the value of userAccountControl with the value 16 (LOCKOUT). This code returns true if — and only if — this value is set. Now if you want to find all the disabled accounts, you can just replace 16 with 2 (ACCOUNTDISABLE), and the code will work.

The bitwise AND compares two values in binary. Only if the bits are both set to 1 does the result equal 1. The reason that this operator can check to see whether a certain flag is set is that if you bitwise AND two numbers and the resulting value is nonzero, a match definitely occurs in at least one of the bits of the two numbers. To understand this situation a bit better, consider the userAccountControl value of 528. You know that the LOCKOUT flag value is 16 (refer to Table 20-1, earlier in this section). You want to check whether the LOCKOUT flag is set in that userAccountControl value. To do this, you perform a bitwise AND of the two values, which looks like this:

```
1000010000 (528 in binary)
0000010000 (16 in binary)
----------
0000010000 (result)
```

You simply line up the binary values, and whenever you see that both values are 1, you put 1 in the result. Because the result contains 1 somewhere, the code found a match for that LOCKOUT flag, so the account must be locked.

Dynamically obtaining a user's distinguishedName

Although it's very convenient to refer to users by using usernames or other attributes in their AD user accounts, when you interact with AD by using ADSI's LDAP provider, you often have to refer to the user object by its distinguishedName (DN) rather than its username. This process can be quite cumbersome, because depending on how you've organized your AD, user objects may move from one container to another, thereby changing their DN. You may have a script that uses a particular user account and can hard-code the DN for that object, but if the DN ever changes, your script will break.

It's far better to generate the DN dynamically based on an AD search for a particular attribute, such as the logon name (sAMAccountName). Here's a very simple function that you can reuse in all your scripts to do just that:

```
function GetUserDN([string]$username) {

    $objADSI = [adsi]""
    $domain = $objADSI.distinguishedname
    $objDomain = [adsi]("LDAP://" + $domain)

    $search = New-Object System.DirectoryServices.DirectorySearcher
    $search.SearchRoot = $objDomain
    $search.Filter = "(sAMAccountName=$username)"
    $search.SearchScope = "Subtree"

    $result = $search.FindOne()
    if ($result -eq $null) {
        return $null
    } else {
        return $result.GetDirectoryEntry().distinguishedName
    }
}
```

This function returns the DN for the given username or $null if it can't find the DN. If you put this function in your script, you can use it like this:

```
$username = "administrator"
$userDN = GetUserDN($username)
if ($userDN -eq $null) {
    Write-Host ("Unable to find " + $username)
} else {
    Write-Host ($username + " - " + $userDN)
}
```

You can modify the GetUserDN function to accommodate other objects — such as computers, groups, and contacts — simply by changing the DirectorySearcher filter criteria and adjusting your function parameters accordingly.

Modifying Object Attributes

Modifying object attributes in Active Directory by using Windows PowerShell is a lot easier than you might think. It consists of three steps:

1. Get a DirectoryEntry object that represents the object you want to modify.

2. Use the `DirectoryEntry` object's `put` method to assign the new value.

3. Commit the changes by using the `SetInfo` method.

To demonstrate just how straightforward this process really is, here's a simple script that modifies a user's first name, last name, display name, and description:

```
$user = [adsi]"LDAP://CN=testuser,ou=test,dc=testlab,dc=local"
$user.put("givenName","Chris")
$user.put("sn","Laile")
$user.put("displayName","Laile, Chris")
$user.put("description","Master of Disaster")
$user.SetInfo()
```

Even though I chose to use a user object in the example, this same procedure works for groups and organization units — in short, for any object in Active Directory. The `put` method takes the attribute name as the first parameter and the value as the second parameter. You can change only attributes that actually exist for the kind of object you're changing. If you try to change an attribute that doesn't exist, an error will be raised.

Attribute names themselves aren't case sensitive, although it's good practice to adhere to case-sensitive attribute names so that you get used to them, because you'll need those names for things like LDAP filters.

The `SetInfo` method does the actual work of making the changes in Active Directory. If you forget this step, you'll find that none of your changes are reflected in Active Directory, even though Windows PowerShell doesn't complain, because any property changes you make are done in memory in a cached mode.

Only when you call the `SetInfo` method after making changes in an object are those changes committed to Active Directory.

Updating Group Membership

Although you can handle all attributes by using the `put` method, the process isn't quite that simple when it comes to group membership. In general, when you do things manually, you have two ways of removing a user from a group: open the group and remove the user as one of its members, or open the user and remove the group from the list of member groups. The easiest way to add a user to a group is to manipulate the group directly by using ADSI, like this:

```
$user = "cn=testuser,ou=test,dc=testdom,dc=local"
$group = [ADSI]"LDAP://cn=MyGroup,cn=Users,dc=testdom,dc=local"
$group.add("LDAP://" + $user)
$group.SetInfo()
```

When adding a user to a group, you have to specify the full DN for the user object. In practice, knowing the exact DN for the user object you want to add isn't very convenient so you'll want to use something like the GetUserDN function to dynamically obtain the object's DN for you.

You can remove a user from a group just as easily as you add a user to a group. In fact, you use the same code except that you use the remove method instead of the add method, like this:

```
$user = "cn=testuser,ou=test,dc=testdom,dc=local"
$group = [ADSI]"LDAP://cn=MyGroup,cn=Users,dc=testdom,dc=local"
$group.remove("LDAP://" + $user)
$group.SetInfo()
```

Getting to the Raw ADSI Object Using psbase

Whenever you connect to AD by using ADSI and LDAP, what you're really getting is a .NET-based type adapter that allows you to communicate through the .NET Framework and with the ADSI provider. The problem used to be that to access the raw ADSI object lying underneath, you had to go through the psbase hidden object built into the ADSI type adapter. In other words, in Windows PowerShell 1.0, you had to do this to get to the children of a given container:

```
$ou = [adsi]"LDAP://cn=users,dc=testlab,dc=local"
$ou.psbase.children
```

In Windows PowerShell 2, if you try to access any of the methods and properties that fall under this psbase class, you can do so directly without first having to refer to psbase, which means that this code is perfectly valid:

```
$ou.children
```

The caveat is that if you run Get-Member on the ADSI type adapter object, it doesn't return the full list of supported properties and methods of the underlying ADSI object. If that's the case, how would you know whether an OU has a property called children? The trick is to run Get-Member on the psbase object instead. You can see the difference clearly if you run these two commands:

```
$ou | get-member
$ou.psbase | get-member
```

The call to Get-Member on the psbase object reveals all the "hidden" features of the raw ADSI object.

Chapter 21

PowerShell Lockdown

· ·

In This Chapter

▶ Taking advantage of Windows PowerShell security features

▶ Creating a code-signing certificate

▶ Perusing the certificate store

▶ Signing the scripts you create

▶ Using Windows PowerShell to control the Windows Firewall

· ·

Security has been a hot topic in recent years, and Windows PowerShell is just one of the products designed to closely follow Microsoft's Trustworthy Computing Initiative. What is security, really? I think a lot of people have the misconception that you're either secured or you're not. The reality is that security consists of layers that act as hurdles for anyone trying to get to whatever it is you're trying to secure.

Now, I don't claim to be a security expert, but it really just takes a bit of common sense to understand that nothing is absolutely secure — although you can take measures to make things more secure. Even though most cars have door locks, for example, many people still install car alarms and other theft-deterrent devices. Do they work? Yes! Are they foolproof? No! Locks, alarms, and other theft-deterrent devices simply make your car less interesting to thieves because they have to work harder to get to the prize. The whole philosophy behind security is that the cost or effort required to break the security exceeds any returns a person can get for doing so.

Windows PowerShell is designed with several layers of security that can be used in concert to ensure that its power can be controlled (ideally, by you). In this chapter, you get to know the different security measures Windows PowerShell has in place by default to help prevent unwanted script execution and how you can adjust these settings to better suit your environment. You'll also get to use PowerShell to manipulate the Windows firewall. Keeping your systems secure while having the ability to leverage something as powerful as Windows PowerShell can no longer be an afterthought, and knowing how to take appropriate security measures can go a long way towards protecting yourself from malicious users.

PowerShell Security Features

With all the flak Microsoft has received about security — or, rather, the lack of security — over the years, it comes as no surprise that anything new that Microsoft has developed (including Windows PowerShell) has some very good built-in security features. Mind you, these features aren't foolproof, but they stop some very common techniques that people use to exploit unsuspecting users.

Getting rid of the current directory loophole

One trick that hackers use is putting malicious commands and scripts in regular places, such as your home directory, that have the same names as commonly used benign commands. If you happen to be in the tainted directory when you type the command name, you run the malicious script instead. Windows PowerShell protects you against this lame but unfortunately effective attack by not including the current directory in the search path when you enter commands. Instead, if the script is in the current directory, you have to prefix it with . \ to tell PowerShell explicitly to look in the current directory, as in this example:

```
PS C:\scripts>.\myscript.ps1
```

Stopping the double-click blues

Another method that tricks users into running malicious scripts is getting them to double-click the malicious file. The file can be an e-mail attachment or a file that was somehow dropped into the file system somewhere, such as in the user's start-up folder. Fortunately, you have some protection against this tactic as well. Unlike a Windows Shell script or one written in VBScript, a Windows PowerShell script doesn't run when you double-click it. Instead, Windows PowerShell scripts open in Notepad when they're double-clicked, because the file extension .ps1 is associated with Notepad.

Protecting through ExecutionPolicy

Another security enhancement is the use of execution policies to define what kind of scripts are allowed to run and, more specifically, where. Windows

PowerShell defines four `ExecutionPolicy` levels, listed in Table 21-1, with the default policy being the most restrictive.

Table 21-1	Windows PowerShell ExecutionPolicy Levels
Level	*Description*
Restricted	This level is the default policy level. The name is appropriate because you're not allowed to run any Windows PowerShell scripts, not even if all they do is display Hello World. The only things you can run on a host on which ExecutionPolicy is set to Restricted are built-in Windows commands and Cmdlets. *Note:* Even your Windows PowerShell profile script won't run when ExecutionPolicy is set to this level unless you sign it. (I discuss signing scripts in the next section.)
AllSigned	This policy allows you to run scripts, but only if the scripts have been signed with a digital signature from a trusted publisher. Ideally, in secure corporate environments, this level is what you want your setting to be, because it's the most secure level that allows scripts to be run. The only downside is that you have to sign all your scripts; otherwise, they won't be allowed to run.
RemoteSigned	If you believe that your system is secure against someone logging in and launching a Windows PowerShell window, this level makes life a bit easier but sacrifices a bit of security. This level allows any script to run, but only if it's launched from a local drive; otherwise, the script must be signed with a digital certificate from a trusted publisher.
Unrestricted	This policy level is a free-for-all level. When ExecutionPolicy is set to this level, it behaves the same way as the regular Windows command prompt or Windows Scripting Host, in that absolutely nothing is required to be signed for the script to run, regardless of location. I highly recommend that you *don't* set ExecutionPolicy to this level.

You can set and get the ExecutionPolicy by using the Get-Execution Policy and Set-ExecutionPolicy Cmdlets. The recommended way, however, is to download the administrative template from Microsoft (http://go.microsoft.com/fwlink/?LinkId=102940), which allows you to set the execution policy centrally through Active Directory by using a Group Policy Object (GPO). I discussed Active Directory in Chapter 20.

Generating a Code-Signing Certificate

I've been talking about the need to sign your scripts with a digital signature, but what does that mean? You need to have a Class III Microsoft Authentication code-signing certificate generated by a trusted publisher to sign your scripts. You can purchase one of these certificates through any number of commercial Certificate Authorities (CAs) such as thawte, Entrust, and VeriSign, or you can generate one yourself if you have your own in-house CA.

You can find out more about Public Key Infrastructure and how to set it up for yourself in Windows Server 2003 by going to https://www.microsoft.com/windowsserver2003/technologies/pki/default.mspx.

Creating a self-signed certificate

A *self-signed certificate* is one that you generate yourself. Anyone can generate a self-signed certificate, which makes it very easy to use for signing your scripts, but to be used on another computer, your self-signed certificate must first be imported on that computer to make it trusted. You use makecert. exe, which is part of the Windows Platform SDK, to generate a self-signed certificate.

You can find more information about makecert.exe by visiting http://go.microsoft.com/fwlink/?LinkId=108538.

Generating a self-signed certificate is a two-part process:

1. Create a local trusted certificate authority.
2. Generate a code-signing certificate from that certificate.

You can generate your own local trusted CA by running

```
makecert.exe -n "CN=MyLocalCertRoot" -a sha1 -eku 1.3.6.1.5.5.7.3.3 -r -sv root.
        pvk root.cer -ss Root -sr LocalMachine
```

You'll be prompted to enter the password to use for the private key and confirm it (shown in Figure 21-1). Then you'll have to enter the password one more time to read the key you just generated and add it to the store (see Figure 21-2). For more on the certificate store, see "Browsing the Certificate Store" section later in this chapter.

Figure 21-1:
The Create Private Key Password prompt during certificate generation.

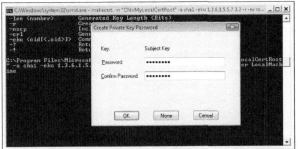

Figure 21-2:
The Enter Private Key Password prompt to load the certificate into the store.

Two files are created in the directory from which you ran `makecert.exe`. These two files are `root.pvk` (the private-key file) and `root.cer` (the certificate/public-key file seen in Figure 21-3). You're probably wondering what the `-eku 1.3.6.1.5.5.7.3.3` part of the command is for. The `-eku` switch specifies enhanced-key-use object IDs (OIDs) for this certificate, and that unique number is the OID for a code-signing certificate.

Before you can sign one of your scripts, you have to create a personal code-signing certificate derived from this trusted root certificate. You do that by using this command:

```
makecert.exe -pe -n "CN=My PowerShell Cert" -ss MY -a sha1 -eku 1.3.6.1.5.5.7.3.3
             -iv root.pvk -ic root.cer
```

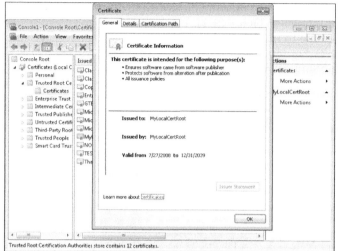

Figure 21-3:
The newly created trusted root certificate.

You see that familiar code-signing OID again, along with references to the root private key and certificate. When you enter the password for the private key, you generate a new certificate that will be stored in the Personal Certificates store. Figure 21-4 shows what a personal signing certificate looks like.

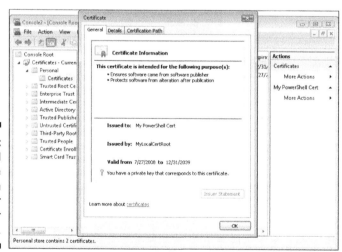

Figure 21-4:
Personal certificate that can be used for signing your scripts.

Requesting a certificate from your Enterprise CA

If you happen to have a Microsoft Enterprise CA in place in your environment, generating a code signing certificate is a much easier process. First, you must make sure that users who want to generate their own code-signing certificate have the necessary permissions on the Code Signing certificate template. Assuming that everything is in place and ready to go, then you must follow these steps:

1. **As the user, open the certificate's Microsoft Management Console (MMC) snap-in.**
2. **Right-click on Personal and select Certificates.**
3. **Choose All Tasks⇨Request New Certificate.**
4. **Select the Code Signing template and then click the Enroll button (see Figure 21-5).**

   Your certificate is generated by the server and automatically imported into your Personal Certificates store. Figure 21-6 shows what this certificate will look like.

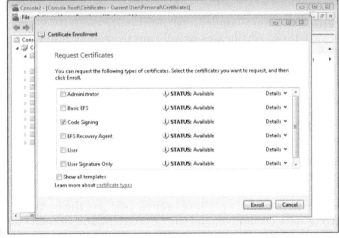

Figure 21-5: Requesting a code-signing certificate from an enterprise CA.

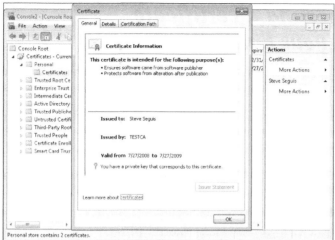

Figure 21-6:
The
Personal
Certificate
from an
enterprise
CA that you
can use to
sign your
scripts.

As you can see by comparing Figure 21-4 and Figure 21-6, there's no functional difference between these two certificates. The one issued by the enterprise CA has the advantage, however, because it's derived from the certificate of the trusted root certificate issuer within your organization. This means that if you sign your script with this certificate, the script will be trusted by other hosts in your domain.

Using a certificate from a commercial, third-party trusted CA can come in useful because these certificates usually are trusted by other organizations as well. You can easily sign a script with your commercial certificate and send it off to a different organization, and the script should run there as well.

Browsing the Certificate Store

In keeping with Windows PowerShell's virtual drive paradigm, the *certificate store* itself is treated as a virtual PowerShell drive. You access it by going to the CERT: drive. The two main braches are CurrentUser and LocalMachine. The CurrentUser branch contains the certificates attached to the current user credential, and the LocalMachine branch contains certificates stored for the entire computer.

Whether you used the self-signing method or requested a certificate from your CA to generate your code-signing certificate, you should now have a certificate in your personal certificate store. This is how you query your personal certificate store for any installed code-signing certificates:

```
Get-ChildItem cert:\CurrentUser\My -codesigning
```

Normally, you have only one certificate in your store based on what you used to generate your certificate, but it's entirely possible to have more than one code-signing certificate. I have two certificates on my computer, for example. I created one by using `makecert.exe` and generated the other one by sending a request to my enterprise CA.

Signing Your Scripts

Before you can sign your scripts with these certificates, you have to be able to get a reference to your certificate from within Windows PowerShell. If you have only one certificate, you do this by running

```
(Get-ChildItem cert:\CurrentUser\My -codesigning)[0]
```

This code assumes that you have only one certificate for code signing, so it may not work as you expect if you have more than one certificate. This little piece of code grabs the first certificate in the list, but that certificate may not be the one you want to use to sign your scripts. If you have more than one certificate, a much better method is to explicitly select the certificate you want to use for signing.

Each certificate has a `Subject` attribute. You can use this attribute to select which certificate you want to use by passing your personal certificate store through the `Where-Object` Cmdlet and explicitly naming the subject of the certificate you want to use. In this example, I'm explicitly choosing the certificate that has the subject `"CN=My PowerShell Cert"` (which, you may recall, is the name of the certificate I use to create a certificate with `make cert.exe` in "Creating a self-signed certificate," earlier in this chapter):

```
Get-ChildItem cert:\CurrentUser\My -codesigning | Where-Object {$_.Subject -eq
    "CN=My PowerShell Cert"}
```

I know it seems that I've taken a really long road to get to this point, but the fact is that signing your script is easy as long as you have a certificate ready to go. The most complicated part of the process is obtaining a certificate to use.

You sign scripts by using the `Set-AuthenticationSignature` Cmdlet. This Cmdlet takes two parameters: the name of the script and the certificate to use to sign it. You'd run this command to sign a script called `signme.ps1`, using the certificate with the subject `"CN=My PowerShell Cert"`:

```
Set-AuthenticationSignature c:\scripts\signme.ps1 (Get-ChildItem cert:\
          CurrentUser\My -codesigning | Where-Object {$_.Subject -eq "CN=My
          PowerShell Cert"})
```

If you open your signed script, you find that it now contains an additional
commented section at the very end, with this section containing the signature block. Here's how the signme.ps1 script looks after you sign it with
your certificate:

```
Write-Host "My Sign Me Script"

# SIG # Begin signature block
# MIIEAAYJKoZIhvcNAQcCoIID8TCCA+0CAQExCzAJBgUrDgMCGgUAMGkGCisGAQQB
# gjcCAQSgWzBZMDQGCisGAQQBgjcCAR4wJgIDAQAABBAfzDtgWUsITrck0sYpfvNR
# AgEAAgEAAgEAAgEAAgEAMCEwCQYFKw4DAhoFAAQUe9+1h6HWnhddsp/7T49CVbF0
# 7q6gggIcMIICGDCCAYWgAwIBAgIQfgk+sX3GA5JNBIJCH9VmQzAJBgUrDgMCHQUA
# MBoxGDAWBgNVBAMTD015TG9jYWxDZXJ0Um9vdDAeFw0wODA3MjgwMjUxMjFaFw0z
# OTEyMzEyMzU5NTlaMB0xGzAZBgNVBAMTEk15IFBvd2VyU2hlbGwgQ2VydDCBnzAN
# BgkqhkiG9w0BAQEFAAOBjQAwgYkCgYEA1xE3HmkLuygF4a1HxAYME6dgWzxJb2h/
# LEuv+rcwMSDW6t733yNir7rK8VRpBE7RKXPYdkF/dG1/5ydk05lOFLbkLti62GD2
# 7qEmK+OvB9iLr/isr1B1JF/0u6K+YzMr2YSbTHoKLhqBn+Klayqx3emQsfiiWWuf
# Bk6bNy0+flkCAwEAAaNkMGIwEwYDVR0lBAwwCgYIKIwYBBQUHAwMwSwYDVR0BBEQw
# QoAQgC2qP6VoJ5ygfxxoNmooR6EcMBoxGDAWBgNVBAMTD015TG9jYWxDZXJ0Um9v
# dIIQ1XXwiiRdJIhBW39Hw2Q8/jAJBgUrDgMCHQUAA4GBAENH1nQjNE4ojzG1vWkB
# AnZ7S4OFMgYjVyQ9rD9WAL566sFoy+OaQUGjR3Q51rRxrfw16u9K6vFw3QoGfJBN
# KuLYF9NnUYZNyXOCjyVS1061PC81iHUZwOoEDmIWzPPrkkIzNjBLX64csW0FNicA
# ahl4n6zcFaSGliiE0/OOaMy5MYIBTjCCAUoCAQEwLjAaMRgwFgYDVQQDEw9NeUxv
# Y2FsQ2VydFJvb3QCEH4JPrF9xgOSTQSCQh/VZkMwCQYFKw4DAhoFAKB4MBgGCisG
# AQQBgjcCAQwxCjAIoAKAAKECgAAwGQYJKoZIhvcNAQkDMQwGCisGAQQBgjcCAQQw
# HAYKKwYBBAGCNwIBCzEOMAwGCisGAQQBgjcCARUwIwYJKoZIhvcNAQkEMRYEFFJm
# Ut/wSfvkIWJUof2VfpXfE1zMMA0GCSqGSIb3DQEBAQUABIGAHsHfqq3HWq51uKob
# b0CNkAoH4irbN4mA8ukoYXE93e0SiOPee93wS8pojUQh/5eEKBYBNYPRQXBhvz4M
# 8/5KNRfVcH/IffpMCr/7Z5guajYelj9NOGAquM7Ls7K/dyCJwXRBJbbr19cC/Nj2
# iv05yfrioKcqxdHT3AP5RIdcF7A=
# SIG # End signature block
```

If you try to modify this script, Windows Powershell reads this as an invalid
signature, and the script won't be allowed to run.

If you want to save yourself from having to type these commands each and
every time you sign your scripts, you can create a function to automate this
process for you and stick this function in your profile script for use any time.
Here's an example:

```
function SignScript([string]$script)
{
    Set-AuthenticationSignature $script Get-ChildItem cert:\CurrentUser\My
              -codesigning | Where-Object {$_.Subject -eq "CN=My PowerShell
              Cert"}
}
```

Now if you want to sign the `signme.ps1` script again, you just need to run

```
SignScript "c:\scripts\signme.ps1"
```

Managing the Windows Firewall

One of the best ways to protect your operating system is to put it behind a firewall. Ideally, the operating system should sit behind dedicated hardware firewalls, but even a software-based firewall such as the built-in Windows Firewall is an added level of security that can help you keep your system protected. Before I go on, I'm going to make the assumption that you already know what the Windows Firewall is and how it works.

You can manage the Windows Firewall through the `HNetCfg.FwMgr` Component Object Model (COM) object. The most basic setting is whether the firewall is enabled in the first place. You can easily determine this status by running this bit of code:

```
$objFW =  New-Object -com hnetcfg.fwmgr
$objFW.LocalPolicy.CurrentProfile.FirewallEnabled
```

If the firewall is turned off (in which case the value of `FirewallEnabled` will be `false`), you can turn it on by entering this code:

```
$objFW.LocalPolicy.CurrentProfile.FirewallEnabled = $true
```

Although you can enable the firewall by using this method, Windows won't let you turn it off by using the COM interface, which is probably a good thing. Otherwise, it would be a really easy way for malicious code that someone was able to run on your computer to shut off the firewall.

The firewall's current profile is the key to reading and configuring all the firewall settings. The two other general settings that you may want to configure are whether exceptions are allowed and whether you want to be notified whenever the firewall blocks a new program. To configure these settings, you set the `CurrentProfile`'s `ExceptionNotAllowed` and `NotificationsDisabled` properties, respectively. The default value for both of these properties is `false`, which means that exceptions are allowed and notifications are enabled.

One of the most common changes people make is to allow *ping requests* (inbound Internet Control Message Protocol [ICMP] echo requests) to go through. This capability isn't allowed by default, but people like the capability to determine whether a host is up. To enable this capability, you have to configure it through the `IcmpSettings` of the current profile, like this:

```
$objFW.LocalPolicy.CurrentProfile.IcmpSettings.AllowInboundEchoRequests = $true
```

In general, it's fine to enable this setting when the host is on your internal network. If the host is exposed directly to the Internet, disabling ICMP echo requests is good practice; when you do, malicious users on the Internet can't easily detect that your host is online.

Another popular option is enabling remote administration of the firewall by setting the `Enable` property of the `RemoteAdminSettings` property to `true`, like this:

```
$objFW.LocalPolicy.CurrentProfile.RemoteAdminSettings.Enabled = $true
```

The three collections in the `CurrentProfile` of significant interest are `GloballyOpenPorts`, `Services`, and `AuthorizedApplications`. If exceptions are allowed, the rules defined in any of these three collections ultimately determine whether a certain connection is allowed.

Defining globally open ports

Depending on what you've installed on your computer, you may have some globally open ports already defined. In simple terms, *globally open ports* define what ports are globally allowed to be used on your system for communicating with other hosts. You can list them all by getting the contents of the `GloballyOpenPorts` property of the current profile with this code:

```
$objFW.LocalPolicy.CurrentProfile.GloballyOpenPorts
```

You can create your new `GloballyOpenPorts` rules by creating a `HNetCfg.FWOpenPort` object, setting its various properties, and then adding it to the `GloballyOpenPorts` collection. Here's a code snippet that lets you add a rule to open port 8080 for Transmission Control Protocol (TCP) traffic:

```
$objFW =  New-Object -com hnetcfg.fwmgr
$portRule = New-Object -com hnetcfg.fwopenport
$portRule.Name = "MyHTTP"
$portRule.Protocol = 6
$portRule.Port = 8080
$portRule.Enabled = $true
$objFW.LocalPolicy.CurrentProfile.GloballyOpenPorts.Add($portRule)
```

As you can see, this code is really straightforward. The only property that needs explanation is the `Protocol` property, which defines whether the rule is for TCP or UDP. To configure this rule for TCP, set this value to 6; to configure this rule for UDP, set this value to 16.

Listing firewall services

Windows also has a set of defined services it can provide, such as file and Printer Sharing, Network Discovery, and Remote Desktop, that are all blocked by the firewall by default. These services are associated with one or more `GloballyOpenPorts` rules. You can get a list of all these services and their associated ports by running this bit of code.

```
$objFW = New-Object -com hnetcfg.fwmgr
foreach($service in $objFW.LocalPolicy.CurrentProfile.Services) {
   Write-Host ("Service Name: " + $service.Name)
   Write-Host ("Service Type: " + $service.Type)
   Write-Host ("Service Customized: " + $service.Customized)
   Write-Host ("Service IP Version: " + $service.IpVersion)
   Write-Host ("Service Remote Addresses: " + $service.RemoteAddresses)
   Write-Host ("Service Enabled: " + $service.Enabled)
   foreach($port in $service.GloballyOpenPorts) {
      Write-Host ("`tPort Name: " + $port.Name)
      Write-Host ("`tPort number: " + $port.Port)
      Write-Host ("`tPort Protocol: " + $port.Protocol)
      Write-Host ("`tPort Enabled: " + $port.Enabled)
   }
   Write-Host "`n"
}
```

When you enable one of these services, the associated `GloballyOpenPorts` rules also become enabled. This makes your life easier since enabling complicated services like File and Print Services only requires enabling one service and you don't have to worry about knowing which ports you have to open — they're all defined in the `GloballyOpenPorts` property of the service and are automatically taken care of for you. Here's a simple bit of code you can use to enable File and Printer Sharing through the Windows firewall:

```
$objFW = New-Object -com hnetcfg.fwmgr
$service = $objFW.LocalPolicy.CurrentProfile.Services | Where-Object {$_.Name
            -eq "File and Printer Sharing"}
$service.Enabled = $true
```

Now, if you rerun the little script to list the services defined in the firewall, you'll see that File and Printer Sharing along with all associated port policies have been enabled.

Allowing applications to get through

Application firewall policies are really easy ways you can allow applications to work through the firewall without having to know every port the application uses. Rather than defining rules based on ports, you simply provide the name of the application's executable name and where it's allowed to talk to and you're all set — the Windows firewall is intelligent enough to take care of the rest. There aren't any applications allowed by default, but if you've allowed applications to go through, you can find out what they are by querying the AuthorizedApplications property of the current profile.

```
$objFW = New-Object -com hnetcfg.fwmgr
$objFW.LocalPolicy.CurrentProfile.AuthorizedApplications
```

You can create new application policies by creating a new HNetCfg.
FwAuthorizedApplication COM object, populating the various properties that define the application, and then adding it to the AuthorizedApplications collection for the profile. Here's an example for allowing ftp.exe to go through the firewall:

```
$objFW = New-Object -com hnetcfg.fwmgr
$objApp = New-Object -com hnetcfg.fwauthorizedapplication
$objApp.Name = "FTP Command Line"
$objApp.ProcessImageFileName = "C:\windows\system32\ftp.exe"
$objApp.RemoteAddresses = "*"
$objApp.Enabled = $true
$objFW.LocalPolicy.CurrentProfile.AuthorizedApplications.Add($objApp)
```

Chapter 22

Converting Your Old Scripts: Out with the Old, In with the New

*I*f you've been in the business of Windows administration for any amount of time, you probably already have a collection of scripts that you use to make your life easier. More than likely, these scripts are written in Windows Shell Scripting (also known as *batch files*) or in VBScript or JScript for Windows Scripting Host (WSH). Most of the time, it makes the most sense to continue using those scripts in their current form and to use Windows PowerShell for any new scripts you create.

Although that system is the path of least resistance, when it comes to understanding a new scripting language, nothing is better than revisiting old scripts and converting them to the new language. For starters, it gives you the opportunity to go over your old code to see where you can improve. I've done this a couple of times, only to find myself chuckling over rookie mistakes and, in some cases, finding dramatic changes that increase the script's performance and reliability. The other benefit is that you already know the logic of the old script, so the exercise of converting it to Windows PowerShell is purely that of understanding how to do the same thing in a new language.

In this chapter, you explore techniques for migrating your existing Windows Shell or Windows Scripting Host scripts to Windows PowerShell. Although I can't promise that converting your scripts to Powershell will make those scripts run faster, I can confidently say that it won't get any more complicated. In fact, in many cases, you'll find that it's much easier to accomplish the same things in PowerShell.

Converting a Windows Shell Script to Windows PowerShell

I usually get laughed at whenever I use the term *Windows Shell Script* in talking about batch files in Windows 2000 and later, but the difference is important. Batch files are designed to run a series of commands in sequence with very limited (almost nonexistent) logic statements to control how things run. In Windows 2000 and later, a lot more keywords and constructs were added to the Windows command shell, making it possible to do things like construct `for` loops and use `if/else` statements to run more than a single command if a particular condition is met.

Windows Shell Scripting is a fairly weak scripting language, but its biggest advantage is that it's supported out of the box in every Windows operating system without your having to install anything. You can overcome its limitations by taking advantage of powerful command line utilities. Converting these scripts to Windows PowerShell is as simple as it gets, because there are only a few things you can do in Windows Shell Scripting that you'll have to translate to Windows PowerShell.

Echoing to the screen

The ability to display something onscreen for the user to read is the most basic form of user feedback. You do this by using the `Echo` command, which has existed forever. You accomplish the same task in Windows PowerShell by using the `Write-Host` Cmdlet, so these two commands are equivalent:

```
Echo Hello World
Write-Host "Hello World"
```

The `Echo` command is so widely used that in Windows PowerShell, `Echo` is the alias for `Write-Host`, so you can continue to use `Echo` if you're really stubborn.

Many of the aliases that link back to old commands were created by the Windows PowerShell developers to help with the transition to Windows PowerShell. Although these aliases are convenient, and the likelihood that they'll go away is very slim, you probably shouldn't rely on them. Instead, use the real Cmdlet names when converting your scripts. Hey, those names even look fancier, so this practice may have the side effect of making you look smarter to the uninitiated!

Using conditional statements

The most basic way to branch out into different parts of your Windows Shell Script is to use `if/else` clauses. The two most common uses for `if/else` clauses are to compare values and to check whether a file or folder exists. The first use is simple; it's just a check to see whether two values are the same (or, in the case of numbers, whether one value is greater or less than the other). This check often looks like this:

```
set a=test
if %a%==test Echo The value is test!
```

You can also throw in an `else` statement, like this:

```
set a=2
if %a% EQU 2 (
    Echo The value is two!
) else (
    Echo The value is not two!
)
```

Both of these examples compare whether two values are equal. The difference between the double equal sign in the first example and `EQU` in the second example is that the double equal sign is used to compare strings, whereas `EQU` is used to compare numbers.

Converting this to Windows PowerShell is just child's play:

```
$a = 2
if ($a -eq 2)
{
    Write-Host "The value is two!"
}
else
{
    Write-Host "The value is not two!"
}
```

Windows Shell Scripting also has the ability to compare one number with another by using a few different operators. Table 22-1 shows you how these operators map to the equivalent PowerShell operators.

Table 22-1	Value Comparison Operators	
Windows Shell Scripting	*Windows PowerShell*	*Meaning*
EQU	-eq	Equal
NEQ	-ne	Not equal
LSS	-lt	Less than
LEQ	-le	Less than or equal
GTR	-gt	Greater than
GEQ	-ge	Greater than or equal

Migrating that FOR command

One of the tricks in Windows Shell Scripting is to use the FOR command to take the contents of a file or the output of a command and then do something with it. Because you'd use the Windows Shell Script FOR command in many scenarios, I'm going to address each scenario and show you how to do exactly the same thing in Windows PowerShell.

Performing some action for each line in a text file

This scenario is by far the most common reason to use the FOR command. Suppose that you have a text file containing a bunch of computer names, one on each line, and want to perform some action on them (such as pinging those computer names). Here's a quick example of a Windows Shell Script that pings each computer listed in a text file called computers.txt located in the current directory and, if the computer responds, copies a file called processed.txt to the top of the C: drive:

```
FOR /F %%i in (computers.txt) do call :dosomething %%i
goto :EOF

:dosomething
set compname=%1
ping %compname% | find "Reply" > NUL
IF %ERRORLEVEL% NEQ 0 goto :EOF
copy processed.txt \\%compname%\c$
goto :EOF
```

Here's how you accomplish the same thing by using Windows PowerShell:

```
$data = Get-Content computers.txt
foreach($line in $data)
{
```

```
$pingresult = Get-WmiObject -query "select * from win32_pingstatus where
        address='$line'"
if ($pingresult.StatusCode -eq 0)
{
    Copy-Item processed.txt \\$line\c$
}
}
```

The main difference is that the `foreach` command in Windows PowerShell can't read directly from a file, so you have to use the `Get-Content` Cmdlet to read the contents of the file. Then you use a `foreach` loop to loop through the contents, because the return value of `Get-Content` is an array of objects, with each object representing a line in the file. To ping the host, you use the `Get-WmiObject` Cmdlet to query the `Win32_PingStatus` WMI class. If the `StatusCode` property of the resulting object is 0, the hostname you supplied was pinged successfully, so you can go ahead and copy the file to that computer.

Another method of pinging a host involves using the `System.Net.NetworkInformation.Ping` .NET class. The only difference is that if the .NET class can't ping the host because it can't resolve the name to an IP, it throws an exception (error), which you have to handle.

Using a FOR loop to split text

Another popular use of the FOR loop in Windows Shell Scripting is tokenizing a string. *Tokenizing* means that you want to split some text by using a delimiter to mark where the string should be split. You may have a text file that contains some information such as username, last name, and first name in comma-separated values (CSV) format, and you want to extract the last name and first name from each line and combine them to form a full name. Here's what the input file may look like:

```
sseguis,Seguis,Steve
bstewart,Stewart,Bryan
bfranklin,Franklin,Bob
```

The Windows Shell Script to extract the last name and first name (second and third columns) of this file and put them together looks like this:

```
for /f "Tokens=2,3 delims=," %%i in (users.txt) do call :makedisplayname %%i %%j
goto :EOF

:makedisplayname
set lastname=%1
set firstname=%2
echo %firstname% %lastname%
goto :EOF
```

You actually have two ways to solve this problem in Windows PowerShell. The long way is to use Get-Content to grab the contents of the file, run it through a foreach loop, and then use the string's split method to chop the string into its parts. The preferred method is to use the Import-CSV Cmdlet, as it encapsulates what you're trying to achieve:

```
$header = "username","lastname","firstname"
$contents = Import-CSV users.txt -header $header
foreach($user in $contents)
{
    Write-Host $user.firstname $user.lastname
}
```

Notice how much more straightforward that code looks. Import-CSV assumes that the first line in the file contains the header information (names of each of the columns), so if you don't have a header, as is the case here, you have to supply the header information yourself by using the -header parameter. The best part is that each line of the file is automatically parsed and converted to an object, with each row being assigned its appropriate header name, so it's easy to refer to the firstname and lastname fields as needed.

That entire PowerShell code snippet can be replaced by a single line of Windows PowerShell code, if you really want to impress:

```
Import-CSV users.txt -header "username","lastname","firstname" | Select-Object
         "lastname","firstname" | ForEach-Object {Write-Host $_.firstname
         $_.lastname}
```

Although Import-CSV is designed to parse files that are comma delimited, one of the enhancements of this Cmdlet in Windows PowerShell 2 supports a -Delimiter parameter, allowing you to specify what the delimiter in the file should be. This is how you'd import a users.txt file that's delimited by the pipe character (|) rather than a command:

```
Import-CSV users.txt -header $header -delimiter |
```

Converting a Windows Scripting Host Script to Windows PowerShell

Windows Scripting Host (WSH) has been around for several generations of Windows now, and has been installed and included by default since Windows 2000. As a result, it has become the most popular platform to script on for work with any of the Windows operating systems. You may have downloaded WSH scripts or written a few from scratch yourself. I'm fairly certain that no Windows shops out there are without some kind of WSH script.

WSH scripts are usually written either in VBScript or JScript. Whether you use one or the other is purely preference. Personally, when using WSH, I write in VBScript 99 percent of the time and use JScript for things that just happen to be easier to do in JScript.

Because WSH is a large topic, and many books have been written on it, there's no way I can cover everything you need to know to convert all your WSH scripts to Windows PowerShell. If the stuff you have is really compli-cated, it makes far more sense to examine how the script works and rethink it in Windows PowerShell than to try to do a verbatim conversion. Interestingly enough, the vast majority of WSH scripts use only a few different, important techniques, which are reused in many ways. I focus on those scripts in this section. After all, when you know how to do something one way, it's easy to figure out how to apply that technique to similar tasks.

Comparing the basics

You already know how to do simple things like echoing something to the screen and using if statements and for loops. (If not, you may want to refresh a bit by taking a look at Chapter 6.) All the looping and switching con-structs in WSH have direct counterparts in Windows PowerShell. Both WSH and Windows PowerShell have variables that can be *variant,* which means that they can take the value of any data type.

The biggest difference between the two is that WSH scripts are compiled in real time, when you run them, whereas Windows PowerShell scripts are inter-preted. Why should you care? Because WSH scripts are compiled just before execution, you can do things like put functions and subprocedures anywhere in the script file and use them within your script normally. In Windows PowerShell, because it's interpreted, any function that you want to create and use has to be defined *before* it can be used. What this generally means is that you have to write all your functions at the top of the script before you can actually use them; otherwise, Windows PowerShell spits out an error saying that the function is not recognized when it gets to that point within your script.

In case you don't know, a clear distinction exists between functions and sub-procedures in VBScript. The main difference is that functions can return a value, whereas subprocedures can't. Windows PowerShell doesn't have such a distinction.

Working with COM objects

One of the most attractive features of WSH, and one that makes it very popu-lar, is that WSH makes it easy to create instances of Component Object Model

(COM) objects and interact with them. Anything installed in Windows that has a COM interface (such as Microsoft Office) can be manipulated through WSH. Windows PowerShell is no different — and can interact easily with .NET objects as well.

The COM object that I see most commonly in WSH scripts is `Scripting.FileSystemObject`. You use that object to manipulate files within the file system, including reading from and writing to files. In Windows PowerShell, you don't have to rely on this COM object to do this job, because plenty of Cmdlets can do it for you. I cover this topic a bit later in this chapter, in the section "Handling I/O."

An example of the need to use COM even in Windows PowerShell is when you interact with Microsoft Office applications. It's quite popular to take input from a Microsoft Excel document or even use Excel to generate and format reports from data collected by your script. Here's a simple WSH script that creates an instance of Excel, adds a workbook, makes the workbook visible, and then populates the first ten rows of the first column:

```
Set objXL = CreateObject("Excel.Application")
objXL.workbooks.add
objXL.Visible = TRUE

For x = 1 to 10
    objXL.Cells(x,1).value = x
Next

Set objXL = Nothing
```

When you convert that piece of code to Windows PowerShell, it looks like this:

```
$objXL = New-Object -ComObject Excel.Application
[void]$objXL.Workbooks.Add()
$objXL.visible = $true

for($x = 1; $x -le 10; $x++)
{
    $objXL.Cells.item($x,1) = $x
}

Remove-Variable objXL
```

You can see that the two pieces of code are almost mirrors, except that depending on the COM object you're using, you may have to accommodate some idiosyncrasies of Windows PowerShell. The `Excel.Application`'s `workbooks.add` method returns a `Workbook` object, for example. You can assign it to some variable for use later in both VBScript and Windows PowerShell. The assignment of this return value is purely optional. The difference is that in Windows PowerShell, if you don't assign this returned value to a variable, the default behavior occurs, which is to output that object (or, rather, the properties of that object) to the screen. To prevent this result, you cast the call to the `add` method as `[void]`, which sends that output to a virtual black hole.

Any time you do anything in Windows PowerShell that returns a value, and you don't want to store the value in a variable or display it to the screen, you can always prefix it with `[void]` to suppress it.

Another difference between WSH and Windows PowerShell is how you interact with the cells within a worksheet. In VBScript, you just specify which cell you want to act on by specifying the row and column to the `Cells` object and then access its `value` property to read or set its value. In Windows PowerShell, you refer to a cell through the `Cell` object's `item` method, which takes the same row and column values as its VBScript counterpart.

If you run the VBScript and Windows PowerShell versions of that script side by side, you'll find that the VBScript version runs faster than Windows Power Shell. Whereas VBScript interacts with COM objects directly, Windows PowerShell, which is built on top of the .NET Framework, has to use little connectors called *interop assemblies* to allow it to talk to non-.NET objects. This additional layer incurs a performance penalty. For best performance when migrating code that uses COM, see whether a .NET class does the same thing, and if so, use that class instead.

Understanding the difference between CreateObject and GetObject

One detail I gloss over in the preceding section is how to use the `New-Object` to create an instance of a COM object, just like `CreateObject` does in VBScript. The reason is that in VBScript, you can use two methods to interact with and connect to a COM object: `CreateObject` and `GetObject`. The easiest way to understand the subtle but important difference between the two methods is that `CreateObject` creates an instance of a COM object that doesn't exist, whereas `GetObject` references an object that does exist.

You see, whenever you call `CreateObject`, you create a new instance of that object. If you write a script that runs `CreateObject` on `Excel.Application` three times without quitting each instance and then look at Task Manager, you' see three separate Excel processes running — one for each time you called `CreateObject`. This is why `CreateObject` maps itself directly to the `New-Object` Cmdlet with the `-ComObject` switch.

What about GetObject? In practice, GetObject is mostly used for two things in WSH: Windows Management Instrumentation (WMI) and Active Directory Services Interfaces (ADSI). Windows PowerShell simply doesn't have GetObject functionality. Microsoft's Script Center has some hacky workarounds, but again, try to rethink this scenario. If you find yourself longing for the GetObject function because you have scripts that use WMI, when you try to migrate that function to Windows PowerShell, you really should be using the Get-WMIObject Cmdlet instead. This Cmdlet is not only designed to fulfill all your WMI needs, but also uses native .NET assemblies, so it runs faster in Windows PowerShell than COM ever will.

As for relying on GetObject to access ADSI providers such as Lightweight Directory Access Protocol (LDAP) for Active Directory or WinNT to access local security accounts, you don't need to use GetObject for that purpose either. Windows PowerShell is fully capable of talking to ADSI sources directly via the [ADSI] type adapter. A *what* adapter? No Get-ADSIObject, Get-LDAPObject, or Get-WinNTObject Cmdlet is similar to Get-WMIObject. Instead, the way you connect to an ADSI source effectively by casting an ADSI string with the [ADSI] type adapter. Still confused? Don't fret — it's much easier than it sounds. Here's a classic example of a VBScript-based WSH code snippet that uses the ADSI LDAP provider to get the distinguished name for all objects in the users container in Active Directory (I cover Active Directory scripting in greater detail in Chapter 20):

```
strDomain = "DC=testdom,DC=local"
Set objUsersContainer = GetObject("LDAP://cn=users," & strDomain)
For Each objUser in objUsersContainer
    WScript.Echo objUser.Get("distinguishedName")
Next
```

In Windows PowerShell, you bypass the GetObject method and do this instead:

```
$strDomain = "DC=testdom,DC=local"
$objUsersContainer = [ADSI]("LDAP://cn=users," +
        $strDomain)
foreach($objUser in $objUsersContainer.children)
{
    Write-Host $objUser.Get("distinguishedName")
}
```

By prefixing the LDAP string with the [ADSI] type adapter, you're effectively telling Windows PowerShell to go ahead and use the ADSI LDAP provider, which it does natively rather than trying to use the old GetObject method. The only other change is minor and occurs within the for loop: You have to tell the foreach loop explicitly that you want to get to the children of the container object. Otherwise, the script will display simply the distinguished name of the container, not its contents.

Handling I/O

If you want to read/write files or do anything file-system-related, you almost always use `Scripting.FilesystemObject` in WSH to help you out. Luckily, Windows PowerShell makes it just as easy (if not easier) to work with files, so rather than present a bunch of mini scripts for you to compare, I thought it best to present Table 22-2, which shows you how to accomplish a file-system task in WSH and in Windows PowerShell. For the WSH examples, assume that the variable `fso` is an instance of `Scripting.FileSystemObject`.

Table 22-2	Comparing File-System Commands	
Purpose	*WSH (VBScript)*	*Windows PowerShell*
Check whether a file exists	`Fso.FileExists("C:\myfile.txt")`	`Test-Path "C:\myfile.txt"`
Check whether a folder exists	`fso.FolderExists("C:\myfolder")`	`Test-Path "C:\myfolder"`
Check whether a drive exists	`fso.DriveExists("C:")`	`Test-Path "C:"`
Get the filename	`fso.GetFileName("C:\myfile.txt")`	`(Get-ChildItem "C:\myfile.txt").basename`
Get the file extension	`fso.GetExtensionName("C:\myfile.txt")`	`(Get-ChildItem "C:\myfile.txt").extension`
Get the parent folder name	`fso.GetParentFolderName("C:\myfolder\otherfile.txt")`	`(Get-ChildItem "C:\myfolder\otherfile.txt").DirectoryName`
Read the entire contents of a file	`fso.OpenTextFile("C:\myfile.txt", ForReading) contents = fso.ReadAll fso.close`	`$contents = Get-Content "C:\myfile.txt"`

(continued)

Table 22-2 *(continued)*

Purpose	WSH (VBScript)	Windows PowerShell
Read one line of a file	`fso.OpenTextFile("C:\myfile.txt",ForReading) line = fso.ReadLine fso.close`	`$linecontent = Get-Content "C:\myfile.txt" -totalcount 1`
Write a line to a file	`fso.OpenTextFile("C:\myfile.txt",ForWriting,true) fso.writeline("This is a line of text!") fso.close`	`Out-File "C:\myfile.txt" -input "This is a line of text!"`
Append a line to a file	`fso.OpenTextFile("C:\myfile.txt",ForAppending,true) fso.writeline("This is a line of text!") fso.close`	`Add-Content "C:\myfile.txt" -value "This is a line of text!"`

Working with ActiveX Data Objects (ADO)

In the past few years, there has been a significant trend toward using ActiveX Data Objects (ADO) within WSH scripts, not always to access data sources (such as Microsoft SQL), but to take advantage of something called disconnected recordsets. You can think of *disconnected recordsets* as being database tables that you create in memory. The rationale for using ADO is that if you can grab data and put it in tabular format so that it can be inserted into a disconnected recordset, you can take advantage of ADO features to do all kinds of data operations, such as sorting and filtering. These functions are highly efficient, and this technique has proved to be highly effective for those who write complex WSH-based data processing scripts.

ActiveX is the product name, if you will, that Microsoft gave to its Component Object Model, which today is referred to simply as COM. ActiveX and COM are one and the same thing.

ADO is COM–based, as its name implies, so it's tempting to use the New-Object Cmdlet with the -ComObject switch to create ADO objects and do as you please. The problem, of course, is that any time you work with COM from Windows PowerShell, performance is a bit on the slow side, and in many cases in which existing ADO–based scripts are used, you notice a marked and possibly unacceptable performance decrease if you try to port this script directly to Windows PowerShell as is. You get around this performance bottleneck by saying good-bye to ADO and saying hello to ADO.NET.

Leveraging ADO.NET to your advantage

As the name implies, ADO.NET is a .NET version of your old friend ADO. It takes the ADO functionality and puts it into .NET–managed code by creating a well-defined set of .NET classes that duplicate and then improve on the old ADO concepts. I wouldn't exactly call it ADO on steroids, but certainly, from Windows PowerShell's perspective, ADO.NET is the more civilized and well-mannered version of its COM–based sibling.

The upside of using ADO.NET is that it's faster, uses well-defined .NET data types, and works predictively like other .NET classes in terms of the names of the methods and properties used. The downside exists only if you're trying to bring over code written to use the old ADO, because you first have to figure out how to do the same thing in ADO.NET by using its new classes and methods. The hard reality is that even if you try to fudge by reusing your ADO code directly, you inevitably run into strange little Windows PowerShell idiosyncrasies that force you to look up the Windows PowerShell method anyway.

An ADO `RecordSet` is typically the data returned as a result of some query. A disconnected recordset occurs when you disconnect from the source such as the SQL database) while keeping the recordset in memory. You can keep using the recordset without having to stay connected to the source, which is a really good thing, because you don't have to tie up a connection to use the data. You can also create a disconnected recordset manually, which allows you to store data in memory in a very convenient tabular format.

You create a disconnected recordset manually by creating an instance of the `ADODB.Recordset` object. Next, you use its `Fields.Append` method to define the various columns in your recordset. Then you read in some generally structured data (such as those in a CSV-value or XML flat file) and insert that data into the recordset. When all your data has been converted from whatever format it's in to the columns you've defined in your recordset, you can take advantage of sort and filtering methods to extract the data you want from it.

Generally, WSH scripts that use ADO are very long. The next example contains all the elements I just talked about, but I keep it as simple as possible so that you can focus on how to convert it rather than wasting brain cells trying to figure out what I'm doing in the script in the first place. The script in the example creates a recordset with three columns — username, firstname, and lastname — defined as columns of the `varchar` (variable number of characters) data type and having a length of 100 characters. I add a few rows to the recordset, display its contents first in current unsorted order, and then display the contents again after sorting by the username column. Finally, I create a filter so that only usernames starting with the letter b get included and then output the recordset again. Here's the example:

```
CONST adVarChar = 200

Set objADORS = CreateObject("ADODB.Recordset")
objADORS.Fields.Append "username",adVarChar,100
objADORS.Fields.Append "firstname",adVarChar,100
objADORS.Fields.Append "lastname",adVarChar,100
objADORS.Open

objADORS.AddNew
objADORS("username") = "sseguis"
objADORS("firstname") = "Steve"
objADORS("lastname") = "Seguis"
objADORS.Update

objADORS.AddNew
objADORS("username") = "bstewart"
objADORS("firstname") = "Bryan"
objADORS("lastname") = "Stewart"
objADORS.Update

objADORS.AddNew
objADORS("username") = "bfranklin"
objADORS("firstname") = "Bob"
objADORS("lastname") = "Franklin"
objADORS.Update

WScript.Echo "Unsorted..."
objADORS.Movefirst
While Not objADORS.EOF
   WScript.echo objADORS("username") & " - " & objADORS("firstname") & " " &
            objADORS("lastname")
   objADORS.Movenext
Wend
WScript.Echo ""
WScript.Echo "Sorted by username..."
objADORS.Sort="username"
objADORS.Movefirst
While Not objADORS.EOF
   WScript.echo objADORS("username") & " - " & objADORS("firstname") & " " &
            objADORS("lastname")
   objADORS.Movenext
Wend

WScript.Echo ""
WScript.Echo "Filtered for usernames starting with the letter B..."
```

```
objADORS.Filter="username LIKE 'b*'"
objADORS.Movefirst
While Not objADORS.EOF
   WScript.echo objADORS("username") & " - " & objADORS("firstname") & " " &
                objADORS("lastname")
   objADORS.Movenext
Wend

Set objADORS = Nothing
```

The output of this script is

```
Unsorted...
sseguis - Steve Seguis
bstewart - Bryan Stewart
bfranklin - Bob Franklin

Sorted by username...
bfranklin - Bob Franklin
bstewart - Bryan Stewart
sseguis - Steve Seguis

Filtered for usernames starting with the letter B...
bfranklin - Bob Franklin
bstewart - Bryan Stewart
```

ADO.NET doesn't have a `RecordSet` object; instead, you use the `System.Data.DataTable` class to achieve the same effect. To achieve the same effect as the preceding WSH–based script, you have to

1. Create an instance of `System.Data.DataSet`.

2. Add a table (`System.Data.DataTable`) to the dataset.

3. Add columns (`System.Data.DataColumn`) to the tables.

4. For each entry you want to add to the tables, create a new row (`System.Data.DataRow`), populate the data, and then add the row to the table.

You display the row in the `DataTable` object by looping through it, using a `foreach` loop. The only caveat is that unlike ADO's `RecordSet` object, a `DataTable` object can't be sorted or filtered. ADO.NET separates the data from its presentation, so sorting and filtering are actually done by changing these properties for the view (`System.Data.DataView`) associated with the `DataTable`. The result is equally fast code with exactly the same output:

```
$objDS = New-Object system.Data.DataSet
$objDS.Tables.Add("userlist")
[void]$objDS.Tables["userlist"].Columns.Add("username",[string])
[void]$objDS.Tables["userlist"].Columns.Add("firstname",[string])
[void]$objDS.Tables["userlist"].Columns.Add("lastname",[string])
```

```
$objDR = $objDS.Tables["userlist"].NewRow()
$objDR["username"] = "sseguis"
$objDR["firstname"] = "Steve"
$objDR["lastname"] = "Seguis"
$objDS.Tables["userlist"].Rows.Add($objDR)

$objDR = $objDS.Tables["userlist"].NewRow()
$objDR["username"] = "bstewart"
$objDR["firstname"] = "Bryan"
$objDR["lastname"] = "Stewart"
$objDS.Tables["userlist"].Rows.Add($objDR)

$objDR = $objDS.Tables["userlist"].NewRow()
$objDR["username"] = "bfranklin"
$objDR["firstname"] = "Bob"
$objDR["lastname"] = "Franklin"
$objDS.Tables["userlist"].Rows.Add($objDR)

Write-Host "Unsorted..."
foreach($row in $objDS.Tables["userlist"])
{
   Write-Host ($row["username"] + " - " + $row["firstname"] + " " +
               $row["lastname"])
}

Write-Host "`nSorted by username..."
$objDV = $objDS.Tables["userlist"].Defaultview
$objDV.Sort = "username"
foreach($row in $objDV)
{
   Write-Host ($row["username"] + " - " + $row["firstname"] + " " +
               $row["lastname"])
}

Write-Host "`nFiltered for usernames starting with the letter B..."
$objDV.RowFilter = "username LIKE 'b*'"
foreach($row in $objDV)
{
   Write-Host ($row["username"] + " - " + $row["firstname"] + " " +
               $row["lastname"])
}
```

On additional thing to point out is that ADO.NET uses standard .NET data types, so when you define the columns, you don't use data types like `varchar` and define the columns' length. Instead, you tell ADO.NET to use the `String` data type, which grows automatically to accommodate text of any length.

Part VI
Configuring and Reporting Via PowerShell

The 5th Wave   By Rich Tennant

©RICHTENNANT

"Great goulash, Stan. That reminds me, are you still scripting your own Web page?"

PowerShell

In this part . . .

I'm rounding off the book with topics that I feel are important to discuss but don't fit cleanly into the other parts of this book. I cover managing your network configuration through Windows PowerShell in Chapter 23. Gathering hardware info and connecting to printers is addressed in Chapter 24. I also talk a bit about using Windows PowerShell to generate simple reports from the data retrieved by Cmdlets or even your own scripts in Chapter 25. Even if you don't necessarily have the need for this kind of functionality today, I recommend going over these chapters anyway because many of the techniques I use in these chapters apply to all kinds of situations, so there's a lot in there to pick up from.

Chapter 23

Controlling Your Network Configuration

C omputers are pretty cool by themselves, but they show their true potential when they're networked. Have you ever been without Internet connectivity for a week? How about a day? Did you feel lost and disconnected from the world? No, this discussion isn't the prelude to an antidepressant drug commercial; I'm merely pointing out that getting online has become as important to people as having their morning coffee.

Network settings are often configured automatically through the use of a Dynamic Host Configuration Protocol (DHCP) server, which dishes out IP addresses and DNS addresses to requesting hosts such as your computer. This DHCP server functionality can exist in your home router that connects you to the Internet or, in corporate environments, run on servers. Either way, the result is the same: You plug in your Ethernet cable or set up your wireless connection, and your computer automatically gets the settings it needs to talk to other computers on your network and even out on the Internet.

In this chapter, you explore Windows PowerShell's ability to query and make changes to your network configuration. You also use the HNnetCfg.FwMgr COM object to control the Windows Firewall.

Managing Your Network Settings

In some cases, you may want to manually configure the network settings on the host directly. This scenario is typical for servers that need fixed IP addresses so that other computers can locate them and for computers that have special requirements (such as your home computer, if you want to set up features like port forwarding on your router so that applications like video-conferencing or certain games work correctly). Whatever the reason, you can manage your network settings through the Windows GUI or, if you're a bit more savvy, through command line tools or even Windows PowerShell.

Command line tools such as *netsh* (network shell) are often used to perform command line configuration of network interface settings. This tool works great, but the downside is that netsh has no real scripting or programming capabilities built in. If you want to do something unique, such as configure the DNS server's IP address based on a computer name, netsh can't help you directly. You still have to rely on scripting languages such as Windows Shell Scripting or Windows Scripting Host (WSH) to do this logic for you and then run netsh with the parameters you derive.

Familiarizing yourself with Win32_ NetworkAdapterConfiguration

Now comes the juicy part. You can manipulate your TCP/IP settings by using Windows PowerShell in two ways:

- ✔ Because Windows PowerShell is capable of running regular command line executables, you can simply use it to run netsh for you.

- ✔ The other method involves taking advantage of the `Win32_ NetworkAdapterConfiguration` class of Windows Management Instrumentation (WMI), a very powerful class that has properties and methods for reading and modifying the network configuration of any of the network adapters on your computer.

To get a taste for what this WMI class can do for you, look at Table 23-1 and Table 23-2 to see some highly useful methods and properties.

You can think of a *method* as being a function that belongs to a class and is used for interacting with it. If you think of this WMI class as a cellphone, the methods are the equivalents of the buttons that tell the phone what to do, such as hang up or increase the volume.

Table 23-1	Important Methods for Win32_NetworkAdapterConfiguration
Method	**Purpose**
EnableDHCP	Configures the adapter to use DHCP to obtain its settings
EnableDNS	Enables DNS to be used for this network adapter
EnableStatic	Configures the adapter to use a static (manually set) IP configuration rather than DHCP
ReleaseDHCPLease	Releases the DHCP lease of the network adapter
ReleaseDHCPLeaseAll	Releases the DHCP leases of all the network adapters
RenewDHCPLease	Renews the DHCP lease of the network adapter
RenewDHCPLeaseAll	Renews the DHCP leases of all the network adapters
SetDNSDomain	Sets the DNS domain
SetDNSServerSearchOrder	Defines the order for DNS lookups
SetDNSSuffixSearchOrder	Defines the DNS suffix order

Table 23-2	Important Properties for Win32_NetworkAdapterConfiguration
Property	**Purpose**
DefaultIPGateway	Returns an array of IP addresses representing the default gateways used by the computer.
Description	Describes the network interface.
DHCPEnabled	Returns whether DHCP is enabled.
DHCPLeaseExpires	Returns the date and time when the DHCP lease expires.
DHCPLeaseObtained	Returns the date and time when the DHCP lease was obtained.
DHCPServer	Returns the IP address of the DHCP server from which the IP address was obtained.

(continued)

Table 23-2 *(continued)*

Property	Purpose
DNSDomain	Returns the DNS domain for the computer.
DNSDomainSuffixSearchOrder	Returns an array of DNS suffixes in the current search order.
DNSHostName	Returns the hostname of the computer used by DNS.
DNSServerSearchOrder	Returns an array of IP address of DNS servers in the order in which they are contacted.
IPAddress	Returns an array of all IP addresses of the computer. In Windows Vista or Windows Server 2008 and later, this property can return IPv6 as well as IPv4 addresses.
IPEnabled	Returns whether TCP/IP is enabled for the network interface.
IPSubnet	Returns the subnet mask associated with the current network adapter.
MACAddress	Returns the Media Access Control (MAC - physical layer) address of the network interface.
MTU	Returns the Maximum Transmission Unit (MTU) for the network interface.
ServiceName	Returns a short version of the product name of the network adapter.

Retrieving your TCP/IP settings

You have to know where you stand before you can get anywhere, so retrieving your TCP/IP settings is the first skill you need to master before making any changes. You get the DNS hostname by querying Win32_NetworkAdapter Configuration for adapters on which TCP/IP is enabled and then retrieving the DNSHostName property. If you have multiple network adapters on your computer, each one has a DNSHostName property, but all these properties have the same value, so to suppress the duplicates, you filter the code through the Select-Object Cmdlet to grab only unique values. The result is

```
$myhost = Get-WmiObject Win32_NetworkAdapterConfiguration -filter "IPEnabled =
           true" | Select-Object DNSHostName -unique
Write-Host $myhost.DNSHostName
```

Similarly, to get the description, IP address, subnet mask, and default gate-way for each IP–enabled network adapter, you can run

```
$netconfig = Get-WmiObject Win32_NetworkAdapterConfiguration -filter "IPEnabled
           = true"
foreach($adapter in $netconfig)
{
   Write-Host ("Description: " + $adapter.description)
   Write-Host ("IP Address : " + $adapter.IPAddress[0])
   Write-Host ("Subnet Mask: " + $adapter.IPSubnet[0])
   Write-Host ("Gateway    : " + $adapter.DefaultIPGateway[0])
}
```

Because the IPAddress, IPSubnet, and DefaultIPGateway properties are arrays, you specifically select the first element in the array. On Windows Vista and Windows Server 2008 computers, the first element is usually the IPv4 address, whereas the second element is the IPv6 address. You can leave off the array index, if you want, and Windows PowerShell automatically displays all the values for that property.

You can use the same procedure to obtain any of the properties listed in Table 23-2, earlier in this chapter. The most important thing is to make sure that you put the filter in for IPEnabled = true. Many interfaces that Windows sees aren't what you and I would consider to be typical network interfaces, and they generally won't be configured with any TCP/IP configuration, so you want to exclude those interfaces by using that filter before trying to access any of the properties that are TCP/IP–specific.

Manipulating your TCP/IP settings

When you're mucking around with your TCP/IP settings, you're usually trying to achieve one of two things:

- ✔ Troubleshoot a connectivity problem (maybe you didn't get an IP address from your DHCP server)
- ✔ Change your TCP/IP settings because now you're on a different network

I'm going to start with the troubleshooting scenario, which is probably more common.

Troubleshooting connectivity

In many cases, your network adapter is configured for DHCP, and for some reason, your computer didn't get its TCP/IP settings from the DHCP server, or you already have a DHCP server configuration but need to obtain new settings because the server settings have changed. In both cases, the best thing to do is to release and then renew your IP configuration. This technique forces the network adapter to clear its current IP configuration and acquire a new one from the DHCP server.

Most computers have only one network interface in use at a time, so the easiest way to accomplish this task is to release and renew the IP address for all interfaces. The quirk is that releasing and renewing the DHCP configuration for all network adapters has to be done through the Win32_ NetworkAdapterConfiguration class directly, not through one of its instances. You do this by using Get-WmiObject to list all the WMI objects and then select the one called Win32_NetworkAdapterConfiguration. Then, using this object, you can run ReleaseDHCPLeaseAll() and RenewDHCPLeaseAll(), like this:

```
Write-Host "Releasing IP Configuration... "
$retVal =(Get-WMIObject -list | Where-Object {$_.Name -eq "Win32_
            NetworkAdapterConfiguration"}).ReleaseDHCPLeaseAll()
if ($retVal.ReturnValue -eq 0) {
   Write-Host "Successfully released IP Configuration!"
   Write-Host "Renewing IP configuration..."
   $retVal = (Get-WMIObject -list | Where-Object {$_.Name -eq "Win32_
            NetworkAdapterConfiguration"}).RenewDHCPLeaseAll()
   if ($retVal.ReturnValue -eq 0) {
      Write-Host "Successfully renewed IP configuration!"
   } else {
      Write-Host "ERROR: Unable to renew IP configuration!"
   }
} else {
   Write-Host "ERROR: Unable to release IP configuration!"
}
```

You can also release and renew the IP configuration on a per-adapter basis. You simply reuse the code from the preceding section to retrieve IP settings, but instead of looking up a property, you use it to call the ReleaseDHCPLease() and RenewDHCPLease() methods. You can even specify which adapter by using Where-Object to select the adapter you want, based on the description of the network interface. My laptop, for example, has both a wired and a wireless network interface. One interface is Intel-based, and the other is Broadcom-based. To make sure that I'm releasing and renewing only the Intel-based interface, I can use this code:

```
$adapter = Get-WmiObject Win32_NetworkAdapterConfiguration -filter "IPEnabled =
            true" | Where-Object {$_.Description.StartsWith("Intel")}
$adapter.ReleaseDHCPLease()
$adapter.RenewDHCPLease()
```

If you have a network interface with its IP configuration statically set, and you want to change it to DHCP, you can use the `EnableDHCP` method for that instance, as follows:

```
$adapter = Get-WmiObject Win32_NetworkAdapterConfiguration -filter "IPEnabled =
        true" | Where-Object {$_.Description.StartsWith("Intel")}
$adapter.EnableDHCP()
$adapter.SetDNSServerSearchOrder(@())
```

It's important to set the DNS server search order to an empty array to clear any DNS settings that were manually configured. This allows Windows to use the settings that were obtained from the DHCP server.

Changing TCP/IP settings

In the second scenario, you move the computer's network interface to another network that doesn't support DHCP, or you'd like to use your own settings instead. To do this, you have to disable DHCP and use static entries. Unlike setting `EnableDHCP`, which you set and are done with, setting your IP configuration manually means supplying all the TCP/IP settings that it needs. Here's some code that sets the IP address, subnet mask, default gateway, and DNS servers:

```
$adapter = Get-WmiObject Win32_NetworkAdapterConfiguration -filter "IPEnabled =
        true" | Where-Object {$_.Description.StartsWith("Intel")}
$adapter.EnableStatic("172.16.0.10","255.255.255.0")
$adapter.SetGateways("172.16.0.1")
$adpater.SetDNSServerSearchOrder(@("172.16.0.2","172.16.0.3"))
```

You can use the same technique to set additional network configuration settings, such as Windows Internet Name Service (WINS) addresses (if you still use WINS). Just make sure that you use the appropriate methods for each of the properties.

Managing Your Windows Firewall

Computer firewalls add a layer of extra security by controlling what kind of network traffic can come into (and, in many cases, out of) the computer. A software-based firewall isn't a replacement for a good hardware firewall, but I consider Windows Firewall to be a good last line of defense. The first iteration of Windows Firewall came with Windows XP Service Pack 2. It was a minimal implementation of a firewall; nevertheless, some security is better than none. It really gave you only a bit of control for incoming traffic based on port or application.

Windows Vista continued to build on Windows Firewall technology, providing the same on-and-off switch that existed in Windows XP Service Pack 2 and, of course, the same capabilities for creating exceptions, but the Service Pack added the ability to create outbound rules as well. Windows Server 2008 and Vista share these enhancements of Windows Firewall. You can not only create very granular inbound firewall rules, but also define outbound rules, further restricting what leaves your server in the first place.

Getting to know the Windows Firewall COMmander

The gatekeeper of Windows Firewall automation is the COM object called `HNetCfg.FwMgr`. Unfortunately, a native .NET version of this COM object doesn't exist, but that's not going to stop you. You create an instance of `HNetCfg.FwMgr` just as you would any COM object, by using the `New-Object` Cmdlet with the `-com` switch, like this:

```
$fwmgr = New-Object -COM HNetCfg.FwMgr
```

Using this COM object, you can query your firewall settings or even make changes, if you want, by interacting with a set of methods and properties. Table 23-3 lists most of the ones you're going to be interested in.

Table 23-3	Methods and Properties of HNetCfg.FwMgr	
Name	**Purpose**	**Accessed Through**
`Authorized Application`	Read-only collection of authorized applications for a given profile	`CurrentProfile` or a profile retrieved from `GetProfileByType`
`CurrentProfile`	Read-only value that points to the profile currently in use	`LocalPolicy` property
`Current ProfileType`	Read-only value that defines the type of profile currently in use	Directly from COM object
`Exceptions NotAllowed`	Read/write value that defines whether exceptions to the firewall policies are allowed	`CurrentProfile` or a profile retrieved from `GetProfileByType`
`FirewallEnabled`	Read/write value that defines whether the firewall is enabled	`CurrentProfile` or a profile retrieved from `GetProfileByType`

(continued)

Name	Purpose	Accessed Through
GetProfile ByType	The profile based on the given Windows Firewall type	LocalPolicy property
Globally OpenPorts	Read-only collection of globally open ports defined in a given profile	CurrentProfile or a profile retrieved from GetProfileByType
IcmpSettings	The ICMP settings for a given profile	CurrentProfile or a profile retrieved from GetProfileByType
Notifications Disabled	Read/write value that defines whether users are notified if something wants to gain access through the firewall	CurrentProfile or a profile retrieved from GetProfileByType
RemoteAdm inSettings	The settings for remote administration	CurrentProfile or a profile retrieved from GetProfileByType
Services	Read-only collection of services for a given profile	CurrentProfile or a profile retrieved from GetProfileByType
Type	Windows Firewall type of a profile	CurrentProfile or a profile retrieved from GetProfileByType

For a detailed listing of all the methods and properties supported by HNetCfg.FwMgr, as well as methods and properties for some of the additional objects used within this COM object, such as Internet Control Message Protocol (ICMP) settings, search for *Windows Firewall tools and settings* on Microsoft's TechNet site (http://technet.microsoft.com).

Enabling and disabling the Windows Firewall

You can disable or enable Windows Firewall by modifying the FirewallEnabled property of the firewall's current profile. Likewise, you can query this property if you want to find out what its current state is. Here's some code that enables Windows Firewall, if it isn't already enabled:

```
$objFirewall = New-Object -COM HNetCfg.FwMgr
if ($objFirewall.FirewallEnabled -eq $false) {
    #Enable the Windows Firewall
    $objFirewall.LocalPolicy.CurrentProfile.FirewallEnabled = $true
}
```

Disabling the firewall works the same way, except instead of setting
`$objFirewall.LocalPolicy.CurrentProfile.FirewallEnabled` to
`$true`, you set it to `$false`.

Windows Vista and Windows Server 2008 allow you to manage Windows
Firewall settings remotely. The default setting is to not allow this behavior, so
if you want to take advantage of it, you need to enable this function explicitly
by running this code:

```
$objFirewall = New-Object -COM HNetCfg.FwMgr
$objFirewall.LocalPolicy.CurrentProfile.RemoteAdminSettings.Enabled = $true
```

Making yourself visible

Internet Control Message Protocol (ICMP) is designed mostly for getting error
states. The best-known of all these states is the ICMP *echo response,* otherwise known as the *ping,* which is often used as quick test to see whether a
host is up. The concept is simple: Send the host an ICMP echo packet, and if
you get a response, the host must be up. This technique is great for home or
office use because it's a quick-and-dirty way to see whether a computer is on
the network.

A ping might be disadvantageous on the Internet, however. If your laptop
is connected directly to the Internet, and someone is scanning the Internet
for computers that are available (perhaps with malicious intent), your ICMP
echo response is a dead giveaway that your computer is "alive" and listening.
This behavior is undesirable, so the default setting in Windows Firewall is to
disallow inbound ICMP echo requests but you may want to enable it anyway
if you're on a well-secured network and your computer is behind some other
firewall (such as a hardware firewall) anyway. You enable this by changing
the `AllowInboundICMPEchoRequest` property of the current profile's
`ICMPSettings` like this:

```
$objFirewall = New-Object -COM HNetCfg.FwMgr
$ICMPSettings = $objFirewall.LocalPolicy.CurrentProfile.ICMPSettings
$ICMPSettings.AllowInboundechoRequest = $true
```

Getting a list of all authorized applications

The most basic firewalls control access by limiting what gets through based
on source or target IP and port information. Windows Firewall can also control firewall access on a per-application basis, so you don't have to know

which ports the application uses. You simply allow an application to go through the firewall, and Windows lets it communicate regardless of which port it wants to use. You can get a list of all authorized applications by running

```
$objFirewall = New-Object -COM HNetCfg.FwMgr
$authorizedApps = $objFirewall.LocalPolicy.CurrentProfile.AuthorizedApplications
Write-Host "Authorized applications... "
foreach($app in $authorizedApps)
{
    Write-Host ("`nName          : " + $app.Name)
    Write-Host ("Executable    : " + $app.ProcessImageFileName)
    Write-Host ("Remote Address : " + $app.RemoteAddresses)
    Write-Host ("Enabled       : " + $app.Enabled)
}
```

Getting a list of all globally open ports

Globally opened ports are ports that have been opened to allow network traffic through. They're the holes in your firewall, so to maximize your security profile, your goal should be to limit the number of open ports to those that are absolutely necessary. To find out what's currently open, you can run this code:

```
$objFirewall = New-Object -COM HNetCfg.FwMgr
$openPorts = $objFirewall.LocalPolicy.CurrentProfile.GloballyOpenPorts
Write-Host "Globally open ports... "
foreach($port in $openPorts)
{
    Write-Host ("Name           : " + $port.Name)
    Write-Host ("Port           : " + $port.Port)
    Write-Host ("Protocol       : " + $port.Protocol)
    Write-Host ("Remote Address : " + $port.RemoteAddresses)
    Write-Host ("Enabled        : " + $port.Enabled)
    Write-Host ("Built-In       : " + $port.Builtin)
}
```

Using the big reset button

So you've been playing around with HNetCfg.FwMgr, gotten excited, and made all kinds of changes — and suddenly, something that used to work over your network interface stopped working. You've already closed your Windows PowerShell window, of course, so you can't just go back to the history to see what commands you've run, and you really don't remember what you did, so you're not sure what to revert to anyway. Luckily for you, a big reset button is built into Windows Firewall to put it back to its default settings. Using this button is as simple as running

```
$objFirewall = New-Object -COM HNetCfg.FwMgr
$objFirewall.RestoreDefaults()
```

It's very important to understand that RestoreDefaults() takes Windows Firewall's settings back to their "out of the box" state. It doesn't roll back your changes. If you customized your Windows Firewall settings before screwing everything up, RestoreDefault wipes out those changes as well.

Chapter 24

Managing Your Hardware

. . . .

. . . .

*Y*ou can argue that software is what really makes a computer, but without the hardware, software would have no foundation to stand on. Even though virtualization has really taken off in recent years, in the end, you're still limited in functionality to the hardware that the software can access. This means that getting to know what hardware you're on can be very important.

In practice, you typically want to query hardware information for only two reasons: to generate an inventory of what devices you have installed or to find out whether some piece of hardware is installed to determine whether you should take some other action. If you can determine whether a device is a laptop based on the hardware installed, for example, you can do fancy things like run certain commands based on whether your PowerShell script is running on a laptop or a desktop.

In this chapter, you interrogate your hardware by querying a number of different WMI classes that deal with the different kinds of hardware on a computer. This is extremely important if you want to create proactive monitoring scripts that keep an eye on hardware errors. It's also very useful for generating hardware inventory if you want to create a crude asset management script. I also delve a bit into working with printers, including the ever-important monitoring of print queues (ever notice the chaos around the office when people can't print?).

Polling Your Hardware

I'm willing to bet that 99 percent of the time, when you want to write a script that deals with hardware, it isn't because you're trying to change those hardware configurations but to find out what hardware you have and, possibly, what state it's in. You can poll almost anything about your computers by using Windows Management Instrumentation (WMI), which you can use as a basis for inventory reports.

In my experience, polling hardware is also critical for managing systems that aren't on your network all the time. These systems can be laptops or desktops that aren't always connected to your main network and may use a Virtual Private Network (VPN) connection to connect remotely. Some organizations have a rule that if you're connected via VPN through one network device, all other network devices should be disabled to prevent the computer from acting as a bridge for other computers to connect through. In this case, you can write a script to make sure that if the user is connected to the network via a wired connection such as Ethernet, you can disable the other network interfaces, such as wireless.

VPNs are made by connecting one network to another by transmitting the data through other networks (such as the Internet), which are often out of your control and potentially unsecure. The data itself is secured by encrypting the data as it's sent, so even if the data is intercepted by someone sitting in the network in between, he can't find out what the original data is. Because the data is shielded by encryption while it's in transit, VPN connections are also called *VPN tunnels* when they're established.

Finding out what hardware you have

The PC world has been blessed and cursed by the hundreds of kinds of hardware and the seemingly infinite combinations of these items to end up with a computer that can run Windows. Although many standards have come into place to make talking to different kinds of devices much easier, in the end, it would be a real pain if you had to remember how to talk to hardware from one vendor versus another.

Your best friend in this case is WMI. You can use WMI to query all kinds of things about the hardware that you have. WMI creates a level of abstraction that allows you to do things like get your BIOS version without having to know who manufactured the BIOS in the first place.

Creating a hardware inventory script

Because so many kinds of devices might be attached to a computer through one of its many ports and internal connections, you're probably not going to be interested in all of them. When you create a hardware inventory script, you're going to want to cherry-pick the ones that you care most about, which usually are

- Manufacturer
- Model
- BIOS version
- Serial number
- CPU type
- Number of CPUs
- Total amount of physical memory
- Drives installed, including capacity
- Video card manufacturer/model
- Network interfaces

Having all this hardware information without a few key pieces of software information might not be very useful, so in addition to the list of hardware I just enumerated, here are a few pieces of software information that you should gather:

- Computer name
- Operating system (including build number and Service Pack)
- Logical partitions (including size and free space)

I'm sure that you can come up with even more things to add to this list, but try to stay focused on these major things for now. Listing 24-1 provides a script that uses WMI to gather and then display all the information listed in the two preceding bulleted lists.

Listing 24-1:   Querying Computer Information Using WMI

```
$strComputer = "."

$objBIOS = Get-WMIObject -class "Win32_BIOS" -namespace "root\CIMV2"
foreach($item in $objBIOS)
{
   $manufacturer = $item.Manufacturer
   $biosver = $item.BIOSVersion
```

(continued)

Listing 24-1 *(continued)*

```
   $serialnum = $item.SerialNumber
}

$objCompSys = Get-WmIObject -class "Win32_ComputerSystem" -namespace "root\
             CIMV2"
foreach($item in $objCompSys)
{
   $compname = $objCompSys.Name
   $model = $objCompSys.Model
   $physicalRAM = [Math]::Ceiling($item.TotalPhysicalMemory / 1MB)
   $numProcs = $item.NumberOfProcessors
}

$objOS = Get-WMIObject -class "Win32_OperatingSystem" -namespace "root\CIMV2"
foreach($item in $objOS)
{
   $OS = $item.Caption + " Build " + $item.BuildNumber + " " + $item.CSDVersion
}

$objProc = Get-WMIObject -class "Win32_Processor" -namespace "root\CIMV2"
foreach($item in $objProc)
{
   $procType = $item.Name
   $procSpeed = $item.MaxClockSpeed
}

Write-Host ("Name           : " + $compname)
Write-Host ("OS             : " + $OS)
Write-Host ("Manufacturer   : " + $manufacturer)
Write-Host ("Model          : " + $model)
Write-Host ("BIOS Version   : " + $biosver)
Write-Host ("Serial Number  : " + $serialnum)
Write-Host ("CPU            : " + $procType)
Write-Host ("CPU Speed      : " + $procSpeed)
Write-Host ("No. CPUs       : " + $numProcs)
Write-Host ("Physical RAM   : " + $physicalRAM + " MB")

Write-Host "`nPhysical Disks:"
$objDiskDrive = Get-WMIObject -class "Win32_DiskDrive" -namespace "root\CIMV2"
             -filter "MediaType Like 'Fixed%'"
foreach($item in $objDiskDrive)
{
   Write-Host ("   * Manufacturer: " + $item.Manufacturer)
   Write-Host ("     Model        : " + $item.Model)
   Write-Host ("     Size         : " + [Math]::Ceiling($item.Size / 1MB) + "
             MB")
}

Write-Host "`nLogical drives:"
$objDrives = Get-WMIObject -class "Win32_LogicalDisk" -namespace "root\CIMV2"
             -filter "DriveType='3'"
```

Listing 24-1

```
foreach($item in $objDrives)
{
   Write-Host ("   * Drive Letter: " + $item.DeviceID)
   Write-Host ("      Volume Name : " + $item.VolumeName)
   Write-Host ("        Capacity    : " + [Math]::Ceiling($item.Size / 1MB) + "
            MB")
   Write-Host ("        Free Space  : " + [Math]::Ceiling($item.FreeSpace / 1MB) +
            " MB (" + `
            [Math]::Ceiling(($item.FreeSpace/1MB) / ($item.Size/1MB) * 100)+
            "%)" )
}


Write-Host "`nVideo Cards:"
$objVideo = Get-WMIObject -class "Win32_VideoController" -namespace "root\CIMV2"
foreach($item in $objVideo)
{
   Write-Host ("   * Name         : " + $item.Caption)
   Write-Host ("      VRAM        : " + [Math]::Ceiling($item.AdapterRAM / 1MB) +
            " MB")
}


Write-Host "`nNetwork Adapters:"
$objNetwork = Get-WMIObject -class Win32_NetworkAdapter -namespace "root\CIMV2"
foreach($item in $objNetwork)
{
   Write-Host ("   * Name         : " + $item.ProductName)
   Write-Host ("      Type        : " + $item.AdapterType)
   Write-Host ("      MAC Address : " + $item.MACAddress)
}
```

As you can see, you have to use different WMI classes depending on the kind of information you want. The procedures are the same for any kind of property that is available through WMI.

I'd like to highlight a few techniques in this example. When querying for physical disk drives, for example, I added an extra filter to the WMI query:

```
$objDiskDrive = Get-WMIObject -class "Win32_DiskDrive" -namespace "root\CIMV2"
            -filter "MediaType Like 'Fixed%'"
```

The reason is that the `Win32_DiskDrive` WMI class returns fixed internal drives as well as drives with removable media, such as DVD-ROM drives. To get only internal, physical disks, you have to filter for objects in which the `MediaType` starts with the word `Fixed`. If you go online to find examples of WMI queries for `Win32_DiskDrive`, you might find examples in which the value of `MediaType` is `Fixed hard disk`. This is fine in Windows NT/2000/XP and Windows Server 2003, but in Windows Vista and Windows Server 2008,

Microsoft changed the media types to differentiate fixed hard drives from external hard drives and removable media drives. By checking for only the first part of the string, you can have a query that works in every version of Windows that supports WMI.

Another technique I use in the script calculates disk sizes and free space. Because almost all the WMI classes return the sizes of disks and memory in bytes, it's often better to convert these values to megabytes (MB) before displaying them to the user. In the past, you had to do this by dividing the value by 1024 to get the number of kilobytes (KB) and then dividing the number of kilobytes by 1024 to get the value in megabytes. Windows PowerShell provides a shortcut by allowing you to divide values with special modifiers to calculate the size automatically in KB, MB, or gigabytes (GB). (I'm so glad the Window PowerShell developers are just as lazy as me.) This shortcut is

```
$physicalRAM = [Math]::Ceiling($item.TotalPhysicalMemory / 1MB)
```

To convert a value that's in bytes to megabytes, just divide the bytes by 1MB; Windows PowerShell does all the dirty work for you. Whenever you divide a number, there's a good chance that you'll end up with additional decimal values. To keep the output as clean and simple as possible, you can use the `[Math]::Ceiling` function to round the value automatically to the next whole integer.

If you want to include a few decimal places in the resulting value, you can use the `[Math]::Round` function instead. This function takes two parameters. The first parameter is the value you want to round off, and the second parameter is the number of decimal places you want to keep. If you want to display the physical RAM in megabytes and show up to two significant digits after the decimal place, you can use this code:

```
$physicalRAM = [Math]::Round($item.TotalPhysicalMemory /
        1MB, 2)
```

Detecting whether the computer is a laptop

As I mention at the beginning of this chapter, having a script that's intelligent enough to detect whether it's being run on a laptop is quite useful. You may want to run a script that changes the power settings on the computer — but only if the computer is a laptop. The correct way (if there is such a thing) to check whether a machine is a laptop is to query the `Win32_SystemEnclosure` WMI class and then get the values for the `ChassisTypes` property, which can be one or more of 24 numeric values that describe the kind of chassis the computer is in. Table 24-1 breaks down the 24 numeric values.

Table 24-1	Win32_SystemEnclosure ChassisTypes Values
Value	*Definition*
1	Other
2	Unknown
3	Desktop
4	Low Profile Desktop
5	Pizza Box
6	Mini Tower
7	Tower
8	Portable
9	Laptop
10	Notebook
11	Hand Held
12	Docking Station
13	All in One
14	Sub Notebook
15	Space-Saving
16	Lunch Box
17	Main System Chassis
18	Expansion Chassis
19	SubChassis
20	Bus Expansion Chassis
21	Peripheral Chassis
22	Storage Chassis
23	Rack Mount Chassis
24	Sealed-Case PC

As you can see, this classification can a bit silly. After all, what's really the difference among a laptop, a notebook, and a subnotebook? Honestly, I don't even know what some of these things are. Sometimes. I think Microsoft stuck some values in there just to see if we're paying attention. Do you know what a chassis type of 16 (Lunchbox) means, for example? Are we sending kids to school now with computerized lunchboxes that keep track of their peanut butter and jelly sandwiches?

To get detection to work properly by using this method, you actually have to check whether the ChassisTypes values contain any different values that could denote a laptop, such as checking whether the chassis type is a laptop or a notebook. In Windows PowerShell, you can determine whether a computer is a laptop by using the Win32_SystemEnclosure class like this:

```
$objEnclosure = Get-WmiObject -class Win32_SystemEnclosure -namespace "root\
             CIMV2"
$chassisTypes = $objEnclosure.ChassisTypes
if (($chassisTypes -contains 8) -or `
    ($chassisTypes -contains 9) -or `
    ($chassistypes -contains 10) -or `
    ($chassisTypes -contains 14))
{
   Write-Host "This is a laptop!"
} else {
   Write-Host "This is NOT a laptop!"
}
```

It's really up to the PC manufacturer to return the correct value, so minimally, you'll want to check whether ChassisTypes contains the values for Portable, Laptop, Notebook, and Sub Notebook.

Another way is simply to check whether the computer has a battery. Technically, this method isn't accurate, because I'm sure there could be a computer that has a battery but isn't a laptop — such as a server with a smart Uninterruptible Power Supply (UPS). To use this shortcut method, you have to look at the computers in your environment and assess whether this simplification will work for you. I'd say that 99 percent of the time, this check will be more than sufficient:

```
$objBattery = Get-WMIObject -class Win32_Battery -namespace "root\CIMV2"
if ($objBattery -ne $null) {
   Write-Host "This is a laptop!"
} else {
   Write-Host "This is NOT a laptop!"
}
```

Whether you can get away with this simplification depends purely on the computers you have in your environment. If you know that you don't have batteries attached to anything but your laptops, this check is one way to keep things simple. If it doesn't work for you, but you know that all your laptops have PCMCIA devices, you can use the same code, but instead of checking for Win32_Battery, look for Win32_PCMCIAController by running

```
$objBattery = Get-WMIObject -class Win32_PCMCIAController -namespace "root\
          CIMV2"
if ($objBattery -ne $null) {
   Write-Host "This is a laptop!"
} else {
   Write-Host "This is NOT a laptop!"
}
```

Finding any connected USB disk drives and memory sticks

In business, a company's success is often the result of some advantage over
its competitors. This advantage can be purely financial (which company
has deeper pockets), but in many cases, it can involve intellectual property
or some kind of technology that makes one company more efficient than
another. It's no surprise that there's been a trend toward implementing solutions that detect possible compromises of your company's information. If
you're already monitoring e-mail and Web traffic, a simple and cost-effective
method is to prevent unauthorized use of USB disk drives and memory
sticks on your computers so that the data can't simply be copied from those
devices.

To do this, you can run a script on a computer periodically to check for any
attached USB disk drives or memory sticks. Then you can write this information to the event log for auditing later. If you want to be proactive, you can
even pop up a message to inform the user that he or she has inserted an
unauthorized device into the computer and that the IT department has been
notified. Just don't be surprised when your popularity rating in the company
drops as a result of your "Big Brother" antics.

Aside from security detection, there are several reasons why you may want
to detect the existence of a USB disk drive or memory stick. If you want your
My Documents folder to be synchronized automatically with your USB drive
whenever you insert it, for example, you can use a script that detects USB
drives to initiate this process for you. To check for USB drives, query the
`Win32_DiskDrive` WMI object and look for instances where the `Media` type
starts with the word `Removable` and contains the word `USB` in its caption,
like this:

```
$usbDevices = Get-WmiObject -class Win32_DiskDrive -namespace "root\CIMV2"
          -filter "MediaType Like 'Removable%' AND Caption Like '%USB%'"
if($usbDevices -eq $null){
   Write-Host "No USB drives detected!"
} else {
   Write-Host "USB drives detected:"
   foreach($item in $usbDevices) {
      Write-Host ("   * " + $item.Caption)
   }
}
```

Checking hardware state

Knowing what hardware you have is a good start, but sometimes, just knowing that some piece of hardware is connected isn't sufficient. Checking for the state of your hardware is just as important. Most hard drives sold today have something called Self-Monitoring, Analysis, and Reporting Technology (SMART). A drive with this technology can try to diagnose itself and warn you of a predicted failure so that you have adequate time to replace the drive before it fails (and drives tend to magically fail at the worst possible moment). You do pay attention to warnings, right?

You can make a quick health check of the drives on your computer by querying the status property for `Win32_DiskDrive`, like this:

```
Get-WMIObject -class Win32_DiskDrive | Select-Object caption,status
```

In fact, two properties in almost all WMI classes deal with logical devices and are useful for getting state information. These properties are `availability` and `status`. These properties aren't guaranteed to have a value for all your devices, so you'll have to check the values to see which ones apply to the WMI class you're interested in. If it's defined, you can use the `availability` property to check for the power state of a device. The `availability` property can take an integral value from 1 through 17, but the most common values are

- ✔ 3: Running or Full Power
- ✔ 7: Power Off
- ✔ 13: Power Save (Unknown)
- ✔ 14: Power Save (Low Power Mode)
- ✔ 15: Power Save (Standby)

The `status` property should contain the general state of the device as a string. Although different WMI classes define different possible values for `status`, the ones you'll run into most often are

- ✔ OK
- ✔ Error
- ✔ Degraded
- ✔ Unknown
- ✔ Pred Fail (indicates a predicted failure or malfunction of the device)
- ✔ Starting
- ✔ Stopping

Controlling Your Printers

The digital age was supposed to put an end to the need for paper. The reality is that computers just make it even easier to generate content to put on paper. Even if you do your best to avoid printing whenever possible, sometimes you simply can't avoid it. You just have to print some things, such as the confirmation e-mail for that e-ticket for your flight to Vegas, just in case the airline's computers suddenly think that you're not supposed to be on that flight.

In my many years of working in IT, I've found that of all the services that people start to freak over when things don't work, printing is near the top of that list (probably after Internet access and e-mail). It's not uncommon to find one printer for every 20–30 people within a company, so if you have a decent-size company, you'll find yourself managing dozens, if not hundreds, of printers. The key to keeping your sanity and being proactive is staying on top of printer management through automation.

Connecting to a shared network printer

If you're lucky enough to have tech-savvy users, it's easy to show them how to find and connect to network printers. Unfortunately, in most cases, users either want an even easier method for connecting to network printers or to have the printers map automatically when they log in. I've even seen administrators go a step further and write scripts to figure out which is the closest printer based on the printer's IP address or computer description. You add a printer by using the `Win32_Printer` WMI class' `AddPrinterConnection` method, like this:

```
([wmiclass]"Win32_Printer").AddPrinterConnection("\\servername\printershare")
```

Note that you don't use `Get-WMIObject` to access `Win32_Printer` to add the printer connection. You don't do this as a shortcut. The difference is that `Get-WMIObject` returns instances of the `Win32_Printer` WMI class, whereas using the `[wmiclass]` prefix means that you're getting the actual `Win32_Printer` class instead.

In practice, if you run `Get-WMIObject` on `Win32_Printer`, you get a bunch of objects that represent the printers installed on the computer. Well, you don't add printers to printers; you add printers to computers. So `AddPrinterConnection` doesn't make sense in the context of an instance of `Win32_Printer`. Instead, you have to use the `AddPrinterConnection` method on the `Win32_Printer` class directly, so you use the `[wmiclass]` accelerator instead.

Disconnecting a shared network printer

The procedure for removing a connection to a shared network printer is a bit different from adding a printer. There's no `RemovePrinterConnection` method in the `Win32_Printer` class. Instead, you need to use `Get-WMIObject` on `Win32_Printer` to get the instance of the printer you want to remove and call its `Delete` method, like this:

```
$printer = Get-WMIObject -class Win32_Printer -filter "Name='\\\\servername\\
            printershare'"
$printer.Delete()
```

If you use backslashes in a `Get-WMIObject` filter, you have to make sure that you use a double backlash (`\\`) for every actual backslash in the filter string.

Setting the default printer

You commonly find users connected to more than one printer because the other printers have additional capabilities that their default printer doesn't or because they want a backup in case the primary one isn't available. You change the default printer by running the `SetDefaultPrinter` method on the instance that you want to make your default printer, like this:

```
$printer = Get-WMIObject -class Win32_Printer -filter "Name='\\\\servername\\
            printershare'"
$printer.SetDefaultPrinter()
```

Checking up on printer state

Printers are sometimes temperamental (or, as some of my users have said, possessed) and can encounter all kinds of trouble. Being physical devices, printers can experience a lot of bad things. They can run out of ink, run out of paper, or even have a paper jam. On the virtual side, you may have a print job that the print driver can't process correctly. All these things can cause the queue to back up as other jobs wait their turn to be printed as soon as the issue has been cleared.

If you want to write a printer-monitoring script, the first places to check are the `status` and `error` states of the printer itself. Listing 24-2 shows how you do this by reading the `PrinterStatus` and `DetectedErrorState` properties of the `Win32_Printer` WMI class.

Listing 24-2:   Script for Checking Printer Status

```
$objPrinters = Get-WMIObject -class Win32_Printer
foreach($printer in $objPrinters)
{
   switch($printer.Printerstatus)
   {
      1 {$status = "Other"}
      2 {$status = "Unknown"}
      3 {$status = "Idle"}
      4 {$status = "Printing"}
      5 {$status = "Warming Up"}
      6 {$status = "Stopped Printing"}
      7 {$status = "Offline"}
   }

   switch($printer.DetectedErrorState)
   {
      0 {$errorState = "Unknown"}
      1 {$errorState = "Other"}
      2 {$errorState = "No Error"}
      3 {$errorState = "Low Paper"}
      4 {$errorState = "No Paper"}
      5 {$errorState = "Low Toner"}
      6 {$errorState = "No Toner"}
      7 {$errorState = "Door Open"}
      8 {$errorState = "Jammed"}
      9 {$errorState = "Offline"}
      10 {$errorState = "Service Requested"}
      11 {$errorState = "Output Bin Full"}
   }

   Write-Host ("* Name        : " + $printer.name)
   Write-Host ("  Status      : " + $status)
   Write-Host ("  Error State: " + $errorState)
}
```

Keeping an eye on the printer queue

If anything on a print server needs close attention, it's the print queue. Besides checking the printer state to make sure that your printers are functioning normally, you need to determine the number of items in each of your printer queues. You determine this number by querying the `Win32_PerfFormatted Data_Spooler_PrintQueue` WMI class. Whether you have one printer or many printers installed, there'll always be a print queue called `_Total` that contains a total of all the print queues on the system. Although this data can be useful in some instances, in general you're going to want to pay closer to attention to each individual print queue so that you know which printer needs attention. The next example demonstrates how you use the `Win32_PerfFormattedData_Spooler_PrintQueue` WMI object to get information about print queues:

```
$objPrintQueues = Get-WMIObject -class Win32_PerfFormattedData_Spooler_
              PrintQueue -filter "Name <> '_Total'"
foreach($queue in $objPrintQueues)
{
    Write-Host ("* Queue Name         : " + $queue.Name)
    Write-Host ("  Number of Jobs     : " + $queue.Jobs)
    Write-Host ("  Job Spooling       : " + $queue.JobsSpooling)
    Write-Host ("  Job Errors         : " + $queue.JobErrors)
    Write-Host ("  Not Ready Errors   : " + $queue.NotReadyErrors)
    Write-Host ("  Out of Paper Errors: " + $queue.OutOfPaperErrors)
}
```

If you're trying to write a script to check your print queue's health, you can use those error counters as a trigger for some action. If the out-of-paper error count is greater than zero, for example, you can send an e-mail to an admin who can make sure that paper is added to the printer. Also, if the number of jobs just keeps increasing and never goes down, you should take a look at the printer to see whether one of the jobs got stuck or someone suddenly decided to print a thousand-page memoir of life as a cubicle junkie.

Chapter 25

Making Reporting Easy

In This Chapter

▶ Using Cmdlets to tabulate your data

▶ Formatting how your data gets displayed

▶ Generating HTML–based reports that stand out

▶ Employing third-party reporting tools

*I*f you ever watch movies that have a military theme, you'll hear the term "situational awareness" thrown about, or you'll hear someone barking out the need for a SITREP (situation report). Why is this important? Whether you're a battlefield commander or a white-collar manager, you can't make decisions in a void. Instead, what you need is real information about whatever situation you're in so that you can make an educated decision about the direction in which to proceed.

This is why reports are so important. Even if you're not managing people, it's important to be able to get information and put it in a format that turns the information into knowledge. This task can be as simple as combining information in a single, human-readable format or doing something fancy like representing your network's operating system distribution in a pie chart. What matters most is to get the information you're looking for into a readily accessible format.

Then again, I'm sure that you know or have known a manager or two (or twelve) who like to ask for reports simply because the request makes them sound managerial, when the truth is that they really have no clue what you're talking about. It's okay. Just make your reports look pretty, keep talking technical until the manager gets a blank look on his or her face, and then walk away. Who's the dummy now?

In this chapter, you find out how to export information you gather using Windows PowerShell into different formats you can use to generate reports. Although Windows PowerShell by itself doesn't have the ability to generate fancy-looking reports, you can use some very useful Cmdlets to output your results into CSV, XML, and even HTML files with very little effort.

Using Built-In Reporting Cmdlets

Okay, so maybe I'm stretching facts a little by talking about built-in reporting Cmdlets. The Cmdlets I talk about in this section can definitely help you make reports, but they aren't necessarily designed for that purpose alone. For reporting, the Cmdlets you're going to want to pay most attention to are the ones that allow you to format, view, and possibly export data in a specific manner, such as these:

- ✔ `Format-Table`
- ✔ `Export-Csv`
- ✔ `Export-Clixml`
- ✔ `ConvertTo-CSV`
- ✔ `ConvertTo-Html`
- ✔ `ConvertTo-Xml`
- ✔ `Out-GridView`

`Format-Table` is great for creating a tabular representation of data onscreen; you can redirect this data to a text file. `ConvertTo-HTML` is a terrific Cmdlet to use when you want to format your tabular data in an HTML page for easy viewing in your favorite Web browser. `Out-GridView` lets you display data in an interactive, graphical table that you can sort and search in. The other Cmdlets let you export to CSV- and XML-formatted text files, which is a great intermediate format that you can import and reformat using other tools such as Microsoft Excel.

Generating Reports

Your first step in creating reports is gathering the data you want to present. In general, this task involves putting that data in tabular format (if it isn't already) and then outputting it to the screen, a file, or maybe even a printer. A lot of Cmdlets that display useful information (such as `Get-Service` and `Get-ChildItem`) already display the data in tabular format, so why mess with it? The default format is usually well chosen and displays the most important information readily. Sometimes, though, you may want to change a few things, such as replacing the header names with something other than the property names defined by the Cmdlet.

Customizing tabular output with Format-Table

The `Format-Table` Cmdlet gives you additional control of the tabular output for a given object or collection of objects. If you run `Get-ChildItem` against a directory in your file system, you get four properties displayed by default: `mode`, `LastWriteTime`, `length`, and `name` properties. If you want just the `Name` and `Length` properties to be displayed, you can use the `Select-Object` Cmdlet to do that for you. If you want to add some extra formatting, such as displaying `Length` in kilobytes instead of bytes, you really need `Format-Table`. Here's an example:

```
Get-ChildItem C:\Windows | Format-Table -property name,@{Label="Size (KB)";
          Expression={[Math]::Ceiling($_.length/1KB)}}
```

The best part of `Format-Table` is that it gives you the ability to define your own columns, which is how you can display the length (size) of the file in kilobytes instead of bytes. You do this by defining a hash table where you put the property name. This hash table must consist of at least two key/value pairs. The first is the `Label` key, which defines the heading for that column. The second is the `Expression` key, which is a PowerShell expression used to derive the value of each row of the table in this column.

You use the `$_` character sequence when you want to represent the object that'll be dynamically retrieved for each item from the command just preceding this section in the command pipeline.

Another reason for using the hash table `Label/Expression` combo to define your own columns is to rename a column in the output. One Cmdlet that's notorious for using very terse column headers is `Get-Process`. `Working Set Memory`, for example, is abbreviated as `WS(K)` in the default `Get-Process` output. If you want to display the process name, description, ID, and working set in a more user-friendly format, you can define your own column headerswhile keeping the same values. As you can see in the next code snippet, instead of just asking for the `WS` property for the process, I put that property in an expression instead and change the label of the column to `Working Set (Memory - KB)` so that the output is much easier to understand:

```
Get-Process | Format-Table -property name,description,id,@{Label="Working Set
          (Memory - KB)"; Expression={$_.WS}}
```

Setting column width in Format-Table

Format-Table tries to be intelligent. It automatically expands and contracts each column's width so that when the table is displayed, it takes up the entire screen width. Sometimes, this behavior isn't what you want; you want to explicitly control how wide each column is. Besides the Label and Expression properties, you can specify a width value to control how many characters wide the column will be. This is how the last command in the preceding section looks if you want to set the widths of each of the columns:

```
Get-Process | Format-Table -property {@{Label="Name"; Expression={$_.Name};
              width=10}, @{Label="Description"; Expression={$_.Description};
              width=15}, @{Label="ID"; Expression={$_.id}; width=5},@
              {Label="Working Set (Memory - KB)"; Expression={$_.WS}; width=15}
```

Using an interactive data table

One limitation of using Format-Table is that after the output is displayed, you really can't do anything else with it. If you want to sort by a different column, you have to rerun the command through a Sort-Object Cmdlet.

One of the cool new Cmdlets in Windows PowerShell 2 is Out-GridView. The grid view generated by Out-GridView is an interactive table format that you can sort in dynamically; it also has search capabilities that allow you to find data within the data view easily. Getting tabular data to display in a grid view requires nothing more than piping the objects to the Out-GridView Cmdlet, like this:

```
Get-Process | Out-GridView
```

You can see what this looks like in Figure 25-1.

You can sort by any column simply by clicking the column header, just as you'd expect. As soon as you start typing text in the search box, the data view automatically filters for matches (see Figure 25-2).

You can even group the data by right-clicking the column header and choosing the Show in Groups option from the shortcut menu. This technique is particularly useful if you're correlating data based on a specific property — if you're loading data from one of the event logs to the grid view and want to group it by source or level, for example.

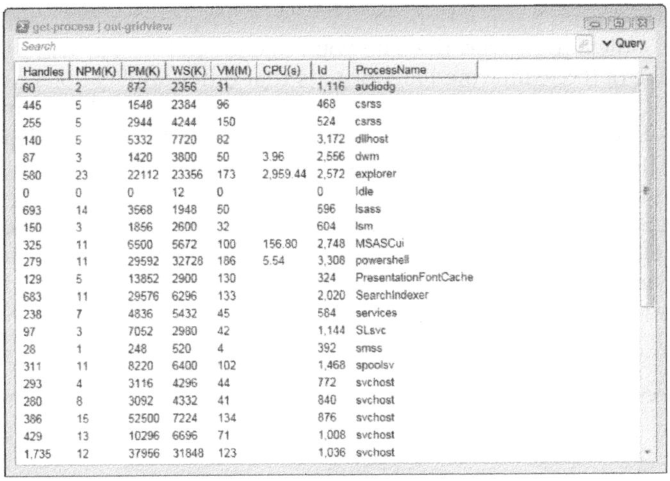
get-process | out-gridview

Search

Query

Handles	NPM(K)	PM(K)	WS(K)	VM(M)	CPU(s)	Id	ProcessName
60	2	872	2356	31		1,116	audiodg
445	5	1548	2384	96		468	csrss
255	5	2944	4244	150		524	csrss
140	5	5332	7720	82		3,172	dllhost
87	3	1420	3800	50	3.96	2,556	dwm
580	23	22112	23356	173	2,959.44	2,572	explorer
0	0	0	12	0		0	Idle
693	14	3568	1948	50		596	lsass
150	3	1856	2600	32		604	lsm
325	11	6500	5672	100	156.80	2,748	MSASCui
279	11	29592	32728	186	5.54	3,308	powershell
129	5	13852	2900	130		324	PresentationFontCache
683	11	29576	6296	133		2,020	SearchIndexer
238	7	4836	5432	45		584	services
97	3	7052	2980	42		1,144	SLsvc
28	1	248	520	4		392	smss
311	11	8220	6400	102		1,468	spoolsv
293	4	3116	4296	44		772	svchost
280	8	3092	4332	41		840	svchost
386	15	52500	7224	134		876	svchost
429	13	10296	6696	71		1,008	svchost
1,735	12	37956	31848	123		1,036	svchost

Figure 25-1: The grid view.

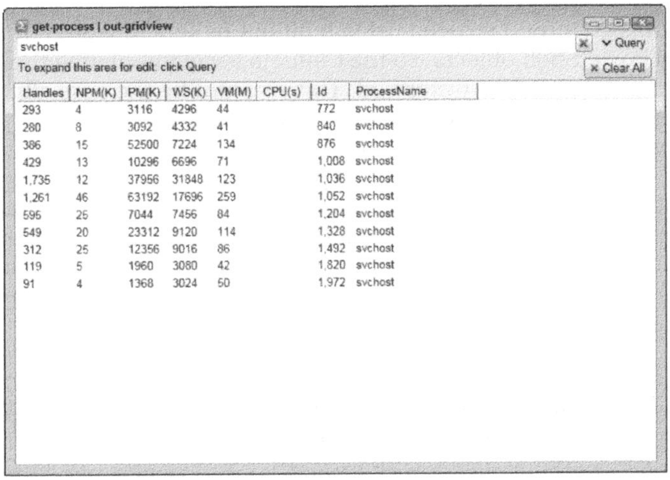
get-process | out-gridview

svchost

Query

To expand this area for edit click Query

Clear All

Handles	NPM(K)	PM(K)	WS(K)	VM(M)	CPU(s)	Id	ProcessName
293	4	3116	4296	44		772	svchost
280	8	3092	4332	41		840	svchost
386	15	52500	7224	134		876	svchost
429	13	10296	6696	71		1,008	svchost
1,735	12	37956	31848	123		1,036	svchost
1,261	46	63192	17696	259		1,052	svchost
595	25	7044	7456	84		1,204	svchost
549	20	23312	9120	114		1,328	svchost
312	25	12356	9016	86		1,492	svchost
119	5	1960	3080	42		1,820	svchost
91	4	1368	3024	50		1,972	svchost

Figure 25-2: Filtered grid view with a query string provided.

Preparing data for other reporting tools

Although Windows PowerShell does have some capabilities for creating reports, you may prefer to use your own reporting software. Microsoft Excel is a great tool for generating reports, for example. The key is getting the data into a format that the reporting software can use, which means getting the data into a structured format that you can import easily into that application. The two best formats for this purpose are CSV (or any other delimited format) and XML. Delimited files, such as CSV files, are perfect for defining relatively simple tabular data, whereas data defined as XML can be more flexible at the cost of being just a bit more complicated.

You use the `Export-Csv`, `Export-CliXml`, `ConvertTo-CSV`, and `Convert To-Xml` Cmdlets to convert the data you've acquired through Windows Power Shell to one of these intermediate formats that other applications can process. `Export-CSV` and `ConvertTo-CSV` are actually the same; they convert Windows PowerShell objects to comma-separated (or any other delimiter) strings. The only difference is that `Export-CSV` expects to write the CSV strings to a file, whereas `ConvertTo-CSV` simply returns the string objects. Likewise, `Export-CliXml` and `ConvertTo-XML` both convert Windows PowerShell objects to a XML representation, the only difference being that the `Export` version outputs directly to a file. This next example shows how you can export the results of running `Get-Process` to either a CSV or XML format:

```
Get-Process | Export-CSV c:\temp\processlist.csv
Get-Process | Export-CliXml c:\temp\processlist.xml
```

Making your data table ready

So far in this chapter, I've been using built-in Cmdlets that already return Windows PowerShell objects, so the Cmdlets for manipulating these objects into tabular data work as described. This may not be the case all the time. If you write a script that extracts data from various sources, such as Active Directory or Windows Management Instrumentation (WMI), and want to combine this data into a tabular format of your own, your initial instinct may be to format the output as a table manually by using `Write-Host` statements. Although that technique works if you're just going to display the information to the screen, it doesn't scale very well. You can't reuse that formatted data if you want to take advantage of any of the other Cmdlets that manipulate tabular data, such as `Export-CSV`.

The solution is to put your data in a PowerShell object. When you create your own PowerShell object, it's like creating your own unique data object. You can add whatever kind of property you want to it and set its values. Now that you have a PowerShell object with properties and values, Cmdlets such as `Format-Table` and `Export-CSV` know how to handle that object, because it's just like every other object they might get from some other Cmdlet. Here's how you create a custom PowerShell object:

```
$objPerson = New-Object PSObject
Add-Member -InputObject $objPerson -MemberType NoteProperty -Name "FirstName"
           -value "Steve"
Add-Member -InputObject $objPerson -MemberType NoteProperty -Name "LastName"
           -value "Seguis"
Add-Member -InputObject $objPerson -MemberType NoteProperty -Name "Description"
           -value "Author"
```

After you run that code, $objPerson points to a PowerShell object that has three properties: FirstName, LastName, and Description, the values of which are Steve, Seguis, and Author, respectively. Now that you have an object, all the other Cmdlets you saw earlier work as you'd expect. In this example, you can see that standard Windows PowerShell Cmdlets can be used with $objPerson because it's treated as any other PSH object:

```
$objPerson | Format-Table
$objPerson | ConvertTo-Csv
$objPerson | Out-GridView
```

Now you know how to create your own PowerShell objects. As you can see, however, when you output $objPerson, it contains only one row of data. You're going to want to have the ability to add rows. Don't bother looking for an AddRow method in PSObject, because there isn't any. Although you can easily display a Windows PowerShell object in tabular format by using each property name as the column header, you really shouldn't think of the object itself as a table. Instead, think of a PowerShell object as a row within the table. In a table, rows share a column header, so to create a table with many rows by using PowerShell objects, you have to create multiple PowerShell objects and put them together in a collection. As long as each object in the collection has the same properties, you can think of the collection as being a table, with each object being treated as a row within that table.

To do this, first you create a collection such as an array; then you loop through all the items you want to add to your table. For each of your rows, you create a new PSObject, which you add to the collection at the end of the loop after you've defined the properties and values for that object. After all the objects have been created and added to the collection, you can do with them as you please, just like any other PowerShell objects returned by Cmdlets like Get-Process. In this case, you're just going to pass the array through Format-Table to make sure that the output does indeed contain ten rows, each with values 0 through 9 and that the square of each of these numbers is listed in the next column:

```
$myColl = @()

for($i = 0; $i -lt 10; $i++)
{
    $myObj = New-Object PSObject
    Add-Member -InputObject $myObj -MemberType NoteProperty -Name "Number" -Value
            $i
    Add-Member -InputObject $myObj -MemberType NoteProperty -Name "Square" -Value
            ($i * $i)
    $myColl += $myObj
}

$myColl | Format-Table
```

The output of this script is

```
            Number                    Square
            ------                    ------
                 0                         0
                 1                         1
                 2                         4
                 3                         9
                 4                        16
                 5                        25
                 6                        36
                 7                        49
                 8                        64
                 9                        81
```

Making Reports Pretty

The way that information in a report is presented can make the difference between a report you can extract useful information from and one that looks like one big data dump. To generate more visually pleasing reports by using nothing but what comes with Windows PowerShell, you have to use the `ConvertTo-Html` Cmdlet. This Cmdlet generates a HTML representation of your data by using nothing other than a HTML table. You can display all your service information in HTML form by running this code (you can see the resulting HTML file in Figure 25-3):

```
Get-Service | Select-Object Name,DisplayName,Status | ConvertTo-Html | Out-File
                c:\temp\services.html
```

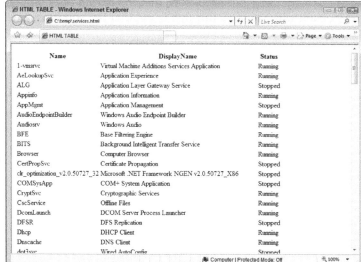

Figure 25-3:
HTML file
generated
by
ConvertTo-
HTML.

Use `Select-Object` before passing the objects to `ConvertTo-HTML` to select the specific properties you want to include in the HTML output; otherwise, by default `ConvertTo-HTML` includes every property defined in the objects it sees which often contains too much information. Alternatively, you can use the `-property` switch in `ConvertTo-HTML` to specify which properties you want.

Converting the output to HTML is certainly a graphical improvement over just having the information displayed in Windows PowerShell, but it still lacks something that makes the output pop when you look at it. The page just looks too generic. For starters, the page is simply called HTML Table; the fonts are generic; and the page is just plain black and white. You can improve this output a little by changing the title and by adding a header and footer so that the report looks more reportlike. You can even throw a splash of color into the header to make it more appealing. Here's an example:

```
$title = "Service Status"
$heading = "<CENTER><H2><FONT Color=Green>Service Status</FONT></H2></CENTER>"
$footer = "<P><CENTER>Generated on : " + (Get-Date) + "</CENTER>"

Get-Service | Select-Object Name,DisplayName,Status | ConvertTo-Html -Title
            $title -PreContent $heading -PostContent $footer | Out-File
            services.html
```

As you may expect, the string you specify in the `-Title` parameter becomes the title of the page. Any HTML code that you put in the `-PreContent` parameter gets placed before any of the objects are converted to a table; then anything you define in the `-PostContent` parameter is appended. With just those few changes, the old HTML page you had on the first go-around is starting to look alive. You can see how that modification changed the way the HTML page looks in Figure 25-4.

Formatting Using Cascading Style Sheets

Cascading Style Sheets (CSS) are files that describe how content within an HTML file should be formatted for display. You can define the fonts, colors, and sizes of the text based on the HTML tags surrounding them. It's a bit out of the scope of this book to discuss CSS in any length, but suffice it to say that CSS files contain formatting directives based on HTML tags (or you can define CSS classes, which you can tag onto different parts of an HTML page to define its formatting).

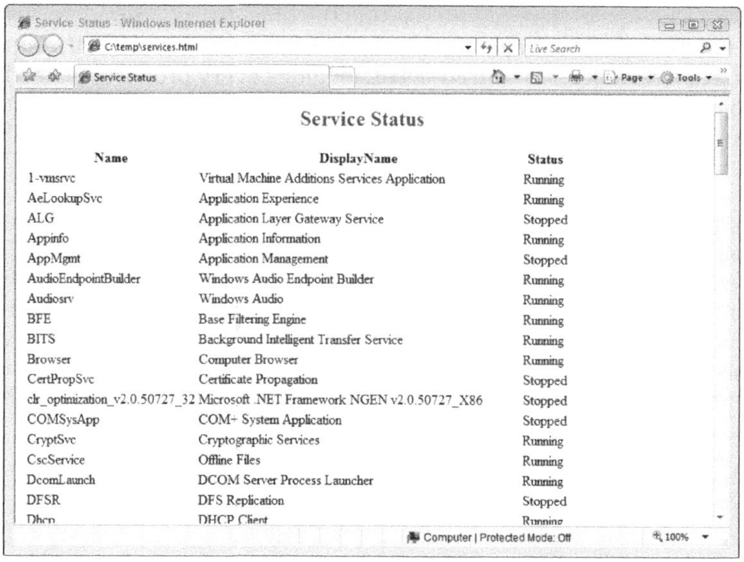

Figure 25-4:
HTML
file using
ConvertTo-
HTML with
some addi-
tional HTML
code.

Here's a simple CSS file that I put together to change the font, size, and color of the column headers (TH tags) and cells (TD tags). The code sets the column header to use a blue Arial 14-point font and each cell to use a green Arial 10-point font:

```
TH
{
    font-family: Arial;
    font-size: 14pt;
    color: Blue;
}
TD
{
    font-family: Arial;
    font-size: 10pt;
    color: Green;
}
```

You save this code as a file with a .css file extension and then tell ConvertTo-HTML to add the appropriate HTML tags in the HTML output to reference this CSS file by using the -CssURI parameter, as I've done here:

```
$title = "Service Status"
$heading = "<CENTER><H2><FONT Color=Green>Service Status</FONT></H2></CENTER>"
$footer = "<P><CENTER>Generated on : " + (Get-Date) + "</CENTER>"

Get-Service | Select-Object Name,DisplayName,Status | ConvertTo-Html -Title
            $title -PreContent $heading -PostContent $footer -CssUri
                "serviceformat.css" | Out-File services.html
```

If you reload the `services.html` file, you'll see that the font style, size, and color have changed, because the file pulls the formatting information from `serviceformat.css` (see Figure 25-5).

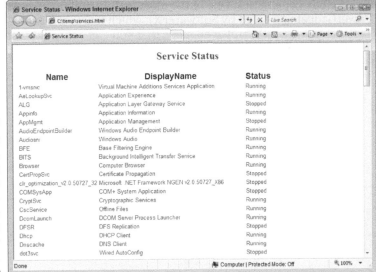

Figure 25-5:
HTML file generated by ConvertTo-Html that uses CSS for formatting.

Now that the report is using the CSS file for its formatting, if you want to change a color or font size, you simply have to change the value in the CSS file, save that file, and reload the HTML page.

You can use CSS files to standardize the look and feel of your HTML reports by defining the formatting in a single CSS file and then having all the reports reference that file. Later, if you decide to change a color or font size, all your reports automatically use the new values; you don't have to regenerate them as you would if you had assigned those values statically.

Using Third-Party Reporting Tools

Right out of the box, Windows PowerShell offers a few useful ways for you to generate simple reports. Unfortunately, management almost always wants reports sliced and diced in many ways, and in those cases, you need something that can be more flexible. One method is to use the export capabilities of Windows PowerShell to put the data in an intermediate format, such as CSV or XML, that can be consumed by other products. Another way is to use ADO.NET to upload the data to a Microsoft SQL database, where you can use powerful SQL reporting tools to your advantage. You can also use COM to create an instance of Microsoft Excel, manipulate the worksheets directly, and use Excel functions and graphing capabilities.

Finally, you can use extensions to add functionality to Windows PowerShell's out-of-the-box capabilities. One of the most mature and popular extensions is PowerGadgets (created by SoftwareFX), which lets you create all kinds of fancy charts, gauges, and even maps that you can control directly from Windows PowerShell. This product is definitely worth looking at if you're interested in more visual reporting.

Part VII
The Part of Tens

The 5th Wave   By Rich Tennant

©RICHTENNANT

Oh come on —
how fatal
can it be?

FATAL
ERROR

In this part . . .

What would a good *For Dummies* book be without a good Part of Tens? After all, it takes weeks of perspiration to weed through mountains of information to bring you these lists of things you absolutely need to know. Find out in Chapter 26 what the top ten Cmdlets are and in Chapter 27, you see the top ten mistakes to avoid. It's okay — I know you're going to flip to the end of this book to take a sneak peek, so go ahead.

Chapter 26

The Ten Most Important Cmdlets

*W*indows PowerShell 2 contains several hundred Cmdlets. All of them are important in one way or the other, so it's hard to pick just ten of them that you'll need the most. I base this chapter on the Cmdlets I feel are the most important based on their utility.

Getting Help with Get-Help

In a command line–driven environment, you don't get the luxury of being able to simply click menus and buttons or to go through dialog boxes in the hope of finding the option or setting you need to do whatever it is you want to do. Instead, you must know not only the command you want to run, but also what parameters it needs and all the other information related to the command.

The Get-Help Cmdlet is your best friend because it helps you find out all the information you need about any particular Cmdlet. It makes command help available at your fingertips any time. You don't need to go online or open any reference help files. Get-Help gets you minimal or detailed information on Cmdlets — and, more important, shows you examples of how to run them because often, the parameters start to make sense only after you see how they're used.

I think it's worth mentioning that a supporting-role award should be given to Get-Command, which is a useful Cmdlet for getting a list of available commands and some basic information about them.

Getting to Know Your Objects with Get-Member

When you want to find out which properties and methods are available for any given object, Get-Member is the Cmdlet to turn to. Unlike other Cmdlets that return or process the value of an object they receive through the pipeline, Get-Member goes straight to the object's structure to give you insider information about what makes that object tick. You also have the option to limit the kind of members that are displayed. If you're interested in the methods but not the properties of objects returned by the Get-Process Cmdlet, for example, you can run

```
Get-Process | Get-Member -membertype Method
```

For each kind of object that it encounters in the pipeline, Get-Member displays the members of that object only once. Whether the command that precedes it in the pipeline returns one or many objects (just as Get-Process returns any number of process objects), Get-Member displays the members for a process object only once, so you don't have to worry that the Cmdlet will spit out the same information many times for the same object type.

Navigating with Set-Location

You've always been able to move around the file system through a command shell, but Windows PowerShell also exposes the Windows registry, variables, environment variables, and even certificates as PowerShell drives that you can navigate just as you would any logical drive. The Cmdlet that lets you move around this virtual drive structure is Set-Location. Typically, this Cmdlet is used with a single parameter: the location that you want the current location to be within your Windows PowerShell window. Set-Location is aliased as CD, because it acts the same functionally as the old Change Directory command in the traditional Windows command prompt.

Reading Text Files with Get-Content

Although Windows PowerShell can consume all kinds of data, thanks to its ability to use .NET classes as well as Component Object Model (COM) objects, simple, plain text files are still the most commonly processed data sources used in scripts. Get-Content makes working with text files extremely easy, because it automatically handles opening the file for reading and pulling in the file contents. Because the file data is automatically converted to a collection of strings, with each line being represented as its own string in the collection, going through each line of a file is effortless.

Most of the time, you'll see Get-Content being used with a single parameter, which is the name of the file to read. It's easy to assume that this Cmdlet is rather simplistic, but if you look at what Get-Content is capable of (by using the oh-so-fabulous Get-Help Cmdlet, which I cover earlier in this chapter), you'll see that this Cmdlet is capable of doing more than just reading in all the contents of a file. It has parameters to specify the encoding of the file so that it's read correctly. You can specify how many lines are read at a time so that if you're processing a file containing thousands of lines, you don't have to wait until the very end before the next command in the pipeline can start using it. You can even configure the maximum number of lines to read.

Writing to a File with Out-File

If you can read a file, you certainly want to be able to write to a file. Windows PowerShell supports the redirection operators (> and >>) that have always been available in the Windows command shell to write or append to a file. Out-File implements that functionality but adds to it much more flexibility. Yes, you can use this Cmdlet to write to and append to a file, just as you use the standard redirection operators, but you can also specify the encoding (such as Unicode and ASCII) or even force writing to a file that has its read-only attribute set.

Out-File can also protect a file from accidental overwrites by aborting the write if the output file already exists, and it has an option to prompt for confirmation before proceeding with the operation. You can also restrict the maximum number of characters in each line of text in the output file, if you need that restriction.

It's important to note that if you use this functionality, any text that exceeds the number of characters you specify gets truncated and is not written to the file.

Leveraging WMI with Get-WMIObject

Windows PowerShell does a great job of including many Cmdlets for doing almost anything you want on your computer, but those Cmdlets don't do everything. For those things you can't do with the native Cmdlets, you always have Windows Management Instrumentation (WMI) to lean on, and harnessing that power is really as simple as running Get-WMIObject. If you read this whole book (okay, maybe just flip through the pages), you see that I often use Get-WMIObject to accomplish many real-world Windows management tasks. It's really that flexible, and the best part is that if you already have a collection of scripts that perform various Windows administrative tasks, you're most likely using WMI already, so migrating its functionality is very easy.

Minimally, you run Get-WMIObject and specify the WMI class you want to connect to. If the WMI class can have many instances (such as Windows services or printers), and you want to grab only particular instances, you can provide filters so that only the ones you're interested in are returned. WMIObject is a very unassuming little Cmdlet, but it's worth its digital weight in gold.

Creating New Objects with New-Object

The Microsoft .NET Framework contains a lot of native classes for working with many aspects of Windows, but you still have to use COM to control some things. You use the New-Object Cmdlet to create instances of both .NET and COM objects. To create an instance of a COM object, you simply run New-Object with the -comobject switch and give it the name of the COM object you want to instantiate. So to create an instance of a Microsoft Excel COM object, you run

```
$objXL = New-Object –comobject "Excel.Application"
```

I also demonstrate in Chapter 25 how you can also use New-Object to create instances of .NET objects like PSObject. The PSObject .NET class is a special one for Windows PowerShell because it gives you the flexibility to tailor it for your own needs by adding properties of your own.

Getting Picky with Select-Object

You use Select-Object whenever you need to be selective about the data you want to obtain from a given object. You can use this Cmdlet to select specific properties of the object, specific objects from an array, and even the first N number of array elements from either the beginning or the end of the array. Usually, you use this Cmdlet as part of a command pipeline in which you filter out specific properties or array elements. Select-Object includes switches that let you

- ✔ Exclude a property from being selected.
- ✔ Expand a property (if the property can be expanded). If the property is really an object, for example, expanding the property displays the properties of that object as well.
- ✔ Select the first and last N number of objects in an array.
- ✔ Select the value of the object in a specific index of an array.
- ✔ Depending on whether the First or Last properties have been specified, skip N number of items from the beginning or the end of the array.
- ✔ Select unique elements in the array.

Going Through Collections with Foreach-Object

When you want to loop through objects in a collection and run some Windows PowerShell code for each object from a pipeline, you use the Foreach-Object Cmdlet and reference each object by using the $_ special variable. It may seem redundant to have a Foreach-Object Cmdlet and a foreach statement that essentially do the same thing. The most noticeable difference is that you use Foreach-Object when you want to act on objects in a pipeline. If you want to display all directories in C:\windows, for example, you can run

```
Get-ChildItem C:\Windows | Foreach-Object {if ($_.Mode.StartsWith("d")) { Write-
           Host ($_.Name + " is a directory")}}
```

The Foreach-Object Cmdlet also has additional parameters that let you run a script block before and after processing all the objects. These parameters can be useful if you want to add header and footer information to the display.

Under the surface, Foreach-Object isn't as efficient as the foreach statement, due to the way that the code eventually gets compiled and converted behind the scenes. This difference may not be significant when you're working with just a few objects, but if you run Foreach-Object against thousands of objects, the time difference becomes noticeable.

Controlling the Pipeline with Where-Object

`Select-Object` lets you pick which properties or array elements should be passed through the pipeline, and `Foreach-Object` lets you loop through elements in a collection, but `Where-Object` is the gatekeeper that determines which objects get to go through. Unlike `Select-Object`, which is designed to handle properties and arrays in a relatively simple fashion, `Where-Object` is designed to let you include a script block to describe what condition must be true for an object to be included in the next step of the pipeline.

The script block, which acts like a pipeline filter, inspects each object that it receives by running it through the code block and then allows it to pass through only if the resulting value is `true`. If you want to get a list of services that have their status property set to `Running`, you can run this code:

```
Get-Service | Where-Object {$_.Status -eq "Running"}
```

Just as you do with `Foreach-Object`, you use the `$_` special variable to reference the current object being inspected. You can put whatever you want in `Where-Object`. The only requirement is that the script block must return `$true` or `$false`.

Chapter 27

Ten Common PowerShell Mistakes

*E*veryone makes mistakes! There's no shame in that fact, especially when you're trying to get your arms around a new scripting language. In this chapter, I talk about some typical mistakes that new Windows PowerShell users make and how you can avoid them.

Forgetting to Change the Execution Policy

The default installation security of Windows PowerShell is one of the first things that newcomers to the language run into when they try to play around with Windows PowerShell on their own. You go online, find a few commands that you like, and try them; they work great. Then you find someone who wrote a script that does exactly what you want. You've read enough to know that the script should be saved with a .ps1 file extension, and when you try to run it, you inevitably run into the exception that prevents anyone from running scripts due to the execution policy.

If you intend to run Windows PowerShell scripts, you must either digitally sign your scripts (as I discuss in Chapter 21) or not require local scripts to be signed by setting the execution policy to RemoteSigned by using the Set-ExecutionPolicy Cmdlet like this:

```
Set-ExecutionPolicy RemoteSigned
```

Using Commas to Separate Parameters When Calling a Function

The way that functions are used in Windows PowerShell often confuses users who have used other scripting languages. Consider this VBScript code snippet, which defines a function that takes two parameters and runs it:

```
call userinfo("Abraham Lincoln",200)

Function userinfo(name, age)
    WScript.Echo "Name: " & name
    WScript.Echo "Age : " & age
End Function
```

In VBScript, as in most other programming and scripting languages, when you call a function with more than one parameter, you use commas to separate the parameters. The preceding code snippet correctly outputs the following:

```
Name: Abraham Lincoln
Age : 200
```

If you convert that function to Windows PowerShell, it looks like this:

```
function userinfo([string]$name,[int]$age)
{
    Write-Host "Name: $name"
    Write-Host "Age : $age"
}
```

Logically, you would assume that to run this function in PowerShell, you can do this:

```
userinfo("Abraham Lincoln",200)
```

The problem is that when you run this code, the output looks like this instead:

```
Name: Abraham Lincoln 200
Age :
```

Oddly enough, the age somehow got included in the name, so Age is blank. In VBScript, when you call a *subroutine* (a function that doesn't return a value), you don't use parentheses. You might try this code to see whether it fixes the problem:

```
userinfo "Abraham Lincoln",200
```

Strangely, even this code returns the same output as the attempt with parentheses. The problem is that the comma in Windows PowerShell is used to create a literal array. Instead of calling userinfo and giving it two parameters, "Abraham Lincoln",200 is actually being treated as a single array object that is converted to a string and passed in as the first and only parameter of the function. The correct way to call a function with more than one parameter is to use a space, as follows:

```
userinfo "Abraham Lincoln" 200
```

Now you get the output you expect!

This aspect of Windows PowerShell has caught many people off guard. As long as you use spaces between parameter values instead of commas, you won't fall victim to this very common mistake.

Defining Functions After You Use Them

Other scripting languages don't care where in the script file the functions are defined, but another peculiarity of Windows PowerShell is that you must always define a function before you can use it. Windows PowerShell scripts are interpreted as they are executed rather than being compiled at run time before being executed. In simple terms, this requirement means that the following script works:

```
function hello([string]$name)
{
    Write-Host "Hello $name"
}

hello "Steve"
```

This next script doesn't work, however, because Windows PowerShell doesn't know what `hello` means until later in the script:

```
hello "Steve"

function hello([string]$name)
{
    Write-Host "Hello $name"
}
```

Treating Pipeline Data as Strings

In almost all the command line–driven shell environments that support pipelines that pass the output of one command to the input of another, the data that goes between pipelines is just pure text. Subsequent commands in the pipeline must parse the output text of the preceding command to extract the data they need. In stark contrast, Windows PowerShell passes objects from one stage of the pipeline to another, which requires a very different mindset when you're stringing commands together. Rather than thinking of string patterns and relying heavily on things like regular expressions, you have to think in terms of collections, objects, and properties.

Here's a good example of how differently Windows PowerShell can behave. This command pipeline gets a list of files and folders in the root of the `C:` drive by using the `Get-ChildItem` Cmdlet and then formats it as a table with the `Name` followed by the last write time:

```
Get-ChildItem C:\ | Format-Table –property Name,LastWriteTime
```

If you want to combine this output with a string and then display it, you might try something like this:

```
"Some random text: " + (Get-ChildItem C:\ | Format-Table –property
            Name,LastWriteTime)
```

Unfortunately, this code doesn't yield the desired results. Instead, the output you get looks like this:

```
Some random text: Microsoft.PowerShell.Commands.Internal.Format.FormatStartData
            Microsoft.PowerShell.Commands.Internal.
Format.GroupStartData Microsoft.PowerShell.Commands.Internal.Format.
            FormatEntryData Microsoft.PowerShell.Commands.Inter
nal.Format.FormatEntryData Microsoft.PowerShell.Commands.Internal.Format.
            FormatEntryData Microsoft.PowerShell.Commands.
Internal.Format.FormatEntryData Microsoft.PowerShell.Commands.Internal.Format.
            FormatEntryData Microsoft.PowerShell.Comm
ands.Internal.Format.FormatEntryData Microsoft.PowerShell.Commands.Internal.
            Format.FormatEntryData Microsoft.PowerShell
```

```
.Commands.Internal.Format.FormatEntryData Microsoft.PowerShell.Commands.
               Internal.Format.FormatEntryData Microsoft.Power
Shell.Commands.Internal.Format.FormatEntryData
```

The problem is that you're combining some text with a collection of format-ted objects, so the string you specify gets displayed by having the ToString method for each object called. For a row in Format-Table, the ToString method simply displays Microsoft.PowerShell.Commands.Internal. Format.FormatEntryData. To get the desired output, you have to convert that formatted table to a string, just as you see it onscreen. To accomplish this task, you use the Out-String Cmdlet. This version yields the desired results:

```
"Some random text: " + (Get-ChildItem C:\ | Format-Table –property
               Name,LastWriteTime | Out-String)
```

If you want to combine formatted text with other text, make sure that you use Out-String to do the correct conversion for you.

Forgetting to Cast Variables as a String

It's a bit funny that I keep talking about Windows PowerShell as being very object-oriented but keep going back to strings. The reason is that when objects are finally displayed, they have to be converted to strings to be humanly readable. One very common mistake has to do with type conversion. When a string and another data type are combined with the plus (+) operator, the other data type is automatically converted to a string via the object's ToString() method. Code like this works automatically:

```
$version = 2
$shell = "Windows PowerShell"
$outputstring = $shell + " " + $version
Write-Host $outstring
```

The output, of course, is Windows PowerShell 2. The implicit type conver-sion works as long as the first data type is a string; otherwise, the conversion will fail. If you reverse $version and $shell, as follows, you end up with an exception:

```
$version = 2
$shell = "Windows PowerShell"
$outputstring = $version + " " + $shell
Write-Host $outstring
```

This exception happens because Windows PowerShell sees that the first variable is an `Integer` and therefore tries to convert the other values it sees being added to it as `Integers`. Because the string `"Windows PowerShell"` is obviously not an integer, it can't be converted, causing the exception to be thrown.

If, for some reason, the string contains only numeric values that could be converted to `Integers`, PowerShell will attempt make that conversion for you.

To fix everything and make sure that what you're combining is treated as a string, you just have to make sure that the first value is a string, and you can do by explicitly casting that value to a string by using the `[string]` prefix. This version doesn't throw any errors:

```
$outputstring = [string]$version + " " + $shell
```

Using Incorrect Comparison Operators

Comparison operators represent another trap for those who have some experience writing code in other scripting or programming languages. Almost all scripting and programming languages use common symbols for comparing values. Table 27-1 shows some of them.

Table 27-1	Typical Comparison Operators
Symbol	*Meaning*
`= or ==`	Equal
`<> or !=`	Not equal
`>`	Greater than
`>=`	Greater than or equal
`<`	Less than
`<=`	Less than or equal

These symbols are generally derived from math, so they're well recognized. It's no surprise that I often find new Windows PowerShell users getting stuck on a script because they don't realize that they've used incorrect comparison operators. The following example is ***not*** the correct way to check whether $x is greater than $y:

```
$x = 5
$y = 2
if($x > $y) {
    Write-Host "$x is greater than $y"
}
```

The > symbol is the redirection operator in Windows PowerShell, just as it is in the Windows command prompt. The preceding code will run without any error, but it won't do what you expect. Instead, the result is that nothing gets displayed onscreen. If you check the current directory, you'll find a new file called 2. The content of 2 is the number 5, because you essentially told Windows PowerShell to output the value of $x to a file called 2 (the value of $y).

In Windows PowerShell, you have to make sure that you use the operators in Table 27-2 when you compare values.

Table 27-2	Windows PowerShell Comparison Operators
Operator	**Meaning**
-eq	Equal
-ne	Not equal
-ine	Not equal; not case sensitive (new in Windows PowerShell 2)
-lt	Less than
-le	Less than or equal
-gt	Greater than
-ge	Greater than or equal

When you use the correct comparison operator, the following code snippet should work properly:

```
$x = 5
$y = 2
if($x -gt $y) {
    Write-Host "$x is greater than $y"
}
```

Trying to Do Too Much in One Pipeline

Windows PowerShell command pipelines are great because you can keep stringing commands together, with each command processing the output of the preceding command. This technique is very powerful because technically, you can put an unlimited number of commands in a pipeline. Often, you'll find that scripts that take several dozen lines in other scripting languages can be done in a single line in Windows PowerShell. The problem is that some new Windows PowerShell users get carried away and want to do all their scripts as one giant pipeline.

There's nothing technically wrong with a very long pipeline, but I suggest that when you find yourself putting more than four commands in a pipeline (especially ones in which you're passing in a long, complex series of parameters), you should start thinking about breaking the pipeline into more manageable segments and storing intermediate values in variables instead. Functionally, this is equivalent to a large pipeline of commands but has the added advantage of being easier to debug and modify if you decide to make a change later.

Even if you know exactly how the pipeline you created works today with the complex sequence of commands you're running, if you look back at the script a few months from now, the process may not be so obvious, and you'll undoubtedly waste time trying to figure out how your own script works. Using smaller command segments makes commands easier to digest when you read the script. Also, picking good variable names can be a self-documenting practice if you're too lazy to write comments in your scripts.

Forgetting About Variable Scope

Windows PowerShell users who don't have any programming knowledge often forget about scope. I'm not talking about the kind of scope that's supposed to make your breath minty fresh, but *scope* in terms of where variables are visible. It's important to understand that any variable you create has a certain scope, depending on where that variable was defined. This behavior is designed to make it possible to use the same variable names in the shell, script, and function, but be unique and have the variable have its own value independent of the other variables with the same name. The best way to understand scope is to see it in action in a simple script:

```
function test()
{
    Write-Host "In function test()..."
    $a = 2
    Write-Host "Value of a is: $a"
```

```
    Write-Host "Leaving function test()..."
}

$a = 1
Write-Host "Value of a is: $a"
test
Write-Host "Value of a is: $a"
```

The resulting output is

```
Value of a is: 1
In function test()...
Value of a is: 2
Leaving function test()...
Value of a is: 1
```

Notice that the value of $a is set to a different value in the function but some-how reverts to its original value after the function is called. There's no magic going on here. The $a defined within the script is actually different from the $a defined in the test function. The first $a defined in the actual script has *script scope level,* meaning that it's visible from anywhere inside the script. If you leave out the $a = 2 line, the test function simply outputs the value of $a from the script itself, which is 1.

If you define $a within the function as I do, however, you actually create a new $a variable within the function that is visible only from within that func-tion. You can do whatever you want with that variable, but as soon as the function is done, that variable no longer exists, and any value you assigned to it within the function is forgotten.

In general, the rule is that variables can be "seen" at any level below the current level, but not vice versa. If you define a variable at the Windows PowerShell prompt, it's visible in any script you run and any function that may be in those scripts. If you define a variable in a function, it isn't visible outside the function. Similarly, variables defined in a script aren't visible when the script finishes running.

Not Using the Debugger

Windows PowerShell 2 includes many new debugging capabilities that make it easier to find bugs in your scripts. If your script is only a couple of lines long (which most scripts tend to be), it's probably easy enough for you to find the source of a bug just by double-checking your code. When you start writing really complicated scripts that are dozens of lines long and contain multiple functions, bugs caused by syntax errors or even variable scope can easily creep in. Use the debugger effectively, and you'll save yourself a lot of headaches later when you're trying to hunt down elusive bugs.

Not Using .NET Classes When Available

This error is probably most common for Windows PowerShell users who have come to rely on using COM objects to interact with the operating system or applications. COM is great in that it's widely supported, and plenty of examples are available to show you how to accomplish almost any task with COM objects. The problem is that interacting with COM through Windows PowerShell is generally a bit slower than using native .NET objects, especially if you compare the speed of using COM in other scripting languages. So whenever possible, before you jump into using COM, do your research; see whether there's another way to do the same thing with .NET classes instead. Your code will run much faster and be better poised to be supportable in the future as in many cases where .NET classes have been made available, they're often full of new features that make working with them easier.

Index

• *X* •

Printed and bound by CPI Group (UK) Ltd, Croydon, CR0 4YY

25/04/2024

14489474-0005